# MASS-MEDIATED TERRORISM

## The Central Role of the Media in Terrorism and Counterterrorism

Brigitte L. Nacos

ROWMAN & LITTLEFIELD PUBLISHERS, INC.
*Lanham • Boulder • New York • Oxford*

ROWMAN & LITTLEFIELD PUBLISHERS, INC.

Published in the United States of America
by Rowman & Littlefield Publishers, Inc.
A wholly owned subsidary of The Rowman & Littlefield Publishing Group, Inc.
4501 Forbes Boulevard, Suite 200, Lanham, Maryland 20706
www.rowmanlittlefield.com

12 Hid's Copse Road
Cumnor Hill, Oxford OX2 9JJ, England

British Library Cataloguing in Publication Information Available

**Library of Congress Cataloging-in-Publication Data**

Nacos, Brigitte Lebens.
  Mass-mediated terrorism : the central role of the media in terrorism and
counterterrorism / Brigitte L. Nacos.
      p. cm.
Includes bibliographical references and index.
  ISBN 0-7425-1082-4 (cloth : alk. paper)—ISBN 0-7425-1083-2 (pbk. : alk. paper)
  1. Terrorism—Press coverage—United States. 2. Terrorism in mass
media. 3. Terrorism and mass media—United States. I. Title.
  PN4784.T45 N35 2002
  070.4'49303625'0973—dc21

                                                                    2002003675

Printed in the United States of America

♾™ The paper used in this publication meets the minimum requirements of American
National Standard for Information Sciences—Permanence of Paper for Printed Library
Materials, ANSI/NISO Z39.48-1992.

For my grandsons Theodore and William,
with the hope that their generation finds ways
to rid the world of terrorism and all political violence

# Contents

# Acknowledgments

RESEARCHING AND WRITING about aspects of terrorism used to be a lonely endeavor: While political violence was a consistent problem in the last several decades—especially for liberal democracies—few social scientists seemed interested in contributing to our understanding of domestic and international terrorism. This changed literally overnight after the terror attacks on the World Trade Center in New York and the Pentagon just outside of Washington, D.C., when terrorism was perceived as the number one threat to the national security of the United States and other countries.

My own interest in terrorism goes back more than a dozen years ago, when I began to test my observation that terrorists are particularly successful in exploiting the links between the mass media, public opinion, and governmental decision making. Along the way, I received encouragement and help from several individuals.

I owe special thanks to my colleague and friend at Columbia University, Robert Y. Shapiro, who has offered generous advice from the outset and has pointed me to valuable resources. I am grateful to Lewis J. Edinger and Donna M. Schlagheck, who read parts of the manuscript and made valuable suggestions that helped me to clarify and improve sections of the book.

Interviewing some of the emergency response specialists, who were involved in the rescue efforts at Ground Zero in New York and experienced terrorism's tragic consequences close-up, strengthened my belief that more terrorism research is needed in order to understand all aspects of political violence and, hopefully, to propose policy applications. I am especially thankful to Keith Johnson, a New York City firefighter and member of Ladder

Company 6, and his wife Dianne for sharing their experiences and feelings. For the same reason I am grateful to Thomas Simmons, a voluntary firefighter and instructor at the Fire Academy of the Bergen County Law & Public Safety Institute, and Wayne Thorsen, a member of the National Guard in New York City.

Brenda Hadenfeldt at Rowman & Littlefield Publishers supported this project from the day she received my proposal. She is a pleasure to work with.

Since my son James E. Nacos is far more computer-literate than his mother, he was the one I called on for figures and tables. Thank you! Last but not least I am thankful to my husband Jimmy for his eternal patience, understanding, and help—especially after 9–11, when I became preoccupied with what he teasingly calls "your terrorism."

# Introduction

A S I ARRIVED at the Brussels airport from New York last year, nervous security agents asked me to open a small gift-wrapped package that had raised their suspicion as my handbag moved through the x-ray machine. The package contained golf balls. A few months later, as I went through a security check at London's Heathrow airport to catch a flight to New York, a security agent unpacked my cosmetic bag and opened a powder compact.

In all of my domestic travels and flights to overseas destinations, the security personnel at U.S. airports never took a second look at my carry-on luggage. Even before the simultaneous hijackings of four commercial airliners and the kamikaze attacks on New York and Washington on September 11, 2001 (referred to ever since as "the events of 9–11," or simply "9–11"), most frequent air travelers were aware of the lax airport security in the United States. Now we know that terrorists notice, too.

Experts in the fields of terrorism, antiterrorism, and counterterrorism had long feared and expected more lethal, international terror on American soil. But few were prepared for the unprecedented attacks on the World Trade Center Towers in New York, the Pentagon in Washington, and the failed attempt on a third target in Washington, most likely the U.S. Capitol, the seat of the Congress. But neither intelligence officers nor terrorism scholars should have been all that surprised. Based on our knowledge of insufficient airport security and of persuasive intelligence that the architect of the first World Trade Center bombing in 1993, the infamous Ramzi Yousef, and some of his fellow terrorists had planned the simultaneous hijackings of American airliners as early as 1995, and that some of these terrorist circles intended to fly a plane into the CIA headquarters near Washington, government officials should have anticipated this sort of super-terrorism.

A few of them actually did. William S. Cohen, then U.S. Secretary of Defense, warned in 1999 of the very real threat that "weapons [of mass destruction] will find their way into the hands of individuals and independent groups—fanatical terrorists and religious zealots beyond our borders, brooding loners and self-proclaimed apocalyptic prophets at home." Moreover, he cautioned that in "the past year, dozens of threats to use chemical and biological weapons in the United States have turned out to be hoaxes. Someday, one will be real."[1] Although appearing in an op-ed piece in the *Washington Post*, the startling statements did not alarm the news media. Neither television news nor the leading print media picked up on or explored the Secretary of Defense's dire prediction. Leslie H. Gelb, President of the Council of Foreign Affairs, commented that he was "astonished" because "none of the television networks and none of the elite press even mentioned it."[2]

While over-covering terrorist incidents, highlighting routine warnings of more devastating terrorism to come, and occasionally pointing to flaws in the counterterrorist preparedness programs, the media did not follow up on serious signs and warnings of the looming terrorist threat as outlined by William S. Cohen's carefully chosen words. After the attacks of 9–11, few in the news media recognized their neglectfulness in this respect. The columnist Richard Cohen was an exception when he wrote:

> I know a guy—never mind his name—who was on one of those government terrorism commissions—never mind which one—and used to say I ought to talk to him. I never did. I was too busy, not just with Bill and Monica but with other things as well, some of them very important. Anyway, I never wrote about the terrorist threat to this country. I was negligent.[3]

This kind of self-examination was scarce and came too late. Nevertheless, as public officials struggled to respond to the attacks on New York and Washington and the plane crash near Philadelphia, the anthrax threat, and the hunt for the perpetrator(s), the media proved indispensable. Television, telephones, radio, newspapers, newsmagazines, and the Internet amounted to a communications network that, at its best, created virtual public meeting places and, at its worst, exploited highlight replays of human evil's most horrific images of destruction.

I began to work on this book long before Osama bin Laden, al-Qaeda, and their associates in terror cells in Europe, the United States, and elsewhere wrote a new chapter in the annals of terrorism on September 11, 2001. Although at the time the most lethal terrorist acts ever, neither the events of 9–11 nor the subsequent anthrax attacks changed my understanding of the mass media's central role in the terrorist scheme. To be sure, these perpetrators exploited the media more shrewdly than other terrorists, but their deeds affirmed my thesis of the media's centrality in the calculus of terrorism, regardless of whether the violent deeds are major or minor in size. Historically, terrorists vied for publicity (having to settle for mouth-to-mouth reporting before the invention of the printing press), now they can exploit far-reaching, instant, and global media networks and information highways to carry the news of their violence along with what has been called "propaganda of the deed."[4] Indeed, as the weeks following the attacks on the World Trade Center and the Pentagon and the U.S. counterattacks on targets in Afghanistan made utterly clear, relatively weak terrorists such as Osama bin Laden and his al-Qaeda terrorist organizations can be formidable players against powerful nations—even the United States, the world's only remaining superpower—in a propaganda campaign triggered by violence.

## A Short Outline for This Book

As it happened, nearly a year before terrorists struck hard inside American borders, the United States suffered a major terrorist attack abroad and the United Kingdom sustained a stunning, if far less harmful terrorist attack in the midst of London. Both of these instances demonstrated the effectiveness of terrorism as far as its perpetrators' publicity goals were concerned. Marking these events in the first year of the twenty-first century as starting points, chapter 1 explains the concept of mass-mediated terrorism and describes how it works in actual terrorist incidents. Although I am aware of the fundamental disagreements over the definition of terrorism, I undertake a new effort to solve this dilemma by suggesting a terminology that links the understanding of terrorism to its perpetrators' deliberate goal—to acquire publicity in the form of media coverage. When the Cold War ended, many foreign policy experts expected less anti-American and anti-Western terrorism in what they envisioned as the "new world order," offering ample opportunities for global cooperation. In order to give the reader a better understanding of the post–Cold War terrorist threat, the chapter traces the developments and reasons for the emergence of more and more lethal terrorism, beginning with the fall of the Soviet Union and the disintegration of the communist bloc.

Never was the news about acts of terrorism as bad and dramatic as it was on September 11, 2001, and thereafter. Chapter 2, although not planned when I began writing the book, examines how the mass media figured into the impact of the 9–11 terrorist events and how the news media reported this unfolding drama and the following anthrax letter scare. In times of major natural and manmade catastrophes, the public depends on the news, especially television and radio reports, for information about the crisis at hand and for instructions about what to do and what not to do. To be sure, much of the information was provided by public officials or members of the business community, but the news media provided generous access to people involved in managing the crisis and/or used these officials as news sources. While it is important to know whether the news served the public interest in this particular respect, one is equally as curious about a host of other questions and issues, such as the reporting patterns during the most acute stages of the crisis and thereafter, whether news organizations became unwittingly the instruments of terrorist propaganda, or whether the media suspended its traditional watchdog role vis-à-vis government in the face of an extraordinary emergency. While some of the most obvious questions and issues of the media coverage were actually raised by critics as the terrorism crisis unfolded, my second chapter provides a comprehensive examination of the news of September 11th and thereafter.

Chapter 3 demonstrates that political violence for the sake of publicity succeeds even when terrorists stage rather modest acts of terrorism. As long as terrorists offer visuals and sound bites, drama, threats, and human interest tales, the news media will report—and actually over-report—on their actions and causes at the expense of other and more important news. Terrorism fits into the infotainment mold that the news media increasingly prefers and offers villains and heroes the promise to attract new audiences and keep existing ones. Here the news is not different from the entertainment industry which thrives on villains and heroes in its search for box-office hits. Moreover, in our celebrity culture, whenever possible at all, terrorists receive celebrity treatment. News reporting made the names of earlier terrorists household words in their immediate target countries, and sometimes beyond. Carlos, the Jackal, Andreas Baader and Ulrike Meinhof of the Red Army Faction, or Arafat in the PLO's terrorist phase come to mind. But more recent terrorists, such as Osama bin Laden and Timothy McVeigh, were treated like legitimate celebrities in the news—in the case of bin Laden, actually before the events of and after 9–11. Because the term *terrorism* has negative connotations, perpetrators of political violence do not like to be called terrorists. As chapter 3 demonstrates, the news media uses the t-word to describe some political violence but avoids the term when reporting on similar incidents of violence for political ends.

A decade ago, when Charles Kegley Jr. wrote, "all terrorism is international" (Kegley 1990). I was not persuaded. Today, if only because of the global nature of the new media, Kegley's earlier conclusion seems far more plausible and convincing. Chapter 4 explores mass-mediated terrorism on the premise that the new means of information and communication in particular offer groups and individuals with violent agendas and messages of hate unlimited, unchecked, and inexpensive opportunities to reach audiences around the globe. In the late twentieth and early twenty-first centuries, groups with terrorist designs communicated with members and supporters via satellite phones, e-mail, and Internet sites while still depending a great deal on the traditional news media to report their violent activities and the causes behind those acts. In addition, the stronger radical movements were able to establish their own radio and television stations and networks. Finally, the relatively easy access to these new means of communication developed into a convenient tool for the recruitment of members or followers and for the solicitation of donations.

Chapter 5 examines how the mass media cover anti- and counterterrorist policies in the American context and how this news figures into decision making regarding the prevention and the countering of terrorism. Because military retaliation and prevention acts are the only responses that are competitive with terrorist acts in terms of reaping publicity, chapter 5 presents case studies of American military strikes in response to terrorism, from the 1983 bombing of Libya to the attacks on al-Qaeda and Taliban targets in Afghanistan following the September 11, 2001 kamikaze attacks in the United States. Since the three cases prior to the retaliatory strikes against Afghanistan were minor, this chapter concentrates on the media's portrayal of this first phase in "the war against terrorism" and on reactions at home and abroad. Moreover, content analyses reveal how the crisis-managing President Bush, who was relentless in his efforts to appeal to the domestic public, to the political elite in Washington, to the international community, and to the world's most prominent terrorist Osama bin Laden (who was in hiding), fared in the news.

As the fears and predictions of mass destruction terrorism grew in the last decade of the twentieth and early years of the twenty-first century, federal, state, and local governments in the United States intensified their efforts to create and/or beef up permanent emergency response agencies. Moreover, programs were established, conferences organized, and emergency simulations and exercises conducted to prepare emergency response professionals from law enforcement, fire departments, emergency medical services, national guard, etc. for dealing with worst-case terrorist attack scenarios. Not surprisingly, in this context, questions were asked about effective public information in the midst of terrorist crises, and the handling of the news media was discussed. When terrorists strike, one of the most important tasks of crisis managers, in particular, and of leaders in the community of emergency response professionals, in general, is that of informing the public and, for this purpose, of dealing with the news media. Based on my studies of media coverage in terrorist and other foreign and domestic crises (Nacos 1990, 1994a, 1996b) and discussions with emergency response professionals, I wrote chapter 6 as a blueprint for effective public information and media relations during terrorist crises. The flip side of the chapter's recommendations could serve as a guide for ethical news coverage in the case of major terrorist incidents.

Finally, the short concluding chapter weighs the positive and negative features of the inevitable links between the mass media, on the one hand, and terrorism as well as counterterrorism, on the other.

## Notes

1. William S. Cohen, "Preparing for a grave new world," *Washington Post*, 26 July 1999, A19.

2. Gelb is quoted here from Joe Klein, "Closework: Why we couldn't see what was in front of us," *The New Yorker* (1 October 2001): 45.

3. Richard Cohen, "The terrorism story—and how we blew it," *Washington Post*, 4 October 2001, A31.

4. Nineteenth-century anarchists and social revolutionaries understood their political violence as "propaganda of the deed" in that they considered their terrorist acts a means of sending messages to both governments and the general public. See Schmid and de Graaf (1982), 11–14.

# 1

# Mass-Mediated Terrorism in the New World (Dis)Order

OCTOBER 12, 2000, SEEMED A PERFECTLY NORMAL DAY in the Yemeni port of Aden, when a U.S. Navy destroyer, the USS Cole, was readied by its crew of 350 to be docked and refueled. Several small boats moved busily around the four-year-old, 9,100-ton, billion-dollar vessel as their occupants hauled the warship's mooring lines around buoys. Shortly after the docking maneuver was accomplished, a lone boat, described later by witnesses as approximately twenty-one to twenty-six feet long, moved toward the Cole's massive hull. Suddenly, the two men in the boat stood up in what seemed like a salute. Seconds later, the boat exploded in a powerful blast, tearing a hole in the port side of the destroyer that was as large as several good-size hotel rooms. Seventeen sailors died and thirty-nine others were injured. The survivors worked furiously to prevent their ship from sinking. They succeeded. What was almost instantly understood as a suicide mission marked a new chapter in the history of anti-American terrorism: A powerful American Navy ship, equipped with guided missiles, machine guns, and the most sophisticated radar equipment, failed to prevent and withstand a rather primitive attack by suicide bombers in a small fiberglass vessel carrying some hundred pounds of explosives.

As the mass media transmitted, highlighted, and replayed pictures of the hole in the Cole's hull, the bloody faces of the injured, the flag-draped caskets of the killed, and the teary-eyed relatives of the victims, all over the globe people saw images that added up to a stunning David and Goliath metaphor: A powerful symbol of the world's most formidable military superpower was incapacitated by members and/or agents of a comparatively weak group unable to fight the mighty United States in open warfare. Even before Yemeni officials charged two Saudi citizens with family roots in Yemen and a history parallel to Osama bin Laden's life along with several Yemenis, American law enforcement officials suspected that bin Laden, already sought by the FBI on terrorism charges, had masterminded this attack against the United States.

While the terror against the USS Cole was far more devastating in terms of its victims and property damage, an attack on the MI6 Intelligence Headquarters in the heart of London on September 20, 2000, presumably by renegades of the Irish Republican Army, was as costly in terms of its effects on the psyche of the English people, who were horrified by the spectacle of someone hurling a rocket from a handheld launcher and a distance of only a few hundred yards onto Britain's foreign intelligence center. While the pictures taken after the audacious attack showed only minimal damage to the well-known MI6 building that once was featured in a James Bond film (*The World Is Not Enough*), they heightened the fear of further violence in London and elsewhere in England.

Aside from the shocking nature of these cases and the security embarrassment they caused for the U.S. and British governments, both incidents had several other factors in common: The deadly bombing of the USS Cole and the small rocket attack on Britain's spy headquarters were highly successful cases of "propaganda of the deed" in that both incidents resulted in massive news reporting and immediate public and elite attention in the targeted countries and in the rest of the world as well. Most importantly, while the precise identity of the perpetrators was not known for a while, the mass media, the public, and government officials speculated about the motives behind the violence and possible remedies. In the process, the grievances of the suspected terrorists were extensively discussed in the mass media. Moreover, chat rooms and message boards on the Internet facilitated lively public debates in the aftermath of these incidents.

Following the bombing of the USS Cole, terrorism became an issue in U.S. politics and especially in American election campaigns in the fall of 2000. Appearing side by side with the Republican presidential nominee, George W. Bush, at a rally in Florida, Senator John McCain seemed to suggest that anti-American terrorism was less likely under the stewardship of Bush than under the leadership of President Bill Clinton and the Democratic presidential candidate, Vice President Al Gore. Referring explicitly to the "tragedy of the USS Cole," McCain said, "We need a steady hand on the tiller, we need the kind of leadership that George W. Bush and Dick Cheney [the Republican vice-presidential candidate] will provide this country so we cannot have those kinds of tragedies happen again."[1]

And in the closing days of the hotly contested U.S. Senate race in New York, between Democrat Hillary Clinton and Republican Rick Lazio, a dispute over terrorism dominated the attacks and counterattacks of both campaigns. Pointing to a fundraising event sponsored by the American Muslim Alliance that had raised fifty thousand dollars for the First Lady, New York State's Republican Party organized phone calls to thousands of eligible voters charging that Mrs. Clinton had accepted campaign donations from an organization that "openly brags about its support for a Mid-East terrorism [sic] group, the same kind of terrorism that killed our sailors on the USS Cole." The calls asked voters to tell Clinton to "stop supporting terrorism" (Riley 2000, A47). The Clinton campaign countered with a television ad that featured a picture of the crippled USS Cole, the sound of taps, and an invisible announcer saying, "Seventeen young American service-men and women on the USS Cole killed by a cowardly act of terrorism. Sadly, Rick Lazio is trying to exploit this tragedy. His campaign is making 500,000 phone calls saying Hillary supports this appalling act of terrorism" (Riley 2000, A61). In truth, the question of Mrs. Clinton and Mr. Lazio's differing methods on Muslim-sponsored terrorism was a nonissue. Even the most passionate pro-Lazio and anti-Clinton circles, and even Lazio's campaign staffers, did not really believe that Hillary Clinton supported anti-Israeli and anti-American terrorism. The *New York Daily News*, a tabloid that endorsed Mrs. Clinton's candidacy, had broken the story of the controversial donations to the First Lady's campaign on its front page, offering Lazio the opportunity to exploit it in hopes of winning additional support among Jewish voters. But Clinton's strong counteroffensive may have been more effective than what a Clinton commercial branded as Lazio's "smear attacks" (Riley 2000, A61).

While nobody knew whether the caustic exchanges between the campaigns of Hillary Clinton and Rick Lazio, or John McCain's remarks in support of George W. Bush, changed voters' minds, it was immediately clear that the candidates and their supporters tried to exploit what was seen at the time as the most spectacular act of anti-American terrorism. The fact that the vast majority of Americans had read, heard, and seen the dreadful images of the attack served as an elucidation that the perpetrators of mass-mediated terrorism had succeeded once again in achieving their most fundamental, media-dependent goal: acquiring the heightened attention of the general public, the political elite, and the decision-making circles in the countries and regions of their choice—and beyond. What a feast it must have been for the designers of the USS Cole attack, when they learned about the incident's elevation to a heated campaign issue in the target country, the United States; from their perspective this was mass-mediated terrorism at its best.

## Mass-Mediated Political Violence or Terrorism

The preceding paragraph introduced the term *mass-mediated terrorism* and indicated an existential link between terrorism and publicity via the mass media. What is the precise meaning of *mass-mediated terrorism*? Starting with the Oxford English Dictionary's definition of violence as "the exercise of physical force so as to inflict injury or damage to persons or property," Sissela Bok defines media violence as "the conveyance or portrayal of such exercises of force in the press or on the radio or the screen" and entertainment violence as including "forms of media violence offered as entertainment" (Bok 1998, 6, 7). These concepts proved useful in Bok's thoughtful examination of the mass media's preoccupation with the most brutal cases of violence, whether they are presented "over and over again" in local and national news reporting or "reflected, repeated, and echoed in endless variations through the lens of entertainment violence" in motion pictures, TV movies, and novels (Bok 1998, 6, 7). Applying Bok's understanding of media violence to terrorism, a particular type of violence, one ends up with a similar but even more compelling concept: media terrorism. To be sure, Bok mentions terrorism in general and the Oklahoma City bombing in particular as she describes television's obsession with images of violence, but her emphasis is on violence as crime—not on violence as political statement. The distinction between criminal violence and the concept of media violence, on the one hand, and terrorism and the concept of media terrorism, on the other, is significant: Most people who commit brutal crimes do not consider their deeds as a means to spread their propaganda or expect to reap publicity for their acts in order to further a political agenda; in sharp contrast, groups and individuals who commit or simply threaten political violence understand their deeds as a means to win media attention and news coverage for their actions, their grievances, and their political ends. For the common criminal, the person he or she chooses as a victim is the target—for the terrorist, as Schmid and de Graaf have pointed out, the "immediate victim is merely instrumental, the skin of a drum beaten to achieve a calculated impact on a wider audience. As such, an act of terrorism is in reality an act of communication. For the terrorist the message matters, not the victim" (Schmid and de Graaf 1982, 14). In other words, unlike common criminals, terrorists have the need to communicate in mind, when they plan and stage their violent incidents; terrorists go out of their way in order to provide the mass media with cruel, shocking, and frightening images. To put it bluntly: when terrorists hurl a rocket into Great Britain's foreign spy headquarters, bomb the hull of the USS Cole, hold hostages in a remote part of the Philippines, or hijack an Indian airliner, they do not simply commit violence—they execute premeditated terrorism that virtually assures a great deal of news coverage.

While the term *media terrorism* captures terrorists' emphasis on communicating their deeds and causes, it could be misunderstood to mean a compliant role on the part of the media. In order to avoid such a misunderstanding, the

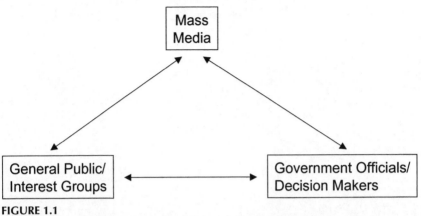

**FIGURE 1.1**
*The Triangle of Political Communication*

term *mass-mediated terrorism* seems more appropriate, capturing the centrality of communication via the mass media in what I call the calculus of mass-mediated political violence or the calculus of mass-mediated terrorism. The idea here is that most terrorists calculate the consequences of their deeds, the likelihood of gaining media attention, and, most important, the likelihood of winning entrance—through the media—to what I call *The Triangle of Political Communication* (see figure 1.1). In mass societies in which direct contact and communication between the governors and the governed are no longer possible, the media provide the lines of communication between public offices and the general public. Indeed, it has been argued that "politics is communication" (Hollihan 2001, chapter 1) and that

> political communication is therefore the means by which people express both their unity and their differences. Through communication we petition our government, plead our unique and special interests, rally those who agree with us to our causes, and chastise those who do not share our world views (Hollihan 2001, 9).

Groups and individuals who feel that they must communicate their causes and grievances precisely because they do not share the mainstream views may not get any access, or, from their point of view, not enough access, to the mass media. The fact is, of course, that the news media are not simply neutral and passive communication conduits, but rather they represent one of the corners in the communication triangle. In that strategic position, the media magnify and minimize, include and exclude. The notion of the news media as gatekeepers is useful in explaining the calculus of mass-mediated political violence; for example, terrorists expect that, in the face of this sort of political violence

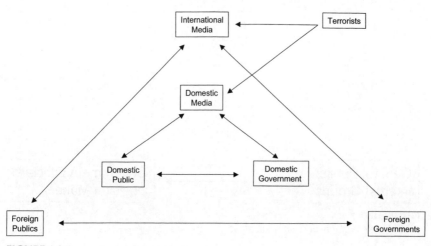

**FIGURE 1.2**
*Terrorism and the Triangle of Political Communication*

(especially spectacular terrorist acts), the media will open their gates for all kinds of incident-related reporting—including the well-calculated messages that terrorists want publicized regardless of whether they claim responsibility for their acts or remain silent. As figure 1.2 indicates, when terrorists strike, their deed assures them the attention of the news media and, as a consequence, of the public and the government in their particular target country. Moreover, given the global nature of the contemporary communication system, the perpetrators of international and domestic terrorist deeds also tap into the international media and thereby receive the attention of publics and governments apart from their immediate target countries as well.

Take the example of Timothy McVeigh, the man convicted for the devastating Oklahoma City bombing in 1995 that killed 168 men, women, and children and injured several hundred more. His act of violence was directed toward the federal government and its agents' deadly force against a sect of antigovernment groups and individuals. While the former U.S. Army sergeant, who shared the ideas prevalent in the right-wing patriot and militia milieu, did not show even a trace of remorse in the years following the bombing and preceding his execution in June 2001, he expressed deep satisfaction that his deed had received attention. He told an interviewer, "I don't think there is any doubt the Oklahoma City blast was heard around the world." McVeigh also revealed that he selected the Murrah Federal Building in Oklahoma City for his attack because it had "plenty of open space around it, to allow for the best possible news photos and television footage." He was determined to "make the loudest statement . . . and create a stark, horrifying image that would make everyone who saw it stop and take notice." So focused on reaping publicity, he had but one regret when he learned that a group of children who attended a day-care center in the building were among his victims: that "the death of innocent children would overshadow the political message of his bombing." And to make sure that the world learned more about his motives, McVeigh left an envelope filled with revealing quotations and documents in his get-away car in case he was killed in the explosion or during his anticipated arrest by law enforcement officers.[2]

Thus, even when terrorists fail to explicitly claim responsibility for acts of violence, the mass media—simply by reporting extensively on such incidents—transmit the perpetrators' messages by warning citizens that even the most powerful governments cannot protect them from this sort of violence. Following the bombing of the USS Cole, for example, neither bin Laden, nor the al-Qaeda group, nor other individuals or groups claimed responsibility. The mass-mediated visuals of the hard-hit and disabled American warship, the pictures of the victims and their families, and the images of frustrated Washington officials were the message that revealed more about the motives than any eloquent claim of responsibility. Not surprisingly, as natural by-products of mass-mediated terrorism, or even as the main or sole goal, perpetrators of terror intend to and often manage to spread fear and anxiety in their target societies. Indeed, this psychological impact on their enemies is for many terrorists high on their list of goals. Palestinians involved in planning suicide attacks on Israelis revealed that, "as a military objective, spreading fear among the Israelis was as important as killing them."[3] Indeed, mass-mediated terrorism is not only an actual act of political violence for propaganda purposes but also the mere threat of such violence.

When terrorists struck in the 1970s and 1980s, they typically claimed responsibility for their deeds. But beginning with the downing of Pan Am flight 103 in late 1988 and continuing with terrorist spectaculars in the 1990s and in the beginning of the new millennium (i.e., the World Trade Center bombing in 1993, the Oklahoma City bombing in 1995, the sarin gas release in the Tokyo subway system the same year, the bombings of U.S. embassies in Kenya and Tanzania in 1998, the suicide attack on the USS Cole in 2000), the perpetrators did not claim responsibility by identifying themselves and/or their affiliations in explicit and timely communications. For this reason, some observers and experts in the field concluded that a new terrorism of expression had emerged. Typically committed by religious or pseudoreligious fanatics, the new kind of political violence has supposedly no media-centered goals, and its perpetrators are said to "lack clearly defined political ends" but give "vent to rage against state power and to feelings of revenge" (Margalit 1995, 19). The point here is that those fight-ing a holy war of terror against an evil enemy do not need to make public claims since they inflict the greatest possible harm, whereas earlier and typ-ically secular terrorists needed to claim responsibility because they were primarily sending powerful messages to their target audiences in order to further their political agenda. Even apart from the alleged emergence of "expressive terrorism," some students of terrorism have questioned the in-evitable relationship between terrorism and communication. Michel Wiev-iorka, for example, has argued that some terrorists do not seek media at-tention and the furtherance of their propaganda.

But whether terrorists claim responsibility for their deeds does not matter at all with respect to media coverage. As Wieviorka recognized, even when perpetrators of political violence seem unconcerned about news coverage, other actors can and do confer media attention upon them—such as the press and government authorities (Wieviorka 1993, 46–47). It is difficult to imag-ine that terrorists who fail to claim responsibility are not aware and pleased that their deeds will be highlighted in the news. I fully agree with Paul Wilkin-son's unequivocal argument that terrorism

> has been a remarkably successful means of publicizing a political cause and re-laying the terrorist threat to a wider audience, particularly in the open and plu-ralistic countries of the West. When one says 'terrorism' in a democratic society, one also says 'media.' For terrorism by its very nature is a psychological weapon which depends upon communicating a threat to a wider society (Wilkinson 2001, 177).

The journalist and columnist Dale Van Atta, who has reported on national se-curity issues for two decades, warned that the press should not buy the sug-gestion of the media's diminished role in the terrorist calculus but argued, "The very act of intending to kill hundreds in airplane and building explo-sions means they [terrorists] seek sensational coverage for their deeds. . . . Like it or not, the media is still an integral part of achieving the terrorist's aim— and therefore must be as judicious and responsible as possible in its re-portage" (Van Atta 1998, 68).

Also, when terrorists do not claim responsibility for a particular act of po-litical violence, they are often aware that they will be recognized as the pri-mary or only suspects and that the news media will report on them and their motives. Thus, following the simultaneous bombings of the U.S. embassies in Kenya and Tanzania in August 1998, bin Laden was covered as the likely ar-chitect of these terrorist strikes, although there was no claim of responsibility on his part. But two months earlier, the Saudi exile told journalists during a press conference in Afghanistan that Americans were "easy targets" and that this would be obvious "in a very short time."[4] And eventually, after the arrest, indictment, trial, and sentencing of several men, the link between the bombings and bin Laden and al-Qaeda was proven.

Pulitzer Prize winner Thomas Friedman suggested that Osama bin Laden "is not a mere terrorist" but a "super-empowered" man with geopolitical inspirations who does not seek headlines but aims to kill as many Americans as possible (Friedman 2002). But according to the Manual of the Afghan Jihad that was used as a training guide for bin Laden's al-Qaeda terrorists, publicity was always the overriding objective. Thus, the manual recommends targeting "sentimental landmarks," such as the Statue of Liberty in New York, Big Ben in London, and the Eiffel Tower in Paris, because their destruction "would generate intense publicity with minimal casualties."[5]

If at all possible, terrorists—just like actors who work in the nonviolent, legitimate political process—prefer to circumvent the media gatekeepers and express their messages directly in front of their target audiences. In the *Minimanual of the Urban Guerrilla*, Carlos Marighela wrote about a twofold approach to the terrorist propaganda scheme and suggested that the

> modern mass media, simply by announcing what the revolutionaries are doing, are important instruments of propaganda. . . . However, their existence does not dispense fighters from setting up their own secret presses and having their own copying machines. . . . The war of nerves—or the psychological war—is a fighting technique based on the direct or indirect use of the mass media.[6]

While Marighela recommended also that "revolutionaries" should tape messages and acquire radio stations to broadcast them, some contemporary terrorist groups own their own radio transmitters and/or television stations. Thus, the Revolutionary Armed Forces of Colombia (FARC), the longest surviving Marxist so-called guerrilla army that controls large parts of the country, fight over the air waves by broadcasting its "Voice of Resistance" with their six mobile transmitters. And the Hizbollah organization broadcasts over its own television station based in Lebanon.

## Defining Terrorism

At this point, the uninitiated reader, and the expert as well, may want to know what *terrorism* means in the context of this book. However, trying to define this term is easier said than done, as students of terrorism well know. While there is no lack of definitions—indeed, whole articles and books have been written about the many efforts to find sound solutions—there is no universally accepted version. Understanding the importance of the term's meaning, Martha Crenshaw has observed,

> It is clear from surveying the literature of terrorism, as well as the public debate, that what one calls things matters. There are few neutral terms in politics, because political language affects the perceptions of protagonists and audiences, and such effect acquires a greater urgency in the drama of terrorism. Similarly, the meanings of the terms change to fit a changing context (Crenshaw 1995, 7).

On one level, the definitional difficulty is rooted in the evaluation of one and the same terrorist act as either a despicable or a justifiable means to political ends, as either the evil deed of ruthless terrorists or the justifiable act of freedom fighters and/or warriors of god. The slogan that "one person's terrorist is another person's freedom fighter" captures these contrasting value judgments. The mass media, mindful of the divergent views and the negative connotations of the terms *terrorism* and *terrorist*, seem uncertain and confused as to when to describe political violence as terrorism and when to choose other labels. Often, reporters and editors tend to take their cue from government officials in this respect. The result is an inconsistent use of several terms describing the perpetrators of terror (terrorist, nationalist, revolutionary, separatist, guerilla, bomber, murderer, criminal, etc.) and their deeds (terrorism, nationalism, revolution, guerilla warfare, bombing, kidnapping, crime, assassination, etc.), a practice in news rooms that I will discuss in detail in chapter 3. Why is it that the mass media called the bombing in the Atlanta Olympic Park during the 1996 Olympic Games "terrorism," but the bombings of abortion clinics and the assassination of abortion providers were called "crimes?"

On another level, controversies over the definition of terrorism are rooted in the disagreements about how to classify the use of force by politically motivated groups or individuals on one hand and by governments on the other. According to this approach, however dissatisfying it may be, "political language divides along the fault line separating mass violence from individual or small-group violence" (Rubenstein 1987, 17). While many, perhaps most, definitions of terrorism speak of political violence against *innocents* or *noncombatants*, this definition would certainly cover acts like the bombing of the U.S. embassies in Kenya and Tanzania and the suicide attack on the USS Cole, but also the unthinkable acts of "state terrorism" committed in Germany under the rule of Adolf Hitler or in the Soviet Union of Joseph Stalin. Even military actions, such as the U.S. air strikes on targets in Afghanistan following the terrorism of September 11, 2001, the bombings of sites in Sudan and Afghanistan in response to the attacks on U.S. embassies in East Africa in 1998, or NATO's air raids on Serbian targets during the conflicts in Bosnia and Kosova in the 1990s, would also qualify under that definition. After all, innocents or noncombatants were victims of all of these acts. Yet, most observers do not consider civilian casualties of declared wars or other military actions as the victims of terrorism. Intuitively, one recognizes a difference here—even if one is severely critical of these acts. As one observer sees it, "In a real sense, terrorism is like pornography: You know it when you see it, but it is impossible to come up with a universally agreed-upon definition."[7] However hard one tries to differentiate, when everything is said and done, to "call an act of political violence terrorist is not merely to describe it but to judge it" (Rubenstein 1987, 17).

Writing before the demise of the Soviet Union, Herman and O'Sullivan tied many of the definitional incongruities to the Cold War biases of western governments, western terrorism experts, and the western media that looked upon the West as the sole victim of terrorist activities. More importantly, they argued that "the Western establishment has defined terrorism so as to exclude governments, which allows it to attend closely to the Baader-Meinhof gang and Red Brigades and to play down the more severely intimidating actions of governments" (Herman and O'Sullivan 1989, 214). In the first case, the authors point out, the nongovernmental actors were called terrorists, in the second case, the governments were "said to be merely violating 'human rights,' not engaging in 'terrorism'" (Herman and O'Sullivan, 214).

The usage of the term *terrorism* has changed greatly over time. In its original definition in the eighteenth century, it meant violent actions from above, by the state, such as those during the Reign of Terror in the wake of the French Revolution, when *terrorism* meant the mass guillotining of the aristocracy and other real or perceived enemies of the state. During the nineteenth century, the definition of *terrorism* expanded to include violence from below, such as the assassinations of prominent politicians by anarchists. In the twentieth century, *terrorism* came to mean mostly political violence perpetrated by non-state actors, such as autonomous or state-sponsored groups and individuals (Vetter and Pearlstein 1991; Hoffman 1998).

It might well be that this latest shift in the definition of terrorism works in favor of violence perpetrated by governments in that they often escape a negative connotation. But short of an unlikely wholesale change in the meaning of terrorism, I suggest a solution that can bridge the definitional controversies. The starting point is the notion of mass-mediated terrorism and its definition as political violence against noncombatants/innocents that is committed *with the intention to publicize the deed, to gain publicity and thereby public and government attention.* This characterization is compatible with definitions put forth by some experts in the field, for example, Schmid and de Graaf (1982, 14) who consider political violence as "an act of communication," or Richardson (1999, 209) who defines terrorism as "politically motivated violence directed against noncombatants or symbolic targets which is designed to communicate a message to a broader audience." The importance of communication in the terrorist design is also implicit in Crenshaw's observation that terrorism "targets a few in a way that claims the attention of many" (Crenshaw 1995, 4). But wouldn't this definition also apply to violence committed by states, by governments? Contrary to groups or individuals that commit or encourage mass-mediated terrorism, governments are not at all interested in publicizing domestic or international acts of violence that harm innocents and noncombatants. In sharp contrast to terrorists, governments, especially in democracies, will speak of civilian casualties as the unintended victims and of damage caused to innocent bystanders as regrettable consequences of war in the hope of less, rather than more, publicity. Moreover, when governments commit or sanction domestic political violence in their own countries or abroad, they (and those who act with their support) do not want to publicize their deeds to a larger audience. One instructive example concerns an incident during the Vietnam War, when former U.S. Senator Bob Kerrey and his squad of Navy Seals, while on one of their dangerous search missions for Vietcong leaders, encountered and killed more than a dozen unarmed Vietnamese civilians, most of them women and children. It took thirty-two years and the persistent questioning of an investigative reporter before Kerrey publicly acknowledged the tragic incident in the village of Thanh Phong.[8] Neither the young Americans who committed this political violence nor the U.S. government officials who sent them into war wanted to publicize the incident then or in the future. Was it an act of political violence? Yes. Was it an act of mass-mediated political violence or, in other words, political violence with publicity in mind, and thus terrorism? No.

As usual, one finds exceptions to the rule. In this context, exceptions apply to governments involved in what they call antiterrorism (preventive measures) or counterterrorism (reactive measures) or the use of force against persons accused of perpetrating political violence. In such cases, publicity may be considered helpful in a government's efforts (1) to discourage further political violence and (2) to satisfy a fearful domestic public that demands protection. In late 2000, for example, Israeli officials acknowledged "publicly, explicitly, and even proudly" (Sontag 2000, A12) that their military was targeting and killing individual Palestinians accused of actual attacks on Israeli citizens or of planning such deeds. While Palestinians spoke of "state terrorism" and "assassinations," a highly placed government official in Israel defended these acts as countermeasures and said that the "most effective and just way to deal with terror is the elimination or incarceration of the people who lead these organizations" (Sontag 2000, A12). After a particular incident that targeted an alleged mastermind behind anti-Israeli terrorism but killed eight Palestinians—

among them two boys—Foreign Minister Shimon Perez reacted angrily when an interviewer used the term *assassination* to characterize the action. "Suicide bombers cannot be threatened by death," he argued. "The only way to stop them is to intercept those who sent them."[9] And Prime Minister Ariel Sharon made clear that "actions to prevent the killing of Jews" would continue.[10] But in the spring of 2002, when Israeli Defense Forces moved into Palestinian towns and refugee camps on the West Bank in response to the most lethal series of suicide bombings inside Israel, the military tried to prevent the news media from covering the use of force that according to Israel's leaders targeted terrorists. These actions also unintentionally harmed civilians—collateral damage in the parlance of military and political leaders of states.

To repeat, then, mass-mediated terrorism understood as violence for political ends against noncombatants/innocents with the intent to win publicity avoids the issue of whether the terrorist label applies to political violence inflicted by governments as well. Mass-mediated terrorism, as defined here, simply does not include political violence committed by states against noncombatants because governments do not want to publicize such incidents but would rather limit media attention and even suppress public disclosure, if they can. By definition, then, mass-mediated terrorism refers to politically motivated deeds perpetrated by groups or individuals for the sake of communicating messages to a larger audience. Their publicity goal does not exclude the terrorists' desire to inflict great harm on their targets. Similarly, it is useful to speak of mass-mediated counterterrorism or mass-mediated antiterrorism, when governments use the mass media to enlist public support for military or other actions in the name of fighting terrorism, to communicate warnings to terrorist foes and to send assuring messages to their own publics (see chapter 5).[11]

### The Terrorist Threat in the Twenty-First Century

Although this book is about the centrality of communication in the scheme of terrorism and about the mass media's obsession with spectacular terrorist incidents at a time of tremendous advances and changes in the media landscape of the early twenty-first century, it seems important to examine and explain how the end of the Cold War might figure into contemporary terrorism and future terrorist threats. After all, a fresh look at political violence as a means to communicate powerful messages is especially urgent, if the likelihood of terrorism is as serious or perhaps even more serious than it was in the past. Actually, no one should have been surprised that the beginning of the new millennium recorded a large number of terrorist incidents in many parts of the world. Numerous experts in the field and government officials, from former

President Bill Clinton to President George W. Bush and CIA Director George Tenet, warned of the unprecedented dangers in the "new era of terrorism," as former U.S. Senator Sam Nunn put it.[12] President George W. Bush and his national security team, as well, recognized terrorism among the major threats to America's national security. In support of the establishment of a National Missile Defense System, Secretary of Defense Donald Rumsfeld said, "We must develop the capabilities to defend against missiles, terrorism and newer threats against our space and information systems."[13] Government officials and scholars pointed to the proliferation of weapons of mass destruction after the disintegration of the Soviet Union, when they made their gloomy predictions as to future terrorist threats. And in an assessment of the post–Cold War threats to the United States' national security, Vice President Richard Cheney summarized these concerns the following way:

> I think we have to be more concerned than we ever have about so-called homeland defense, the vulnerability of our system to different kinds of attacks. Some of it homegrown, like Oklahoma City. Some inspired by terrorists external to the United States—the World Trade towers bombing, in New York. The threat of terrorist attack against the U.S., eventually, potentially, with weapons of mass destruction—bugs or gas, biological, or chemical agents, potentially even, someday, nuclear weapons. The threat of so-called cyberterrorism attacks on our infrastructure (Lemann 2001, 59).

The United States received its first bitter taste of biological terrorism in the form of anthrax spores during the wake of the terrorist attacks on the World Trade Center and the Pentagon in 2001. But the potential for more lethal and, indeed, catastrophic terrorist violence was only part of the alarming story. As the end of the twentieth and the beginning of the twenty-first century demonstrated, most terrorist incidents were orchestrated by groups and individuals who used the same or similar methods as their predecessors in the 1970s, 1980s, and 1990s—hijackings, hostage-takings, bombings, suicide missions, assassinations, and facility assaults. The perpetrators of the attacks on New York and Washington on September 11, 2001, used conventional means—i.e., the hijacking of airlines—and turned them into instruments of mass destruction.

Terrorism is on the rise. To illustrate this point, the U.S. State Department's yearly statistics of international terrorist incidents lists a total of 423 for the year 2000, up from 392 cases in 1999. The number of specifically anti-American acts of terrorism rose from 169 in 1999 to 200 in 2000. While the precise number of incidents may be higher or lower, depending on what cases are counted as international terrorism, the list is valuable. It is even harder, indeed impossible, to get reliable numbers or estimates about domestic incidents that qualify as mass-mediated terrorism because most of these cases are not reported as such. Yet, many of the increasing number of hate crimes fall into the category of mass-mediated political violence or terrorism. Take, for example, the Southern Poverty Law Center's list of hate crimes that describes hundreds of such cases every year. When a self-described white supremacist gang leader threatened a black classmate with violence, when a note reading "KKK White Knights" was left on a black woman's door, when a group of black teenagers yelled racial epithets at white teenagers as they assaulted them, when an armed young man attacked a student as he left an Islamic prayer meeting—these were terrorist threats and actions that frightened the respective targets.

Moreover, it is interesting to note that in 2001 the FBI's list of the "Ten Most Wanted Fugitives" included three terrorists—Osama bin Laden, of the international al-Qaeda group, and Eric Robert Rudolph and James Charles Kopp, of the domestic variety. While bin Laden was widely viewed as a terrorist, Rudolph, who was charged with the deadly bombing of an abortion clinic in Birmingham, Alabama, and the fatal bombing at Centennial Olympic Park in Atlanta, Georgia, and Kopp, who was sought for the assassination of Dr. Barnet Slepian, who provided legal abortions, were widely viewed as criminals. Yet, neither Rudolph nor Kopp were ordinary criminals; they were anti-abortion terrorists who acted according to the political agenda of the most extreme wing of pro-life activists.

When the United States and other western democracies were still the primary targets of terrorism in the 1970s and 1980s, some experts argued persuasively that this kind of political violence was merely a nuisance rather that a serious problem for these target countries (Laqueur 1987). Others warned that the world should brace for a more violent chapter in the long history of terrorism and described eerie scenarios of major terrorist actions that would cause mass disruption and even mass destruction (Kupperman and Kamen 1989). For a short time, the collapse of the Soviet Union and the end of the Cold War fueled hopes of a drastic reduction in terrorism, but the events of the last several years proved the pessimists right. Terrorism did not decline; instead lethal attacks became more common. The World Trade Center bombing in 1993, the Oklahoma City bombing in 1995, and the sarin gas attack in Tokyo's subway system that same year were the opening shots in a salvo of lethal terrorist spectaculars that continued with the bombings of the U.S. embassies in Kenya and Tanzania in 1998, the suicide attack on the USS Cole in 2000, and the kamikaze attacks on the World Trade Center and Pentagon in 2001.

There are several reasons why terrorism remains one of the more serious problems in the post–Cold War world and threatens to become yet a greater menace. First, the collapse of communism and the end of the bipolar world order resulted in the dismantling of a mechanism that, in a strange way, kept terrorism within a manageable range. Before the Iron Curtain fell, the United States, its western European allies, Japan, and assorted regimes in Latin America were frequently the targets of leftist terrorists who fought against the capitalist and imperialist world—especially the United States. During these years, the American superpower was also the primary target of secular and religious groups who opposed Washington's Middle East policies and involvement in the region—particularly in support of Israel. In those years, terrorism made strange bedfellows. The German Red Army faction, for example, teamed up with Palestinian nationalist and Islamic fundamentalists; terrorism sponsor Muammar Gadhafi of Libya and Palestinian groups lent support to the Irish Republican Army; and secular Latin American terrorists cooperated with religious Arabs and left-wing extremists in western Europe. All the while, anti-American and anti-Western terrorists enjoyed significant support from eastern bloc countries in the form of arms, training facilities, and safe havens. The fact that this web of terrorism extended deep into the Soviet bloc and fostered political violence against the West provided, at the same time, a mechanism of restraint: the Soviet Union could use its influence over eastern bloc countries, such as East Germany, and client states, such as Libya, to keep anti-Western and anti-American terrorism beneath a certain threshold, and thus the Soviet Union could avoid the risk of military confrontations with its adversaries in the West.

During this period, leftist terrorists (i.e., the Italian Red Brigades or the German Red Army Faction) and nationalist and religiously motivated groups (i.e., various secular Palestinian and Islamic groups in the Middle East) preferred to target influential persons from the political, business, or military realm rather than innocent victims. When innocent bystanders were targeted, the inflicted harm was not as extreme as in more recent incidents, such as the downing of PanAm Flight 103 in 1988 over Lockerbie, Scotland, the bombings of the U.S. Embassies in East Africa and of the USS Cole, and the terror of 9–11 in New York and Washington. As the Soviet bloc disintegrated and Moscow's power decreased, the restraining mechanism vanished. The surviving and newly emerging movements and groups, poised to use political violence for their causes, were far more autonomous than they were during the previous decades.

Moreover, the Cold War world order limited the likelihood of disproportional counterterrorist strikes by western states, most of all the United States, that did not want to upset the balance-of-power arrangement. It was with this in mind that the Carter administration decided against punitive military strikes in Iran during the Iran hostage crisis and at a time when the Soviet Union had invaded Iran's neighbor, Afghanistan. When the Reagan administration saw the need to strike back at terrorism, they did not choose Iran, then considered the most flagrant sponsor of anti-American terrorism, but the relatively weak Libya as the target of U.S. counterterrorism. No doubt, American decision makers were well aware that the North African state was far less important in Moscow's geopolitical interests than Iran, and that an attack on Libya would not risk a military clash with the Soviet Union. To this end, the 2001 U.S. air strikes against targets in Afghanistan in the hunt for Osama bin Laden and the Taliban leadership would have been inconceivable during the Cold War because of the Soviet Union's proximity to this country.

The second reason why terrorism remains one of the more serious problems is that the end of the old world order unleashed nationalist and religious frictions that were suppressed in the past. The breakup of the Soviet Union into more than a dozen independent states did not end the historic ethnic and religious conflicts within and between those new republics but, rather, allowed them to explode. The conflict between Russia and separatists in the province of Chechnya as well as the ethnic hostilities in Bosnia and Kosova were cases in point. From the outset, terrorist threats and actual violence figured prominently in the Chechen rebels' struggle for independence. Aware of their own weakness in comparison to Moscow's military force, rebel leaders warned as early as 1992 that they would bomb Moscow's subway system and attack nuclear plants (McMullan 1993). Given that terrorism is the weapon of the weak, it was hardly surprising that the continuing conflict between Chechen separatists and the Russian army led to terrorist acts against Russian targets both in the Chechen province and elsewhere in Russia. Similarly, terrorism was part of the ethnic conflicts in Bosnia and Kosovo. The Muslims in Chechnya and Bosnia felt abandoned by the West. In the early 1990s, Sefir Halilovic, the then commander-in-chief of the Bosnian Army, threatened that terrorists would put "European capitals ablaze" unless the West supported Bosnian Muslims (Ranstorp and Xhudo 1994, 210). Andrei Dudayev, a Chechen rebel leader, threatened terrorist attacks against western Europe charging that the West supported Russia's aggression against Chechnya (*New York Times* 1996, A6).

To be sure, militant Muslims were not the only ones preaching, threatening, and committing political violence in these regions. On the contrary, Bosnian Serbs, for example, were the first party to resort to international terrorism in the Bosnian conflict when they seized French members of the United Nations peacekeeping contingent as hostages in order to prevent NATO air strikes. In this particular incident, media considerations played prominent roles in the calculations of both sides. The Serb hostage-holders allowed television crews to film their hostages with the expectation that the French government would not be able to remain firm once the French people saw the faces of their scared countrymen on their television screens. Fearing the impact of these kinds of visual images on the public, decision makers in Paris asked French television networks to obscure the faces of the hostages electronically.

The mobilization and increased activities of religious and pseudoreligious movements and groups increased the likelihood of terrorism that causes far more deaths, injuries, and damages than secular political violence. At a "martyr's wedding"—a ceremony honoring two Palestinian boys who died fighting the Israelis—at Martyr's Square in the Gaza strip, banners and signs congratulated Ahmed and Ibrahim "for dying in the service of God." Ahmed's mother chanted, "I am proud. . . . Thanks be to God" (Finkel 2000, 50). This scene, witnessed by a reporter in the fall of 2000, was not an unusual one. Just like their fathers, uncles, and older brothers, young boys fought and died in the Palestinian intifada for the glory of god. Whether Christian identity adherents in the United States and Canada, militant Jewish fundamentalists in Israel, fundamentalist Muslims in Lebanon, Algeria, the West Bank, and elsewhere, or bizarre sects like the Aum Shinrykio in Japan, "violence first and foremost is a sacramental act or divine duty executed in direct response to some theological demand or imperative" (Hoffman 1995, 272).

Those who consider themselves God's soldiers in a holy war are not bound by the moral imperatives of secular or less zealous religious terrorists. In that light, it is hardly surprising that the most shocking acts of terror in the recent past were the work of religiously motivated groups or individuals—from the first World Trade Center bombing to the Tokyo nerve gas attack, from the deadly attack on Palestinians worshiping in a mosque of Hebron to the suicide attacks on the World Trade Center and the Pentagon. Khadar abu Hoshar, convicted of plotting to bomb tourist sites in Jordan and awaiting his execution in a Jordanian prison, showed no regret but affirmed his decision to devote his life "to the cause of jihad, or holy war, in hopes of bringing to power governments that follow the strict code of Islamic law."[14] For the same reason, suicide terror missions have been far more common among religious or pseudoreligious terrorists, rather than secular terrorists, as are plots to cause the greatest possible harm. As one expert sees it,

> The combination of religion and terrorism can be cited as one of the main reasons for terrorism's increased lethality. The fact that for the religious terrorist violence inevitably assumes a transcendent purpose and therefore becomes a sacramental or divine duty, arguably results in a significant loosening of the constraints on the commission of mass murder" (Hoffman 1995, 280).

Suicide terrorism is not a new phenomenon. In 1983, for example, explosive-laden trucks, driven by suicide bombers, plowed into the U.S. embassy and into U.S. Marine barracks in Beirut, Lebanon, killing a total of 258 Americans. But altogether, suicide terrorism was rare. This changed in the more recent past. Beginning in the mid-1990s, suicide terrorism took on epidemic proportions in the Middle East, when Palestinian terrorists mounted a series of lethal attacks in which they died along with hundreds of victims. The Palestinian terrorists were typically in their early twenties, indoctrinated in fundamentalist mosques and schools and eager to become *shadinin* or martyrs in the *jihad* or holy war against the Jewish state. However, the ringleaders among those nineteen hijackers who died in the attacks on New York and Washington did not fit the profile of a young, poor man with limited education because all of the ringleaders were older, well-educated, and of middle-class backgrounds.

Probably inspired by the perceived success of the attacks on New York and Washington and the Hamas sponsored suicide missions against Israelis, a secular Palestinian group began to target Israeli civilians with "human bombs" in late 2001 and intensified this campaign in the spring of 2002. This was, to be sure, not the first time that secular terrorists had chosen to kill themselves in order to commit violence. Members of the Kurdish Workers Party, for example, undertook suicide missions earlier. But in the case of the al-Aqsa Martyrs Brigade, an offshoot of Yasir Arafat's al-Fatah organization, the choice of lethal suicide missions seemed to emulate the strategies of religiously motivated idols (bin Laden and al-Qaeda) and possible political rivals (Hamas).

Extremists from other religions were also ready to die for their causes. The young fundamentalist Jew Yigal Amir, who assassinated Prime Minister Yitzak Rabin in order to stop the peace process between Israelis and Palestinians, claimed to have acted in accordance with the Torah and Jewish law and God. "Everything I did was for the sake of God," he said (Greenberg 1996, A9). While the assassin was not killed during the incident, he certainly considered the possibility and was ready to die for his cause. The same was true for the Brooklyn-born Dr. Baruch Goldstein, a follower of the Rabbi Meir Kahane and the organizations that survived the militant Jewish leader, who massacred twenty-nine Palestinians as they worshipped in a Hebron mosque. Goldstein was eventually killed in the bloody massacre as well.

While North American fundamentalists with hate-based belief systems drawn from the Christian Identity movement have so far shied away from suicide terrorism, some of these factions have pondered and actually attempted catastrophic measures. Thus, a white supremacy group planned to poison water reservoirs in the American Northwest that supply drinking water to densely populated urban centers. And like-minded extremists tried to release toxic chemicals through ventilation systems into buildings in the Southwest. In both instances, the terrorists failed.

Opposition to the vision of a new world order with greater political, economic, and military cooperation among the family of nations revitalized the leaders and followers of the old white supremacy gospel in the Christian Identity movement and related racist, anti-Semitic, and xenophobic conspiracy theories in the United States (Stern 1996; Kaplan 1995). With Communists and the Cold War threat out of the way, these groups attacked Washington's alleged compliance in the country's takeover by a world government. The prospect of United Nations "storm troopers" and other international fighters eradicating the United States as we know it justifies, in the eyes of these groups, violence against the government and its agents. These sorts of ideas, whether spread by neo-Nazi, militia, patriot, white supremacy, or Christian identity groups (and they converge in their conspiracy theories), are, in one way or another, attractive abroad as well—especially in Canada, Europe, and Australia. The Internet provides the apostles of hate and their adherents a means of communication, where they can promote each other's sites in the hunt for recruits.

Contemporary terrorist organizations have easier access to weapons of mass destruction than in the past. The United States, Germany, and other western industrial powers have long been involved in massive arms exports, especially to countries in the developing world. And during the Cold War era, countries east of the Iron Curtain supplied extremists in the West with arms. The Semtex plastic explosives, for example, that terrorists used to blow up PanAm Flight 103 over Lockerbie, Scotland, were produced in and supplied by Czechoslovakia. But following the dismantling of the eastern bloc and the So-viet Union, stockpiles of nuclear weapons became accessible, and scientists and technicians who developed nuclear arms and chemical and biological agents in Russia and elsewhere in the East were for hire. Whether through un-derground channels, such as the Russian Mafia, or through some unpaid sci-entists, some of these dangerous weapons and some of these experts found their way into countries with known ties to terrorist groups. The idea that ter-rorists might resort to weapons of mass destruction is the ultimate nightmare (Allison et al. 1996; Stern, 1999).

Groups like Japan's Aum Shinrykio and Osama bin Laden's al-Qaeda failed in the past in their efforts to buy highly enriched uranium from sources in Russia and other republics of the former Soviet Union in order to build their own nuclear weapons. However, bin Laden admitted that he did not exclude the use of nuclear, chemical, and biological weapons in his holy war against Is-rael and its supporters; his group allegedly "obtained phials of anthrax and the lethal viral agent botulism" (Reeve 1999, 216). And it does not take the finan-cial muscle of a bin Laden to acquire potent weapons. Just as the U.S. Army lost track of large quantities of explosives stored in military facilities, such as Fort Bragg, it is not impossible that groups or individuals could steal nuclear, biological, or chemical material by breaking into some laboratory.

So real is the threat of catastrophic terrorism that the professional response community did not take a chance—not even before the terror attacks of Sep-tember 11, 2001, and the subsequent anthrax threat. Thus, in the summer of

2000, when eight businesses in New York City received anonymous letters allegedly containing hazardous biological agents, the Mayor's Office of Emergency Management responded swiftly by dispatching and alerting medical and hazardous material specialists and a host of other response specialists. The "day of eight letters" turned out to be a hoax, but the terrorist response professionals knew that it was not an unlikely scenario for a real act of terrorism.[15] But even without getting their hands on weapons of mass destruction, amateurs, whether working alone or in groups, can build crude, homemade bombs by mixing a few hundred pounds of legally sold materials—as the Oklahoma City and the first World Trade Center bombings showed.

Political change in some parts of the world has opened up channels of communication that were controlled and censored in the past by autocratic governments. As a result, mass-mediated terrorism has become a more attractive weapon. Let's return to the example of the long-lasting Russian–Chechen conflict that has involved a great deal of violence on both sides. In late March of 2001, three simultaneous car explosions killed twenty-three and injured more than one hundred civilians in Southern Russia. If this had happened in the old Soviet Union, the state-controlled mass media probably would not have reported the incident. Although Russian authorities were far from granting press freedom along the lines of western democracies and, in fact, threatened at this particular time the very existence of NTV television, the only major channel outside of the Russian government's control, the Russian public and the rest of the world learned about these particular bombings and many similar bombings, hostage situations, and hijackings by extremists among Chechen separatists. Indeed, domestic critics of the Putin government suspected that the government-controlled television channels showed the shocking visuals of terrorism's victims in order to justify and enlist support for Russia's military actions against Chechnya. Whatever the motives, based on their earlier terrorist threats there was no doubt that Chechen leaders welcomed the publicity that their actions received in the Russian and international media.

This last point brings the discussion back to our central theme—the inevitable and primary role of communication and propaganda in the terrorist design and the contemporary mass media's appetite to facilitate the need of virtually all terrorists to have their deeds publicized. Former British Prime Minister Margaret Thatcher had it right when she proclaimed that publicity is the oxygen of terrorism. If anything has changed in the last ten or fifteen years, it is the increased availability of the sort of oxygen Mrs. Thatcher warned of and upon which mass-mediated terrorism thrives.

In the years since the Berlin Wall came down and the Soviet Union crumbled, the mass media of communication have changed in dramatic ways—mostly, but not solely, because of the global reach of the Internet and cellular phones. In the last decade or so, when more and more people connected to and communicated through the Internet, the traditional or old media transformed, too, (1) by establishing their presence on the World Wide Web, and (2) by accelerating mergers and acquisitions that created ever larger megamedia organizations with national, international, and even global character (Alger 1998, Bagdikian 2000). Today, the vastly expanded public spaces provided by the old and new media offer groups that promote and commit political violence far greater opportunities to communicate with their various audiences than in the past. Moreover, the Internet has become a target and a means to inflict damages on governments, businesses, and private citizens. Cyberterrorism, or Internet-terrorism, are real threats to computer-dependent polities and economies. Indeed, it has been argued that virtual attacks represent the new warfare of the twenty-first century, but, by the same token, information attacks are the new terrorism of our time. According to one account, virtual terror is "a free-for-all, with more and more players hurrying to join the scrimmage" (J. Adams 2001, 102).

These developments—from the new terrorism, as Walter Laqueur calls it (Laqueur 1999), to the recent changes in the media market and the technological advances—call for a fresh look at the links between political violence and the mass media. Most comprehensive studies about political violence/terrorism and media/communication were conducted and published before the Internet's breakthrough as a widely used medium of communication and before the significant changes in traditional mass media, such as the United States' preference of cable television to the once dominant broadcast television networks, and the progression from public to additional, and now far more numerous, private broadcast channels in Europe (Schmidt and de Graaf 1982; Schlesinger et al. 1983; Paletz and Schmid 1992; Livingston 1994; Nacos 1996). More recently, some terrorism scholars have examined various aspects of terrorism and the Internet (Arquilla and Ronfeldt 1999; Ronfeldt 1999; Whine 1999a, 1999b; Zanini 1999), but the more systematic studies of terrorism and the mass media published in the 1990s and 1980s dealt typically with newspapers, news magazines, and the evening news programs of the over-the-air television networks.

As serious news organizations move increasingly away from reporting what journalists/gatekeepers deem *important* for the enlightenment of fellow citizens to what profit-oriented corporate managers consider *interesting* for the entertainment of news consumers, "hard" news is increasingly crowded out by "soft" news (Bennett 2001, 12–15). As a result, most news offered in the twenty-first century is essentially a blend between "hard" information and "soft" entertainment—infotainment in the guise of news reporting. The around-the-clock, "all the news all the time," television channels and the proliferation of the news magazine format in television have driven this trend (Seib 2001). Infotainment, far more than informative hard news, strives on the very images and themes that terrorist incidents offer—drama, tragedy, shock, anger, grief, fear, panic—the ideal ingredients for transforming real life terror into breathtaking thrillers or heartbreaking soap operas designed to captivate and stir up audiences.

Journalists are aware of the impact that powerful visual images of terror have on those who are exposed to them. Thus, in a dispatch about the aftermath of five simultaneous bomb explosions in the Philippines in late December 2000 that killed twenty-two people and injured 124 men, women, and children, the Associated Press reported from Manila that "graphic media images heightened the sense of insecurity. Television showed an unconscious boy in the hospital after his leg was amputated, and one newspaper carried a front-page photo of a rescue worker carrying a little girl's mangled body."[16] Whether the deadly bombs were detonated by members of one of the country's Muslim separatist groups, the Moro Islamic Liberation Front or the Abu Sayyaf, or by the left-wing New People's Army mattered less than the fact that the grim media images in the wake of the multiple terror actions shook up the populace, the government, and the law enforcement community—certainly a major goal of the perpetrators, who wanted to undermine the Philippine people's trust in their government's ability to protect them.

To repeat an earlier point: The argument here is not that the news media in general or journalists in particular sympathize with the perpetrators of political violence, but rather that they are *unwitting* accomplices of media-savvy terrorists. This is not a new development. However, as the move from news-as-information to news-as-entertainment continues, especially in television, media organizations seem increasingly inclined to exploit terrorism as infotainment for their own imperatives (i.e., ratings and circulation). More than ever before, terrorists and the media are in a quasi-symbiotic relationship. As Wilkinson suggests,

> The media in an open society are in a fiercely competitive market for their audiences, are constantly under pressure to be first with the news and to provide more information, excitement and entertainment than their rivals. Hence, they are almost bound to respond to terrorist propaganda of the deed because it is dramatic bad news. (Wilkinson 2001, 177).

The attacks in the United States on September 11, 2001, and the subsequent anthrax letters amount to the worst terrorist assaults imaginable and, consequently, to the worst kind of "dramatic bad news" that Wilkinson mentioned as irresistible to the media.

## Notes

1. Tom Raum, "Bush hunts Florida votes." http://dailynews.yahoo.com/h/ap/ 20001025/el/bush_6.html [accessed 25 October 2000]; and Carter M. Yang, "Gore attacks Bush on education." http://dailynews.yahoo.com/h/abc/20001025/pl/ 20001025003.html [accessed 25 October 2000].

2. McVeigh revealed a great deal about his right-wing ideology, his motives, and his desire for publicity in interviews with reporters Lou Michel and Dan Herbeck from the *Buffalo News* in April 2001. See also Lou Michel and Dan Herbeck, *American Terrorist: Timothy McVeigh & the Oklahoma City Bombing* (New York: ReganBooks, 2001), esp. 168, 169, 227, 245, and 382.

3. Nasra Hassan, "An arsenal of believers," *New Yorker* (19 November 2000): 38.

4. Based on what bin Laden said in this particular news conference as well as in other communications, it was not difficult to pinpoint him as the driving force behind the bombings in East Africa. The quotes from his news conference in Khost, Afghanistan, are from Dale Van Atta (1998), 66.

5. See Hamza Hendawi, "Terror manual advises on targets." http://story.news .yahoo.com/news?tmpl=story&u=/ap/20.../afhan_spreading_terror_ [accessed 11 February 2002].

6. Marighela is quoted here from Schmid and de Graaf (1982), 19.

7. Christopher C. Joyner is quoted here from Kegley (1990), 11. See chapter 1 of Kegley for a good discussion of the definitional difficulties. Although his book is about international terrorism, the issues arising from various views about an appropriate definition of the term *terrorism* are applicable to domestic terrorism as well.

8. The Thanh Phong incident was investigated by Gregory L. Vistica, who also interviewed Bob Kerrey. See Gregory L. Vistica, "What happened in Thanh Phong," *The New York Times Magazine* (29 April 2001).

9. Perez is quoted here from Clyde Haberman, "In the Mid-East this year, even words shoot to kill," *New York Times,* 5 August 2001, section 4, p. 3.

10. Ariel Sharon is quoted here from Haberman, section 4, p. 3.

11. The nuclear bombs that devastated Hiroshima and Nagasaki and the destruction of Dresden, Germany, in the last phase of World War II targeted and killed many civilians. In both instances these acts were justified as parts of a declared war and as efforts to end the hostilities quickly to spare the lives of American GIs involved in the battle against Japan and of surviving victims of Nazi terror in Germany's concentration camps. Whether one accepts or rejects such justifications, this sort of violence against civilian populations is dealt with in the context of war—not terrorism.

12. Senator Nunn is quoted here from Christopher Drew, "Japanese sect tried to buy U.S. arms technology, Senator says," *New York Times,* 31 October 1995.

13. This remark was made during Rumsfeld's confirmation hearings before the Judiciary Committee of the U.S. Senate in early 2001. See Charles Aldinger, "Bush Pentagon nominee says missile defense need." http://dailynews.yahoo.com/h/nm/ 20010111/pl/rumsfeld_missiles_dc_2.html [accessed 1 April 2002].

14. The Jordanian on death row was quoted in Judith Miller, "On Jordan's death row, convicted terrorist says he has no regrets." http://www.nytimes.com/2001/01/15/world/15TERR.html [accessed 1 April 2002].

15. This information is based on a description by Richard J. Sheirer, the Director of the Mayor's Office of Emergency Management for the City of New York, at the conference on "Responding to Acts of Terrorism," organized by the National Institute for Government Innovation. Los Angeles, 16–18 July 2001.

16. "Philippine police cite lead in hunt for bombers. http://www.nytimes.com/aponline/world/AP-Philippines-Explosions.html [accessed 31 December 2000].

# 2

# Terrorism as Breaking News: Attack on America

TUESDAY, SEPTEMBER 11, 2001, BEGAN AS A PERFECT DAY along the American East coast. The sun was golden bright. The sky was blue and cloudless. On a clear day like this, the World Trade Center's twin towers resembled two exclamation marks above Manhattan's skyline, and they could be seen from many miles away in the surrounding counties of three states—New York, New Jersey, and Connecticut. At 8:48 A.M., when the workday began for thousands of employees in the offices of the 110 stories of the Center's towers, a hijacked Boeing 767 crashed into the North Tower. Eighteen minutes later, at 9:06 A.M., another Boeing 767 crashed into the South Tower. Just before 10:00 A.M., the South Tower collapsed, and twenty-nine minutes later, its twin fell down. In between these events, at 9:40 A.M., a Boeing 757 dived into the Pentagon; at 10:10, another Boeing 757 crashed in Somerset county near Pittsburgh, Pennsylvania. September 11, 2001 was forever America's "Black Tuesday."

Within eighty-two minutes, the United States suffered a series of synchronized attacks that terminated in the most deadly, most damaging case of terrorism in history. More than three thousand persons were killed, and the damage to properties, to businesses, and to the economic conditions in the United States and abroad was incalculable. With the symbol of America's economic and financial power toppled in New York, the symbol of U.S. military strength partially destroyed in Washington, and a symbol of political influence—most likely the White House or Capitol—spared by courageous citizens aboard another jetliner that crashed near Pittsburgh, Pennsylvania, the impact was cataclysmic. America after the terror attack was not the same as it was before. Although the World Trade Center bombing of 1993 demonstrated that the United States is not immune to international terrorism on its own soil, and the Y2K terrorism alert reinforced that recognition, Americans were stunned by the velocity and audacity of the 2001 strike.

Apart from the relatively small number of people who were alerted by relatives and friends via phone calls from the stricken WTC towers and those eyewitnesses who watched in horror, millions of Americans learned of the news from television, radio, or the Internet. In fact, minutes after the first kamikaze flight into Tower I, local radio and television stations as well as the networks reported first a possible explosion in the WTC, then a plane crash into one of the towers. Soon thereafter, the first pictures of the North Tower appeared on the screens, with a gapping hole in the upper floors enveloped in a huge cloud of dark smoke. As anchors, hosts of morning shows, and reporters struggled to find words to describe what was indescribable, a mighty fireball shot out of Tower II—presumably the result of a second powerful explosion. The towering inferno was eventually replaced by another horror scene: one section of the headquarters of the Department of Defense engulfed in a large plume of smoke. With the cameras again on the WTC, the South Tower collapsed in what seemed like slow motion. Switching again to the Pentagon, the camera revealed a collapsed section of the facade. Amid rumors that a fourth airliner had crashed in Pennsylvania, the cameras caught the collapse of the World Trade Center's North Tower.

For at least part of this unfolding horror, many millions of Americans watched television stations or their related Internet sites. And, ironically, most Americans were familiar with the shocking images: the inferno in a skyscraper, the terrorist attack on a towering high rise, the total destruction of a federal building in the nation's capital by terrorists, the nuclear winter landscape in American cities, Manhattan under siege after a massive terrorist attack. In search of box office hits, Hollywood produced a steady stream of disaster movies and thrillers, often based on best-selling novels about ever more gruesome images of destruction. The entertainment industry's cavalier exploitation of violence was shockingly obvious following the terror strikes, when it was revealed that the "planned cover for a hip-hop album due to be released in November [2001] depicted an exploding World Trade Center."[1]

In a popular culture inundated with images of violence, Americans could not comprehend what was happening before their eyes and what had happened already. The horror of the quadruple hijack and suicide coup was as real as in a movie, but it was surreal in life. As Michiko Kakutani observed, "there was an initial sense of déjà vu and disbelief on the part of these spectators—the impulse to see what was happening as one of those digital special effects from the big screen."[2] The following quotations reflect the reactions of people who escaped from the World Trade Center, witnessed the disaster, or watched it on television:

I looked over my shoulder and saw the United Airlines plane coming. It came over the Statue of Liberty. It was just like a movie. It just directly was guided into the second tower.

—Laksman Achuthan, managing director of the Economic Cycle Research Institute[3]

I think I'm going to die of smoke inhalation, because you know, in fires most people don't die of burning, they die of smoke inhalation. This cop or somebody walks by with a flashlight. It's like a strange movie. I grab the guy by the collar and walk with him.

—Howard W. Lutnick, chairman of Cantor Fitzgerald[4]

I looked up and saw this hole in the World Trade Center building. And I—I couldn't believe it. I thought, you know, this can't be happening. This is a special effect; it's a movie.

—Clifton Cloud, who filmed disaster with his video camera[5]

It's insane. It's just like a movie. It's, it's actually surreal to me to see it on TV and see major buildings collapse.

—Unidentified man in Canada[6]

This is very surreal. Well, it's out of a bad sci-fi film, but every morning we wake up and you're like it wasn't a dream, it wasn't a movie. It actually happened.

—Unidentified woman in New York[7]

Witnessing the calamity from a tenth-floor apartment in Brooklyn, novelist John Updike felt that "the destruction of the World Trade Center twin towers had the false intimacy of television, on a day of perfect reception."[8] Many people who joined newscasts in progress thought that they were watching the promotion for one of several terrorism thrillers scheduled for release later in the month. Whether they realized it or not, and many did not, most people, even eye-witnesses at the disaster scenes, were far from sure whether movies had turned into life, or whether life was now a movie. Updike alluded to this sentiment, when he recalled the experience:

> As we watched the second tower burst into ballooning flame (an intervening building had hidden the approach of the second airplane), there persisted the notion that, as on television, this was not quite real; it could be fixed; the technocracy the towers symbolized would find a way to put out the fire and reverse the damage.[9]

In a seemingly inexplicable lapse of judgment, the German composer Karlheinz Stockhausen characterized the terror attacks on the United States as "the greatest work of art."[10] His remarks caused outrage in his country and the abrupt cancellation of two of his concerts in Hamburg. Perhaps this was a case of total confusion between the real world and the "pictures in our heads" that Walter Lippmann (1949) described long before the advent of television. In particular, Lippmann suggested that "[f]or the most part we do not first see, and then define, we define first and then see."[11] While many people initially identified the horrors of "Black Tuesday" as familiar motion picture images, Stockhausen may have processed the real life horror first as a symphonic Armageddon in his head, when he said: "That characters can bring about in one act what we in music cannot dream of, that people practice madly for 10 years, completely fanatically, for a concert and then die. That is the greatest work of art for the whole cosmos." Following the uproar over his statement, Stockhausen apologized for his remarks saying, "Not for one moment have I thought or felt the way my words are now being interpreted in the press."[12] One can only guess that the angry reactions to his statement brought him back from the pseudo-reality in his head to the real life tragedy and its consequences.

When emotions gave way to rationality, the truth began to sink in. The most outrageous production of the terrorist genre was beyond the imagination of the best special effects creators. This was not simply two hours worth of suspense. Real terrorists had transformed Hollywood's pseudo-reality into an unbearable reality, into real life. This time there was neither a happy ending to be enjoyed nor an unhappy ending that the audience could forget quickly.

Perhaps the temporary confusion was a blessing. Perhaps the fact that reality replaced media-reality in slow motion helped people cope with the unprecedented catastrophe within America's borders. Perhaps the delayed tape in people's heads prevented citizens in the stricken areas from panicking, helped citizens all over the country to keep their bearings.

The greatest irony is that the terrorists who loathed America's pop culture as decadent and poisonous to their own beliefs and ways of life turned Hollywood-like horror fantasies into real life hell. In that respect, they outperformed Hollywood, the very symbol of their hate for western entertainment. After visiting the World Trade Center disaster site for the first time, New York's Governor George Pataki said:

> It's incredible. It's just incomprehensible to see what it was like down there. You know, I remember seeing one of these Cold War movies and after the nuclear attacks with the Hollywood portrayal of a nuclear winter. It looked worse than that in downtown Manhattan, and it wasn't some grade "B" movie. It was life. It was real.[13]

The question of whether imaginative novelists and filmmakers anticipate terrorist scenarios or whether terrorists borrow from the most horrific images of Hollywood's disaster films was no longer academic. Shortly after the events of

September 11th, an ongoing cooperation between filmmakers and the U.S. Army intensified in order to predict the forms of future terrorist attacks. The idea was that the writers who created Hollywood terrorism might be best equipped to conceptualize terrorists' intentions. According to Michael Macedonia, the chief scientist of the Army's Simulation, Training, and Instrumentation Command, "You're talking about screenwriters and producers, that's one of the things that they're paid to do every day—speculate. These are very brilliant, creative people. They can come up with fascinating insights very quickly."[14] However, it was not farfetched to suspect that the perpetrators of the 9–11 terror took special delight in borrowing from some of the most horrific Hollywood images in planning and executing their terrorist scheme.

## The Perfect "Breaking News" Production

From the terrorists' point of view, the attack on America was a perfectly choreographed production aimed at American and international audiences. In the past, terrorism has often been compared to theater. According to this explanation,

> Modern terrorism can be understood in terms of the production requirements of theatrical engagements. Terrorists pay attention to script preparation, cast selection, sets, props, role playing, and minute-by-minute stage management (Weiman and Winn 1994, 52).

While the theater metaphor remains instructive, it has given way to that of terrorism as television spectacular, as breaking news that is watched by record audiences and far transcends the boundaries of theatrical events. And unlike the most successful producers of theater, motion picture, or television hits, the perpetrators of the lethal attacks on America affected their audience in unprecedented and lasting ways. "I will never forget!" These or similar words were uttered over and over.

After President John F. Kennedy was assassinated in 1963, most Americans and many people abroad eventually saw the fatal shots and the ensuing events on television. But beyond the United States and other western countries, far fewer people abroad owned television sets at the time. When the Palestinian "Black September" group attacked and killed members of the Israeli team during the 1972 Olympic games in Munich (using their surviving victims as human shields during their ill-fated escape), an estimated eight hundred million people around the globe watched the unfolding tragedy. At the time, satellite TV transmission facilities were in place to broadcast the competitions into most parts of the world. But nearly thirty years later, a truly global television network, CNN, existed along with competitors that televised their programs across national borders and covered large regions of the world. Thus, more people watched the made-for-television disaster production "Attack on America," live and in replays, than any other terrorist incident before. It is likely that the terrorist assaults on New York and Washington and their aftermath were the most watched made-for-television production ever.

From the perspective of those who produced this unprecedented, terrorism-as-breaking-news horror show, the broadcast was as successful as it could get. Whether a relatively inconsequential arson by an amateurish environmental group or a mass destruction by a network of professional terrorists, the perpetrators' media-related goals are the same: terrorists strive for attention, for recognition, and for respectability and legitimacy in their various target publics (Nacos 1994a, 1996b; O'Sullivan 1986). It has been argued that contemporary religious terrorists, unlike secular terrorists (such as the Marxists of the Red Brigade/Red Army or the nationalists of the Palestinian Liberation Front during the last decades of the Cold War), want nothing more than to lash out at the enemy and kill and damage indiscriminately, to express their rage. But while all of these sentiments may well figure into the complex motives of group leaders and their followers, there is no doubt that their deeds are planned and executed with the mass media and their effects on the masses and governmental decision makers in mind. Unlike the typical secular terrorists, religious terrorists want to inflict the greatest possible pain, but they want a whole country, and in the case of international terrorism, the whole world, to see their act, to understand the roots of their rage, to solidify their esteem in their constituencies, and, perhaps, to win new supporters.

To be sure, publicity via the mass media is not an end in itself. Most terrorists have very specific short-term and/or long-term goals. It is not hard to determine the short-term and long-term objectives of those that planned and executed the suicide missions against the United States. Even without the benefit of a credible claim of responsibility, the mass media, decision makers, and the general public in the United States and abroad discussed the most likely motives for the unprecedented deeds. In the short-term, the architects and perpetrators wanted to demonstrate the weaknesses of the world's only remaining superpower vis-à-vis determined terrorists, to frighten the American public, and to fuel perhaps a weakening of civil liberties and domestic unrest. No doubt, the long-term schemes targeted U.S. foreign policy, especially the American influence and presence in the Middle East and other regions with large Muslim populations. More important, as communications from Osama bin Laden and his organization revealed, those who decided on these particular terror attacks regarded the anticipated strikes by the United States as the beginning of a holy war between Muslims and infidels. Bin Laden, in a fax to Qatar-based al-Jazeera television, called the Muslims of Pakistan "the first line of defense . . . against the new Jewish crusader campaign [that] is led by the biggest crusader Bush under the banner of the cross.[15] The bin Laden statement that was widely publicized in the United States left no doubt that he purposely characterized the confrontation as a battle between Islam and "the new Christian-Jewish crusade."[16]

Whatever else their immediate and ultimate goals were, those who planned the attacks were well aware, as are most perpetrators of political violence, that the mass media of communication is central to furthering their publicity goals and even their political and religious objectives. Without the frightening images and the shocking reportage, the impact on America and the rest of the world wouldn't have been as immediate and intense as it was.

## When Terrorists Strike Hard, They Command Attention

In the past, media critics have documented and questioned the mass media's insatiable appetite for violence; they have explored the effects of this kind of media content on people who are regularly exposed to violence in the news and in entertainment (Gerbner and Gross 1976; Nacos 1996b; Bok 1998; Wolfsfeld 2001). While violence-as-crime and violence-as-terrorism tend to be grossly over-reported, the coverage of terrorist incidents that provide dramatic visuals is in a league of its own in terms of media attention. With few exceptions, ordinary criminals do not commit their deeds to attract cameras, microphones, and reporter's notebooks. But for terrorists, as chapter 1 explained, publicity is their lifeblood and their oxygen. No other medium has provided more oxygen to terrorism than television because of its ability to report the news instantly, nonstop, and in visuals and words from any place to all parts of the globe, a facility that has affected the reporting patterns of other media as well.

When commentators characterized the terrorist events of "Black Tuesday" as the Pearl Harbor of the twenty-first century or the second Pearl Harbor, they ignored one fundamental aspect that separated the surprise attack on December 7, 1941, from that on September 11, 2001: the vastly different communication technologies. Three hours passed from the time the first bombs fell on Pearl Harbor and the moment when people on the U.S. mainland first learned the news from radio broadcasts. More than a week lapsed before the *New York Times* carried the first pictures of the actual damages. Sixty years later, the terror attacks had a live global TV, radio, and Internet audience and many replays in the following hours, days, and weeks.

In September 1970, members of the Popular Front for the Liberation of Palestine (PFLP) simultaneously hijacked four New York-bound airliners carrying more than six hundred passengers. Eventually, three of the planes landed in a remote part of Jordan, where many passengers, most of them Americans and Europeans, were held for approximately three weeks. This was high drama. The media reported extensively, but the reporting paled in comparison to the great attention devoted to equally as dramatic or far less shocking incidents in later years. The communication technology at the time did not allow live transmissions from remote locations. Satellite transmissions were in their early stages and were very expensive. For the PFLP, the multiple hijacking episode ended in disappointment. While the tense situation resulted in media, public, and government attention, no news organization covered the events in ways that might have forced President Richard Nixon and European leaders to act under pressure.[17]

But as television technology advanced further and competition among TV, radio, and print organizations became fiercer, the media became more obsessed with exploiting violence-as-crime and violence-as-terrorism in search of higher ratings and circulation. As a result, the contemporary news media, especially television, have customarily devoted huge chunks of their broadcast time and news columns to major and minor acts of political violence (see chapter 3), supporting media critics' argument that the mass media, as unwitting as they are, facilitate the media-centered terrorist scheme.

There was no need to count broadcast minutes or measure column length to establish the proportion of the total news that dealt with "Black Tuesday" and its aftermath. For the first five days after the terror attack, television and radio networks covered the disaster around the clock without the otherwise obligatory commercial breaks. There simply was no other news. Most sports and entertainment channels switched to crisis news, many of them carrying the coverage of one of the networks and suspending their suddenly irrelevant broadcasts. For example, Fox cable's sports channel in New York simply showed the image of the U.S. flag. Newspapers and magazines devoted all or most of their news to the crisis. Given the warlike dimension of the attacks on America, this seemed the right decision early on. Eventually one wondered whether terrorism coverage needed to be curtailed a bit so that other important news got the attention it deserved. *Newsweek* and *TIME*, for example, devoted all cover stories in the eight weeks following the events of 9–11 to terrorism and terrorism-related themes.

If not the perpetrators themselves, the architects of the terror enterprise surely anticipated the immediate media impact: blanket coverage not only in the United States but in other parts of the world as well. How could the terrorists better achieve their objective than by obtaining the attention of their targeted audiences? Opinion polls revealed that literally all Americans followed the initial news of the terrorist attacks (99% or 100% according to surveys) by watching and listening to television and radio broadcasts. While most on-line adults identified television and radio as their primary sources for crisis information, nearly two thirds also mentioned the Internet as one of their information sources.[18] This initial universal interest in terrorism news did not weaken quickly. Probably affected by the news of anthrax attacks along the U.S. East coast, more than 90% of the public kept on watching the news about terrorism "very closely" or "closely" nearly six weeks after the events of 9–11.[19]

Political leaders as well followed the original terror news, replays, and subsequent crisis reporting. There is no doubt, then, that the terrorists behind the attack on America received the attention of all Americans, the general public, and world leaders alike. This level of media coverage was a perfect achievement as far as the "attention getting" goal in the United States was concerned. The architects of the 9–11 terror were delighted. Referring to the kamikaze pilots as "vanguards of Islam," bin Laden marveled,

> Those young men ( ... inaudible ... ) said in deeds, in New York and Washington, speeches that overshadowed other speeches made everywhere else in the world. The speeches are understood by both Arabs and non-Arabs—even Chinese.[20]

With these remarks, bin Laden revealed that he considers terrorism a vehicle to dispatch messages—speeches in his words. And since he and his circle had followed the news of 9–11, they were sure that their message had been heard.

Not surprisingly, from one hour to the next, the perpetrators set America's public agenda and profoundly affected most Americans' private lives. As soon as television stations played and replayed the ghastly scenes of jetliners being deliberately flown into the World Trade Center and the Pentagon, business as usual was suspended in the public and private sector. All levels of government and vast parts of the business community concentrated on the immediate rescue contingencies and on preventing further attacks that were rumored in the media. Within days, all levels of government and the business community began to implement new anti- and counterterrorist measures. (For a discussion of the politics of counterterrorism, see chapter 5.) All of this was thoroughly reported by the news media, as was the fact that most Americans no longer lived ordinary lives in one respect or another.

Those who were responsible for the acts of terror spread anxiety and fear in a public traumatized by their terror. Fifty-three percent of the American public across the United States, not simply those in the attacked regions in the East, changed their plans and activities for the rest of "Black Tuesday"; four of every ten employed men and women did not go to work that day or quit their jobs.[21] In the days after the assault, nine in ten Americans worried about additional terrorist events in their country, and a majority worried that they themselves, or somebody close to them, could become victims the next time around. Compared with the public's reaction to previous acts of terrorism, these sentiments were stronger than ever before. For example, in the days after the 1995 Oklahoma City bombing, one in four Americans worried that they, or a member of their family, could become victims of terrorism. In the days after the 2001 attacks on New York and Washington, 51% to 58% of the public had such fears.[22] This is precisely what the architect of terror intended. In a videotaped message, Osama bin Laden said about the reactions of Americans to the terror of 9–11, "There is America, full of fear from north to south, from west to east. Thank God for that."[23] These concerns did not evaporate as time passed. Instead, most Americans continued to be concerned about further terrorist attacks and that they, or a member of their family, could become a victim the next time around.[24] However, the number of those who felt depressed and/or had trouble sleeping in the days following the suicide attacks decreased quite dramatically during the following weeks.[25]

When President George W. Bush, New York's Mayor Rudy Giuliani, and other public officials urged Americans to return to quasi-normal lives, the media's crisis coverage did not reflect that public officials in Washington had returned to normalcy. There were pictures of Washington's Reagan National Airport remaining closed because of its proximity to the White House and other government buildings. There was an image of a fighter jet over Washington escorting the presidential helicopter on a flight to Camp David. There were reports explaining Vice-President Richard Cheney's absence, when the President addressed a joint session of Congress and in the weeks thereafter, as a precaution, in case terrorists might strike again. And there were constant visuals of a tireless Mayor Giuliani as crisis-manager before the daunting background of ground zero in Manhattan's financial district, at the funeral of yet another police- or fireman, at a mass at St. Patrick's Cathedral, or at a prayer service in Yankee stadium.

Every public appearance by the President, New York City's Mayor, New York state's Governor George Pataki, U.S. Senators, U.S. Representatives, members of the Bush administration; every hearing and floor debate in the two chambers of Congress; and every publicly announced decision was in reaction to the terrorist attack and was reported in the news. Even weeks after "Black Tuesday" and during the anthrax scare, CNN and other all-news channels interrupted their programs not only to report on President Bush's public appearances but on Mayor Giuliani's activities as well. And when the broadcast networks returned to their normal schedules, the around-the-clock news channels continued to report mostly on terrorism and counterterrorism in the form of military actions against targets in Afghanistan that began on October 7th.

When professional sports competition resumed after a moratorium of several days, watching sports broadcasts did not necessarily mean that fans could forget the horror for a while. Unwittingly the media transmitted constant reminders: Baseball fans in Chicago displaying a "We Love New York" banner; American flags were placed on helmets and caps of competitors; a hockey game was interrupted so that players and fans could hear the presidential speech before Congress; players praised rescue workers at the terror sites and embraced members of a rival team in an expression of unity. The sports pages of newspapers captured the reactions of well-known sports stars; the American flag on the cover of Sports Illustrated signaled that the entire issue following 9–11 was devoted to patriotism.

Entertainment as well was in the grasp of the horrendous acts. When David Letterman resumed his late-night show, he was unusually serious and made no attempts to be funny. Instead of offering hilarious punch lines, he found words of comfort for news anchor Dan Rather who was twice moved to tears when talking about the terror next door. *Saturday Night Live*, Comedy Central, and other entertainment shows were all less aggressive in provoking laughter at the expense of political leaders. Bill Maher of ABC's *Politically Incorrect* was the exception when he told his audience that the suicide bombers were not cowards but that the United States was cowardly by launching cruise missiles on targets thousands of miles away. Maher, who later apologized for his remarks, was criticized by White House spokesman Ari Fleischer and punished by some advertisers who withdrew their sponsorship; some local stations dropped the program. Even poking fun at bin Laden and the Taliban, as Jay Leno and the *Saturday Night Live* performers did, seemed not all that funny. Some publications, such as the *New York Times*, suspended their weekly cartoon section for a while. And when a star-studded cast of entertainers performed in a two-hour telethon to raise funds for the victims of terror, the celebrities told touching stories of innocent victims and real-life heroes. But nothing reminded the American audience more succinctly of the extraordinary circumstances behind the benefit than the sight of superstars Jack Nicholson, Sylvester Stallone, Meg Ryan, Whoopi Goldberg, and other show business celebrities relegated to answer telephone calls of contributors, since the producers had not found slots for them to perform in the program. Finally, even the most outrageous TV and radio talk show hosts toned down their personalities as they embraced the terror crisis story, albeit only for a short time.

When the television series *The West Wing* postponed its scheduled season-opener and replaced it with a special episode in which the White House dealt with the aftermath of a terrorist nightmare, the blur of fact and fiction, life and entertainment, came full circle. After Hollywood's make-believe disasters became reality, when nineteen suicide terrorists struck America, the real-life calamity inspired a television drama and ideas for more such episodes to come.

Whether tuned to the coverage of current affairs, sports news, or even entertainment, Americans had a hard time forgetting about terrorism for a while. Although most people agreed that TV programs about the attacks on the World Trade Center and the Pentagon, and later the news about anthrax bioterror, were depressing and frightening, many people simply could not stop watching terrorism news. While this addiction was true for six of every ten Americans in the middle of September, only one in two Americans were still watching this sort of coverage by mid-October. At the same time, a vast majority felt that watching terrorism news was frightening. Not surprisingly, people who were hooked felt more fearful of future terrorism than those who were not addicted.[26]

Not only Americans but people abroad, too, knew quickly about the terrorist attacks on the United States and were affected by what they saw, heard, and read. The Gallup Organization found, for example, that more than 98% of the Hungarian public knew about the terror soon after it happened. This caused one commentator to conclude, "If there were any remaining doubts about the media's capacity to almost simultaneously disseminate global news, this poll's finding should serve to dispel it."[27] Reacting to the news, the majority of Hungarians (51.2%) were "very" or "somewhat" worried that they, or someone in their family, could become a victim of terrorism.[28] Equally informed, 83% of people in the United Kingdom and 76% of the Russian public shared those fears.[29] Even a cursory examination of the media around the world affirmed what journalists reported from those regions: For weeks after the terror attack on the United States and before the first counterterrorist strikes against targets in Afghanistan, the event, its political, economic, and military implications, and the threat of a major military confrontation in the Middle East, remained highest on the media, public, and elite agenda.

As media organizations, star anchors, and public officials became the targets of biological terrorism and postal workers became the most numerous victims of "collateral damage" in an unprecedented anthrax offensive by elusive terrorist(s), the news devoted to terrorism multiplied—especially in the United States but abroad as well. The aftermath of the 9–11 terror—the anthrax cases, the debate of possibly more biological and chemical agents in the arsenal of terrorists, and the military actions against al-Qaeda and Taliban targets in Afghanistan—crowded out most other events and developments in the news. Terrorists and terrorism had set the media agenda, the public agenda, and the government agenda. To the terrorists, the attention of the mass media, the public, and governmental decision makers was a total victory.

## Why Do They Hate Us?

Sixteen days after the attacks on New York and Washington, the *Christian Science Monitor* published an in-depth article addressing a question that President Bush had posed in his speech before a joint session of Congress: "Why do they hate us?" Describing a strong resentment toward America in the Arab and Islamic world, Peter Ford summarized the grievances articulated by Osama bin Laden and like-minded extremists, but also held by many less radical people in the Middle East and other Muslim regions, when he wrote that

> the buttons that Mr. bin Laden pushes in statements and interviews—the injustice done to the Palestinians, the cruelty of continued sanctions against Iraq, the presence of US troops in Saudi-Arabia, the repressive and corrupt nature of the US backed Gulf governments—win a good deal of popular sympathy.[30]

This lengthy article was but one of many similar reports and analytical background pieces tracing the roots of anti-American attitudes among Arabs and Muslims and possible causes for a new anti-American terrorism of mass destruction. Lisa Beyer offered this summary of grievances in her story in *TIME* magazine:

> The proximate source of this brand of hatred toward America is U.S. foreign policy (read: meddling) in the Middle East. On top of its own controversial history in the region, the United States inherits the weight of centuries of Muslim bitterness over the Crusades and other military campaigns, plus decades of indignation over colonialism.[31]

A former U.S. Ambassador at Large for Counterterrorism wrote,

> Certainly, the U.S. should reappraise its policies concerning the Israeli-Palestinian conflict and Iraq, which have bred deep anger against America in the Arab and Islamic world, where much terrorism originates and whose cooperation is now more critical than ever.[32]

While the print press examined the roots of the deeply seated opposition to U.S. foreign policy in the Arab and Islamic world extensively, television and radio dealt with these questions as well—in some instances at considerable length and depth. Thus, in the two-and-a-half weeks that followed the terrorist attacks, the major television networks and National Public Radio broadcast thirty-three stories that addressed the roots of anti-American terrorism of the sort committed on September 11, 2001, the motives of the perpetrators, and, specifically, the question that President Bush had asked. In the more than eight months before the attacks on New York and Washington, from January 1, 2001 to "Black Tuesday," none of the same TV or radio programs addressed the causes of anti-American sentiments in the Arab and Islamic world.[33] This turnaround demonstrated the ability of terrorists to force the media's hand, to set the media's agenda. Suddenly, in the wake of terrorist violence of unprecedented proportions, the news explored and explained the grievances of those who died for their causes and how widely these grievances were shared even by the vast majority of those Arabs and Muslims who condemned violence committed in the United States. With or without referring to a *fatwa* (religious verdict) that Osama bin Laden and four other extremist leaders had issued in 1998, or to the most recent communications from these circles, the news media now dealt with the charges contained in these statements as well as with additional issues raised by Muslims in the Middle East and elsewhere. The 1998 *fatwa*, posted on the Web site of the World Islamic Front, listed three points in particular:

> First, for over seven years the United States has been occupying the lands of Islam in the holiest places, the Arabian Peninsula. . . . If some people have in the past argued about the fact of the occupation, all people of the Peninsula have now acknowledged it. The best proof of this is the Americans' continuing aggression against the Iraqi people using the Peninsula as a staging post. . . .
>
> Second, despite the great devastation inflicted on the Iraqi people by the crusader-Zionist alliance, and despite the huge number of those killed, which has exceeded 1 million . . . despite all this, the Americans are once again trying to repeat the horrific massacres. . . .
>
> Third, if the Americans' aims behind these wars are religious and economic, the aim is also to serve the Jews' petty state and divert attention from its occupation of Jerusalem and murder of Muslims there.[34]

These specific accusations were among a whole laundry list of grievances that the media explored in the wake of the terrorism in New York and Washington. And the existence of bin Laden's various declarations of hate were reported as news although they were issued as far back as 1996 and 1998.

It has been argued that religious fanatics who resort to this sort of violence are not at all interested in explaining themselves to their enemies because their only conversation is with God. But it was hardly an accident that the leaders among the suicide attackers, who diligently planned every detail of their conspiracy, left behind several copies of their instructions in the hours before and during the attacks. By insuring that law enforcement agents would find the documents, the terrorists must have been confident that America and the world would learn of their cause. They were proven right when the FBI released copies of the four-page, handwritten document to the media for publication. Revealing the pseudoreligious belief that drove the hijackers to mass destruction and their own deaths, the instructional memorandum contained the following sentences:

> Remember that this is a battle for the sake of God. . . .
>     So remember God, as He said in His book: "Oh Lord, pour your patience upon us and make our feet steadfast and give us victory over the infidels." . . .
>     When the confrontation begins, strike like champions who do not want to go back to this world. Shout, "Allah Akbar," because this strikes fear in the hearts of the non-believers. God said: "Strike above the neck, and strike at all their extremities." Know that the gardens of paradise are waiting for you in all their beauty, and the woman of paradise are waiting, calling out, "Come hither, friend of God."[35]

The intent here is not to criticize the media for publicizing such documents, for trying to answer why terrorists hate Americans and why many nonviolent people in the Arab and Islamic world hold anti-American sentiments, but rather to point out that this coverage and the accompanying mass-mediated discourse were triggered by a deliberate act of mass destruction terrorism. After 9–11 there was a tremendous jump in the quantity of news reports about one of the other aspects of developments in the Muslim and Arab world and even more so about Islam. Television news especially paid little attention to these topics before the terror attacks in New York and Washington. But, as table 2.1 shows, the switch from scarce or modest coverage before 9–11 to far more news prominence thereafter occurred in radio and the print press as well. While many of these news segments and stories focused on anti-American

**TABLE 2.1**
**Muslim(s), Arab(s), Islam in the News before and after September 11, 2001**

|           | Muslim Period I | Muslim Period II | Arab Period I | Arab Period II | Islam Period I | Islam Period II |
|-----------|------|------|------|------|------|------|
|           | (N)  | (N)  | (N)  | (N)  | (N)  | (N)  |
| ABC News  | 31   | 163  | 11   | 99   | 1    | 31   |
| CBS News  | 32   | 144  | 27   | 117  | 1    | 27   |
| NBC News  | 9    | 98   | 5    | 90   | —    | 18   |
| CNN       | 23   | 203  | 43   | 200  | 1    | 31   |
| Fox News  | 1    | 100  | 2    | 64   | 1    | 46   |
| N.Y. Times| 345  | 1,468| 345  | 1,272| 216  | 1,190|
| NPR       | 54   | 217  | 53   | 182  | 10   | 84   |

N = Number of news segments/articles mentioning the search words.
*Source*: Compiled from Lexis-Nexis and *New York Times* archives using the search words "Muslim," "Arab," and "Islam."
*Note*: Period I = Six months before the terrorist attacks of September 11, 2001; Period II = six months after the attacks of 9–11.

terrorism committed by Muslim and Arab perpetrators and the role of fundamentalist Islamic teachings, there were also many stories reporting on and examining the grievances of the mass of nonviolent Muslims and Arabs as well as the teachings of mainstream Islam.

Before "Black Tuesday," the news from the Middle East and other Islamic regions was overwhelmingly episodic and focused on particular, typically violent, events. Following the Iran Hostage crisis, one critic noted that "Muslims and Arabs are essentially covered, discussed, apprehended either as oil suppliers or as potential terrorists. Very little of the detail, the human density, the passion of Arab-Muslim life has entered the awareness of even those people whose profession it is to report the Islamic world" (Said 1981, 26). Given the scarcity of foreign news in the post–Cold War era in the American mass media, especially television (Hickey 1998), there was even less contextual news or "thematic" stories (Iyengar 1991) from this part of the world. But it would have been precisely the thematic approach that should have addressed all along the conditions that breed anti-American attitudes in the Arab and Muslim world. It took the terror of "Black Tuesday" for the media to offer a significant amount of contextual coverage along with episodic reporting. In the process, the perpetrators of violence achieved their recognition goal: By striking hard at America, the terrorists forced the mass media to explore their grievances in ways that transcended by far the quantity and narrow focus of their pre-crisis coverage.

### Making the News as Villain and Hero

What about the third goal that many terrorists hope to advance—to win or increase their respectability and legitimacy? Here, the perpetrators' number one audience is not the enemy or the terrorized public, in this case Americans, but rather the population in their homelands and their regions of operation. And in this respect, again, the terror of "Black Tuesday" was beneficial from the view of the architects and the perpetrators of violence. A charismatic figure among his supporters and sympathizers to begin with, Osama bin Laden was the biggest winner in this respect. Whether he was directly or indirectly involved in the planning of the terrorist strikes did not matter. The media covered him as "America's number one public enemy"[36] and thereby bolstered his popularity, respectability, and legitimacy among millions of Muslims. The American and foreign news publicized visuals and reports of the popular support for bin Laden following the terror attack against the United States. A lengthy bin Laden profile in the *New York Times*, for example, contained the following passage: "To millions in the Islamic world who hate America for what they regard as its decadent culture and imperial government, he [Osama bin Laden] is a spiritual and political ally."[37] A page one article in the same edition of the *New York Times* reported from Karachi, Pakistan,

> In every direction in this city of 12 million people, the largest city in a nation that has become a crucial but brittle ally in the United States' war on terrorism, there are cries and signs for Osama bin Laden, for the Taliban, for holy war.[38]

The Associated Press reported that a book about the terrorist-in-chief was a bestseller in the Middle East. The volume contained the complete transcript of an interview with bin Laden that was broadcast in abbreviated form by al-Jazeera television in 1998 and rebroadcast after the terror strike against the United States in September of 2001. Sold out in most bookstores of the region, readers were reportedly borrowing the book from friends and making photocopies.[39]

Bin Laden, his al-Qaeda group, and the closely related web of terror spanning from the Middle East into other parts of Asia, Africa, Europe, North America, and possibly South America, were no match for the American superpower in terms of political, economic, and military power. But, as table 2.2 shows, in the aftermath of the terrorist attacks on New York and Washington and up to the beginning of the bombing of Afghanistan on October 7th, the U.S. television networks mentioned Osama bin Laden more frequently and the leading newspapers and National Public Radio only somewhat less frequently than President George W. Bush. A terrible act of terror turned the world's most notorious terrorist into one of the world's leading newsmakers. The fact that the American news media paid more attention to bin Laden than

**TABLE 2.2**
**News Stories Mentioning President Bush and**
**bin Laden Following the 9/11/2001 Terrorist Attacks**

|  | Pres. G. W. Bush | Osama bin Laden |
|---|---|---|
|  | (N) | (N) |
| ABC News | 175 | 299 |
| CBS News | 210 | 270 |
| NBC News | 159 | 211 |
| CNN | 292 | 469 |
| NPR | 271 | 188 |
| *N.Y. Times* | 655 | 611 |
| *Wash. Post* | 684 | 490 |

N = Number of segments/stories
*Source*: Compiled from Lexis-Nexis data; TV and radio broadcasts for
the period 9/11/2001–10/6/2001; newspaper articles for the period 9/12/2001–10/7/2001.

to the U.S. president, or nearly as much, was noteworthy, if one considers that George W. Bush made fifty-four public statements during this time period (from major addresses to shorter statements to a few words during photo opportunities) compared to bin Laden, who did not appear in public at all, did not hold news conferences or give face-to-face interviews.[40]

Although the American media did not portray bin Laden as a sympathetic figure, he did share center stage with President Bush in the mass-mediated global crisis. Since the 1998 bombings of the U.S. embassies in Kenya and Tanzania, the American media devoted considerable broadcast time and column inches to bin Laden (see chapter 3). But the celebrity terrorist's ultimate ascent to the world stage was more dramatic and forceful than that of Yasir Arafat in the 1970s, the Ayatollah Khomeini and Muammar Gadhafi in the 1980s, Saddam Hussein in the early 1990s, and bin Laden himself in the years and months preceding "Black Tuesday." And through all of this, bin Laden was in hiding, did not hold news conferences or grant interviews. However, the Qatar-based Arab television network, al-Jazeera, aired a videotape made available by al-Qaeda immediately after President Bush told America and the world that military actions had begun in the multifaceted hunt for bin Laden and his terror organization. All U.S. networks broadcast the tape as they received the al-Jazeera feed. Bin Laden's shrewdly crafted speech received the same air time as President Bush's speech. The same was true for a videotaped statement by bin Laden's lieutenant for media affairs who threatened that "Americans must know that the storm of airplanes will not stop. God willing, and there are thousands of young people who are as keen about death as Americans are about life."[41]

In the ten weeks following the attacks of 9–11, *TIME* magazine depicted Osama bin Laden three times and President George W. Bush twice on its cover. During the same period, *Newsweek* carried bin Laden twice on its cover and President Bush not at all. Finally, the cover of *Newsweek*'s eleventh issue after 9–11 featured President George W. and First Lady Laura Bush.

From the terrorists' point of view, it did not matter that bin Laden earned bad press in the United States and elsewhere. Singled-out, condemned, and warned by leaders, such as President Bush and British Prime Minister Tony Blair, Osama bin Laden was in the news as frequently as the world's legitimate leaders, or even more frequently. This in itself was a smashing success from the perspectives of bin Laden and his associates: The mass media reflected that bin Laden and his followers preoccupied not only America and the West but literally the entire world.

In sum, then, by attacking symbolic targets in America, killing thousands of Americans and causing tremendous damage to the American and international economy, the architects and perpetrators of this horror achieved their media-centered objectives in all respects. This propaganda coup continued in the face of American and British counterterrorist military actions in Afghanistan (see chapter 5).

## High Marks for the News Media

In the days following the attacks, when most Americans kept their televisions or radio sets tuned to the news during most of their waking hours, the public gave the media high grades for its reporting. Nearly nine in ten viewers rated the performance of the news media as either excellent (56%) or good (33%). The Pew Research Center for the People & the Press (that keeps track of the relationship between the public and the news media) called this high approval rating "unprecedented."[42] This record approval came on the heels of increasing public dissatisfaction with the mass media and a number of journalistic and scholarly works that identified the degree of and reasons for the increasing disconnect between the public and the news media (Fallows 1996; Patterson 1993). The terrorism catastrophe brought Americans and the press closer together, closer than in recent times of normalcy and during previous crises, in particular, the Gulf War.[43] Five aspects in particular seemed to effect these attitudinal changes: First, the public appreciated the flow of information provided by television, radio, and print either directly or via media organizations' Internet sites. In the hours and days of the greatest distress, television and radio especially helped viewers and listeners feel as if they were involved in the unfolding news. Unconsciously, people took some comfort in seeing and hearing the familiar faces and voices of news anchors and reporters as signs of the old normalcy in the midst of an incomprehensible crisis. At a time when the overwhelming majority of Americans stopped their normal activities, watching television, listening to the radio, reading the newspaper, going online gave them the feeling of doing something, of being part of a national tragedy.

Second, people credited the news media, especially local television, radio, and newspapers in the immediately affected areas in and around New York, Washington, and the crash site in Pennsylvania, with assisting crisis managers in communicating important information to the public. For crisis managers, the mass media offered the only effective means to tell the public about the immediate consequences of the crisis—what to do (for example, donate blood of certain types, where to donate and when) and what not to do (initially, for example, not trying to drive into Manhattan because all access bridges and tunnels were closed). In this respect, the media served the public interest in the best tradition of disaster coverage (see chapter 6).

Third, Americans experienced a media—from celebrity anchors, hosts, and other stars to the foot-soldiers of the fourth estate—that abandoned cynicism, negativism, and attack journalism in favor of reporting, if not participating in, an outburst of civic spirit, unity, and patriotism. From one minute to another, media critics and pollsters recognized a reconnection between the press and the public after years of growing division. As even the most seasoned news personnel couldn't help but show their emotions while struggling to inform the public during the initial hours and days of the crisis, audiences also forgot about their dissatisfaction with the media in a rare we-are-all-in-this-together sentiment. This explains the sudden high approval ratings for the fourth estate mentioned earlier.

To be sure, there were some bones of contention. As Americans everywhere displayed the star spangled banner, images of the American flag appeared on television screens as well. Many anchors and reporters wore flag pins or red, white, and blue ribbons on their lapels. Others rejected this display of patriotism. Barbara Walters of ABC-TV, for example, declared on the air that she would not wear any version of Old Glory.[44] When the news director of a cable station on Long Island, New York, issued a memo directing his staff not to wear any form of flag reproductions, there was a firestorm of opposition from viewers and advertisers. But even this incident seemed to fade after the news director issued an apology and it became obvious that the flag was not banned from the station's coverage.[45]

Fourth, the news provided public spaces where audience members had the opportunity to converse with experts in various fields and with each other, or witness question-and-answer exchanges between others. Whether through quickly arranged electronic town hall meetings or phone-in programs, television, radio, and on-line audiences wanted to get involved in public discourse. Many news organizations facilitated the sudden thirst for dialogue. While television and radio were natural venues for these exchanges, newspapers and newsmagazines published exclusively, or mostly, letters to the editors on this topic and reflected a wide range of serious and well-articulated opinions. Seldom, however, was the value of thoughtful moderators and professional gatekeepers more obvious than in the days and weeks after the terror nightmare. The least useful, often bigoted comments were posted on Internet sites and message boards.

Fifth, news consumers were spared the exasperation of watching reporters and camera crews chasing survivors and relatives of victims, camping on front lawns, shoving microphones in front of people who wanted to be left alone. In the 1980s, when terrorists struck against Americans abroad, the media often pushed their thirst for tears, grief, tragedy, and drama to and even beyond the limits of professional journalism's ethics in their hunt for pictures and sound bites. But this time around, neither the public nor media critics had reason to complain about the fourth estate's insistence on invading people's privacy and exploiting grief-stricken relatives of victims and survivors. This time, many husbands and wives, mothers and fathers, daughters and sons of disaster victims spoke voluntarily to reporters, appeared voluntarily, and in many instances repeatedly, on local and national television to talk about their traumatic losses. Many survivors described their ordeals and their feelings in touching detail. Most of these people were born and grew up in the era of television and seemed comfortable, in some cases even eager, to share their sorrow and their tears, their memories and their courage with anchors, hosts, correspondents—and millions of fellow Americans.

Again, this was not the result of a changed and more restrained media but of a cultural change. Expressing one's innermost feelings, showing one's despair, controlled crying or sobbing before cameras and microphones seemed natural in the communication culture of our time and in the age of so-called reality TV and talk shows with a human touch such as Oprah Winfrey or Larry King. Thus, unlike past TV audiences who were exposed to ruthless exploits of grief during and after terrorist incidents, following the terror attacks of September 11, 2001, viewers participated in mass-mediated wakes, full of collective sadness and shared encouragement.

When the broadcast media played and replayed the recorded exchanges between victims in the World Trade Center and emergency police dispatchers, they exploited the unimaginable suffering of those who were trapped and soon died in the struck towers. Criticizing this practice as "primetime pornography," one commentator wrote,

> Can there be anybody on the planet who failed to immediately grasp the full horror of what went on Sept. 11 that they need to hear, over and over, the emotional mayhem of ordinary people trying to cope amidst overwhelming disbelief, fear and terror—not to mention grief? But in our show-and-tell culture there is nothing so private and sensitive that it can't be exposed and sensationalized—especially where ratings are involved.[46]

One can perfectly agree with this insistence on journalistic ethics, as I do, and still wonder whether the "show-and-tell culture" has not only desensitized broadcasters but also confused the public's distinction between private and public sphere.

### Crisis News: Weaknesses, Questions, and Issues

Twelve days after the kamikaze attacks on the World Trade Center and Pentagon, media critic Marvin Kitman, commenting on the perhaps longest continuous breaking news events in the history of television, wrote:

> They [the TV people] kept on showing those same pictures of the planes hitting, the buildings crumbling. I'm sure if I turned the TV on right now, the buildings would still be crumbling. It never got any better. One picture is worth a thousand words, except in "live" television, where people felt compelled to constantly talk even when they knew very little about what they were talking about.[47]

While the initial emergency coverage, especially in television and radio, deserved high marks, some of the infotainment habits that had increasingly made their way into television news crept rather soon into the presentations of what screen banners called the "Attack on America" or "America Attacked." Recalling the rather trivial headlines and cover stories before 9–11, one expert in the field suggested early on that "suddenly, dramatically, unalterably the world has changed. And that means journalism will also change, indeed is changing before our eyes."[48] As it turned out, this was wishful thinking. There was no longer the feeding frenzy on Congressman Gary Condit's private life, Mayor Rudy Giuliani's nasty divorce, or the meaning of Al Gore's beard for his political future, but that did not mean an end to the overkill and hype that characterized past reporting excesses, whether in the context of the O. J. Simpson murder case and trial or the accidental deaths of Princess Diana and John F. Kennedy Jr. Immediately after 9–11, when a series of unspeakable events were reported as they unfolded, and a day or two thereafter, when the enormity of the attacks and their consequences began to sink in, there was simply not enough genuine news to fill twenty-four hours per day. As a result, television networks and stations replayed the scenes of horror again and again, revisiting the suffering of people over and over, searching for emotions beyond the boundaries of good taste. As noted earlier, in their search for family members or friends who were among the thousands of missing in New York, many people pursued reporters and camera crews with photographs of their loved ones in the hope of some good information, some good news. While highlighting these photographs could be seen as servicing a grieving community, dwelling on picture galleries of the victims was certainly not. One shocked observer recalled that "one of the yokels on Ch. 2 showed pictures she had found in the street after the explosion and cheerfully pointed out 'that these little children may now be without parents.'"[49]

The shock over the events of 9–11 wore off rather quickly in the newsrooms, giving way to everyday routine. Some television anchors welcomed their audiences rather cheerfully to the "Attack on America" or "America's New War" and led into commercial breaks with the promise that they would be right back with "America's War on Terrorism" or whatever the slogan happened to be that day or week.

There were signs of bias that were especially upsetting to Arab and Muslim Americans who felt, for example, that the scenes of Palestinians rejoicing over the news of the attacks in New York and Washington were over-reported and too often replayed. In contrast to Palestinian celebrations, anti-American outbursts in Europe received little or no attention. For example, when fans of a Greek soccer team at the European Cup game in Athens jeered America during a minute of silence for the terrorism victims of 9–11 and tried to burn an

American flag, no television news programs and only a handful of American newspapers (publishing only a few lines in reports about the soccer game on the sports pages) mentioned the incident.[50] But the coverage raised far more serious questions about the proper role of a free press in a crisis that began with the suicide terror in New York, Washington, and near Pittsburgh and intensified when anthrax letters were delivered in states along the U.S. East coast. Three areas, in particular, proved problematic.

The first of these issues concerned the videotapes with propaganda appeals by bin Laden and his lieutenants that al-Qaeda made available to the Arab language TV network al-Jazeera. On October 7, shortly after President Bush informed the nation of the first air raids against targets in Afghanistan, five U.S. television networks (ABC, CBS, NBC, CNN, and Fox News) broadcast an unedited feed from al-Jazeera that gave bin Laden and his associates access to the American public. Two days later, three cable channels (CNN, Fox News, and MSNBC) aired in full a statement by bin Laden's spokesman Suleiman Abu Gheith. Both tapes contained threats against Americans at home and abroad. Bin Laden said, "I swear to God that America will not live in peace before peace reigns in Palestine and before all the army of infidels depart the land of Muhammad, peace be upon him."[51] His spokesman warned that "the storms will not calm down, especially the storm of airplanes, until you see defeat in Afghanistan." He called on Muslims in the United States and Great Britain "not to travel by airplanes and not to live in high buildings or skyscrapers."[52] The Bush administration cautioned that these statements could contain coded messages that might cue bin Laden followers in the United States and elsewhere in the West to unleash more terror. But intelligence experts were unable to identify suspect parts in the spoken text or visual images at a time when Attorney General John Ashcroft, the FBI, and other government officials in Washington warned of more terrorist strikes to come. While the administration's argument that these tapes were vehicles for hidden messages was not credible, it was certainly true that these videos and their transcripts contained terrorist propaganda, which newspapers printed in full. The most damaging effect was that these broadcasts further frightened an already traumatized American public. Students of propaganda have argued that propaganda of fear or the "fear effect" is most effective "when it scares the hell out of people" (Pratkanis and Aronson 1992, 165). But this is not what the administration argued. Prodded by National Security Advisor Condoleezza Rice who warned that the hateful threats from the bin Laden camp could incite more violence against Americans abroad, all American television networks agreed to edit future tapes and eliminate "passages containing flowery rhetoric urging violence against Americans."[53] This argument was just as weak as the suggestion of hidden signs contained in the tapes. After all, al-Jazeera and other television channels aired the material in the Middle East and other regions with Muslim populations. It would have been far more credible to argue that threats from bin Laden and his associates increased the public's anxiety.

The networks' joint decision was not universally applauded because it raised the question whether the networks had given in to pressure from the administration when they agreed to exercise this form of self-censorship. While the argument that the press in a democracy needs to fully inform citizens, especially in times of crisis and great danger, has most weight here, it is also true that the news media make all the decisions on whom and what to include and exclude, or whom and what to feature more or less prominently in their broadcasts. In the case of the al-Qaeda tapes, after the first ones were aired excessively by some cable networks, subsequent tapes were under-covered. All of these videotapes should have been broadcast fully, and their transcripts should have been printed entirely by the press. The public should have learned of bin Laden's propaganda without being exposed to endless replays. The mistake was made initially when passages of the first bin Laden video were broadcast so many times with full screen or split screen exposure, when bin Laden and al-Qaeda loomed too large in the overall news presentations compared to other news sources and developments. The second mistake was the suppression or partial suppression of the content of later videotapes by broadcast and print media.

A similar controversy arose over CNN's decision to join al-Jazeera in submitting questions to Osama bin Laden following an invitation by al-Qaeda and the promise that bin Laden would respond to them. While a face-to-face interview with the man who openly praised the terrorism of 9–11 could have yielded valuable information—especially for U.S. decision makers, the exchange of written questions and answers was a far more questionable journalistic exercise under the circumstances (if only because the media organizations could not be sure whether bin Laden or someone else would answer their questions). Under these circumstances, it was just as well that the answers were never provided.

A second issue concerned the media's sudden obsession with endlessly reporting and debating the potential for biological, chemical, and nuclear warfare in the wake of 9–11. As real and would-be experts filled the air waves, some hosts and anchors were unable to hide their preference for guests who painted doomsday scenarios. As table 2.3 shows, this was common in broadcasts even before the first anthrax case in Florida made the news on October 4, 2001. It was as if anchors and news experts expected the other shoe to drop as they went out of their way to report to the public that the public health system and other agencies were ill prepared to deal with bioterrorism and other mass destruction terrorism.

**TABLE 2.3**
**Biological and Chemical Terrorism and Anthrax in the News**

|            | B/C Terror I | B/C Terror II | Anthrax I | Anthrax II |
|------------|:------------:|:-------------:|:---------:|:----------:|
|            | (N)          | (N)           | (N)       | (N)        |
| ABC News   | 20           | 30            | 2         | 383        |
| CBS News   | 12           | 30            | 0         | 267        |
| NBC News   | 8            | 57            | 3         | 250        |
| CNN        | 17           | 99            | 1         | 567        |
| Fox News   | 23           | 37            | 0         | 103        |
| NPR        | 11           | 37            | 8         | 176        |
| *N.Y. Times* | 76         | 194           | 27        | 729        |
| *Wash. Post* | 55         | 147           | 25        | 465        |

N = Number of segments/stories
*Source*: Compiled by retrieving transcripts and newspaper content from the Lexis-Nexis archives using the
   search words "biological" and "chemical" and "terrorist" for biological and chemical terror and "anthrax."
*Note*: B/C Terror I and Anthrax I segments/stories aired/published from September 11, 2001 to October 3,
   2001 for television and radio, and September 12, 2001 to October 4, 2001 for newspapers.
   B/C Terror II and Anthrax II segments/stories aired/published from October 4, 2001 to October 31,
   2001 for television and radio, and October 5, 2001 to November 1, 2001 for newspapers.

When the news of a Florida man dying of anthrax and subsequent cases
validated these predictions, anthrax terrorism and other forms of bioterrorism moved higher up on the agenda of TV, radio, and print news. In less than
a month, from the discovery of the first case on October 4th to October 31st,
the television networks covered or mentioned the anthrax terror in hundreds
of segments. The leading newspapers published even more stories on anthrax
and other possible threats from biological and chemical agents (see table 2.3).

The most serious bioterrorism attacks in the United States deserved headlines and serious, regular, in-depth coverage, but the attacks did not merit an
army of talking heads who beat the topic to death many times over. In the
process, public officials who tried to mask their own confusion, experts who
scared the public, and media stars who overplayed the anthrax card con-
tributed to a general sentiment of uncertainty. By shrewdly targeting major
news organizations and two of the most prominent television news anchors,
Tom Brokaw of NBC and Dan Rather of CBS (and perhaps Peter Jennings of
ABC, considering that the baby son of one ABC news producer was diagnosed
with exposure to anthrax bacteria following his visit at ABC News headquarters in New York), the perpetrator(s) were assured massive attention even before
the first anthrax letter hit Washington. Along the way, mass-mediated advice
about whether to buy gas masks, take antibiotics, avoid public places, and
speculations over the next form of bioterrorism (smallpox?) or chemical terror warfare (sarin gas attacks, such as Aum Shinrykio's attack in Tokyo's subway system?) fueled the nightmares of those citizens who could not switch off
their television sets since 9–11.

This concern was not lost on a few people inside the media. One political columnist identified the greatest danger of journalism—"our new obsession with terrorism will make us its unwitting accomplices. We will become (and have already partly become) merchants of fear. Case in point: the anthrax fright. Until now, anthrax has been a trivial threat to public health and safety."[54] The same columnist also warned,

> The perverse result is that we may become the terrorists' silent allies. Terrorism is not just about death and destruction. It's also about creating fear, sowing suspicion, undermining confidence in public leadership, provoking people—and governments—into doing things that they might not otherwise do. It is an assault as much on our psychology as on our bodies."[55]

Not many in the media listened. At the height of the anthrax scare, the media kept publicizing far more scary scenarios for terrorism of mass destruction. *Newsweek*'s November 5, 2001 edition was a case in point. The issue's extensive cover story, "Protecting America: What must be done," described the most vulnerable targets for terrorist attacks as "airports, chemical plants, dams, food supplies, the Internet, malls, mass transit, nuclear power plants, post offices, seaports, skyscrapers, stadiums, water supplies." Collapsed into ten priorities "to protect ourselves" in the actual cover story, the described vulnerabilities read more like a target description for terrorist planners than useful information for a nation in crisis.

Finally, in taking a softer stand vis-à-vis the President, administration officials, members of Congress, and officials at lower level governments, the news media made the right choice when encountering a crisis that presented the country with problems it had never faced before. But suspending the adversarial stance of normal times is one thing, to join the ranks of cheerleaders is another. While comparing the hands-on and very effective crisis-managing mayor of New York City with Winston Churchill during World War II was understandable under the circumstances, likening President George W. Bush (on the basis of his speech before a joint session of the U.S. Congress) to Abraham Lincoln during the Civil War and Winston Churchill during WWII, as some media commentators and many cited sources did, was quite a stretch. But nothing demonstrated more clearly that some reporters and editors had lost their footing than an article about Laura Bush as "a very different" First Lady after the terrorist crisis began. When Mrs. Bush's visited New York in her "new role of national consoler," a reporter concluded, "As the need for a national hand-holder has made itself evident, Mrs. Bush's role as a kind of Florence Nightingale at least comes as a natural one."[56] Even more farfetched was a comparison by presidential scholar Michael Beschloss, one of the most frequent guests on political talk TV programs, who, according to the *New York*

*Times*, compared "the first lady's sang-froid to that of Queen Elizabeth the Queen Mother during World War II. (The queen mother refused to leave London, against the wishes of her advisers.)"[57] Given this kind of hyperbole, even in the most respected media, it was hardly surprising that the news media's most important role in the democratic arrangement—that of acting as a governmental watchdog—took a back seat in the weeks after the 9–11 terror attacks and in the first weeks following the anthrax scare.

When the Republican controlled House of Representatives stopped its work after anthrax spores were found in Senator Tom Daschle's office (but were not yet found in the lower chamber of Congress), the *New York Post*, a conservative, pro-Republican daily, called members "Wimps" in a huge front-page headline and chided representatives because they had "chicken[ed] out" and "headed for the hills yesterday at the first sign of anthrax in the Capitol."[58] Even for a tabloid, this choice of words was perhaps not the best; however, the substance proved on the mark in the following days, when government offices from Capitol Hill to the Supreme Court were closed while thousands of fearful postal workers in Washington, New York, and New Jersey were told to continue working because anthrax spores in their buildings and on their mail sorting machines did not pose any danger to their health. At the time, two postal workers in Washington had already died of anthrax inhalation and several others had been diagnosed with less lethal cases. Yet, by and large, the news media did not question what looked like a double standard. In the face of an ongoing terrorism crisis at home and a counterterrorism campaign abroad, the mainstream watchdog press refrained from barking in the direction of public officials.

In late October and early November, when public opinion polls signaled that the American public was far less satisfied with the Bush administration's handling of homeland defense in the face of anthrax bioterrorism than with its military campaign against bin Laden, al-Qaeda, and the Taliban in Afghanistan, columnists, journalists, and editorial writers asked the questions that needed to be answered and voiced criticism that needed to be expressed. In an in-depth piece in the *New York Times*, for example, John Schwartz wrote, "[If] there's one lesson to be learned from the Bush administration's response to the anthrax threat, it's this: People in the grip of fear want information that holds up, not spin control." [59] More specifically, he wrote:

> Critics of the administration say that the reasons for the lackluster response include lack of communication between agencies, a lack of preparedness on the part of the Health and Human Services Secretary, Tommy G. Thompson, a former governor of Wisconsin with little background in medicine or science, and officials' tendency to respond in the same way they would respond to a mere political problem.[60]

This piece, similar news stories, and commentary signaled that the news media began to slowly reclaim their watchdog role with respect to the terrorism of 9–11, the anthrax scare, and related political and policy issues. While nobody yearned for the return of the attack-dog media, the revival of a more critical approach to domestic politics and policies was a signal that the terrorist assaults on America failed in one respect: Even political violence of this magnitude did not for long beat down the fundamental democratic liberties that underlie the watchdog function of the news media—although the news remained muted with respect to the politics of anti- and counterterrorism in the post-9–11 period (see chapter 5).

## Notes

1. Quoted here from Amy Harmon, "The search for intelligent life on the Internet," *New York Times*, 23 September 2001, Week in Review, 2.

2. Michiko Kakutani, "Critic's Notebook: Struggling to find words for a horror beyond words," *New York Times*, 13 September 2001, E1.

3. "A day of terror: the voices," *New York Times*, 12 September 2001, 10.

4. "After the attacks: one man's account," *New York Times*, 15 September 2001, 10.

5. Cloud described his reaction as a guest on NBC's *Today* program on September 12, 2001.

6. The unidentified Canadian made the remark on the Canadian Broadcasting Corporation's program *The National*, 11 September 2001.

7. From *CNN Money Morning*, 14 September 2001.

8. John Updike, untitled contribution in "Talk of the Town," *The New Yorker* (24 September 2001): 28.

9. Updike, 28.

10. Stockhausen's remarks and the reactions they caused in Germany were reported in "Attacks called great art," *New York Times*, 19 September 2001, according to http://www.nytimes.com/2001/09/19/arts/music/19KARL.html [accessed 1 April 2002].

11. Lippmann explores the idea of environment and pseudo-environment (or reality and pseudo- or media-reality) especially in chapters 1 and 6 of his book.

12. Stockhausen is quoted here from Bill Carter and Felicity Barringer, "In patriotic times, dissent is muted," *New York Times*, 28 September 2001. According to the article, the Eastman School of Music's Ossia Ensemble canceled a planned performance of Stockhausen's work "Stimmung" scheduled for early November at New York's Cooper Union.

13. Governor Pataki made these remarks on ABC News' *Nightline* on 14 September 2001.

14. Quoted here from Associated Press reporter Robert Jablon, "Hollywood think tank helping Army," http://dailynews.yahoo.com/h/ap/20011009/us/attacks_hollywood_1.html [accessed 1 April 2002].

15. The statement was written in Arabic, but an English translation was carried by the wire services and widely publicized in the media. See, for example, http://www.msnbc.com/news/633244.asp [accessed 26 September 2001].

16. See http://www.msnbc.com/news/633244.asp.

17. Eventually, the hijackers released most of their hostages. Afterwards, some European governments did free a few terrorists from prison as demanded by the PFLP and thereby resolved the standoff.

18. According to a *Los Angeles Times* telephone poll on September 13–14, 2001, 83% of the respondents said they watched the news "very closely," 15% "closely," and 2% "not too closely." Nobody chose the response option "not closely at all." In a survey conducted September 14–15, 2001, the Gallup Organization found that 77% of the public followed the news "very closely," 20% "somewhat closely," 2% "not too closely," and 1% "not at all." An ABC/*Washington Post* poll on September 11, 2001, found that 99% of the public followed the news on television and radio. Polling on-line adults on September 11 and 12, 2001, Harris Interactive found that 93% identified television and radio as their primary news source; 64% mentioned the Internet as one of their primary sources.

19. According to a survey conducted by the Pew Research Center for the People & the Press on October 17–21, 2001, 78% of the respondents said that they watched terrorism news very closely, 16% watched closely, 4% not closely, 1% gave no answer. This result was nearly the same level of interest as in mid-September (13–17) when 74% of survey respondents revealed that they watched terrorism news very closely, 22% closely. In fact, more Americans watched this kind of news very closely in the second half of October than in mid-September.

20. The quote is taken from the translated transcript of a videotape, presumably recorded in mid-November 2001, and retrieved from http://www.washingtonpost .com/wp-srv/nation/specials/attacked/transcripts/binladentext_121301.html [accessed 13 December 2001].

21. These figures were reported in an ABC/*Washington Post* survey on September 11, 2001.

22. These statistics are the results of surveys conducted by the Gallup Organization, April 21–23, 1995, and September 14–15, 2001. A Gallup survey conducted on September 11, 2001, reported that 58% of Americans expressed fears of more terrorism.

23. See "Text: Bin Laden's Statement." http://www.guardian.co.uk/waronterror/ story/0,1361,565069,00.html [accessed 7 April 2002].

24. According to surveys conducted by the Pew Center for the People & the Press in mid-October 2001, 52% of the respondents were "very" or "somewhat" worried that they or a member of their family would become a victim of terrorism. In mid-September, 53% had those concerns. However, the number of people who were "very concerned" actually increased from September to October. See http://people-press.org/midoct01rpt.htm [accessed 24 October 2001].

25. Surveys conducted by the Pew Research Center for the People & the Press found that seven in ten Americans felt depressed following the 9–11 terrorist attacks, but, in mid-October, only 29% of respondents revealed that they felt depressed. During that same time period, those having trouble sleeping decreased from 33% to 12%.

26. A survey conducted on September 13–17, 2001, by the Pew Center for the People and the Press revealed that 63% of the respondents could not stop watching terrorism reports; on October 17–21, 49% said that they were hooked on terrorism news. In the September poll, 77% of the respondents said that watching terrorism news was frightening; in the October poll, 69% said the same.

27. Richard Burkholder Jr., "Initial reaction to the attacks on America: Polls from Hungary, the United Kingdom, Australia, New Zealand, France and Russia." The Gallup Organization, http://www.gallup.com [accessed 22 September 2001].

28. This statistic is from surveys conducted by the Gallup Organization on September 12, 2001.

29. These statistics are from surveys conducted by MORI (Roy Morgan International) on September 14, 2001, and by the ROMIR (Russian Public Opinion and Market Research) on September 12, 2001.

30. For the full text, see Peter Ford, "Why do they hate us?" *Christian Science Monitor*, http://www.csmonitor.com/2001/0927/p1s1-wogi.html [accessed 1 April 2002].

31. Lisa Beyer, "Roots of Rage," *TIME* (1 October 2001): 44–47.

32. Philip C. Wilcox Jr., "The Terror," *The New York Review of Books* (18 October 2001): 4.

33. To retrieve relevant transcripts from the Lexis-Nexis database, the following search words were used: "why they hate us," "roots" and "terrorism," and "motivations" and "terrorism." Each transcript was examined as to the relevancy of its content. While all transcripts retrieved for the post-attack period (September 11, 2001–September 29, 2001) addressed the reasons for anti-American sentiments in the Arab and Muslim world, those retrieved for the pre-attack period (January 1, 2001–September 10, 2001) did not include a single record that dealt with this problem.

34. For the full text of the document, visit http://www.fas.org/irp/world/para/docs/980223-fatwa.html [accessed 1 April 2002].

35. The document was written in Arabic. This translation was taken from "Full text of notes found after hijackings," *New York Times*, http://www.nytimes.com/2001/09/29/national/29S/FULL-TEXT.html [accessed 1 April 2002].

36. Quoted here from *People* magazine on CNN, 29 September 2001.

37. Robert D. McFadden, "Bin Laden's journey from rich, pious boy to the mask of evil," *New York Times*, 30 September 2001, B5.

38. Rick Bragg, "Streets of huge Pakistan city seethe with hatred for U.S.," *New York Times*, 30 September 2001, 1.

39. The sudden bestseller was Jamal Abdul Latif Ismail's *Bin Laden, Al-Jazeera—and I.* For more on this book, see Donna Abu-Nasr, "Bin Laden's past words revisited." http://dailynews.yahoo.com/htx/ap/20010928/wl/bin_laden_s_words_2.html [accessed 1 April 2002].

40. George W. Bush's fifty-four public statements during the period were retrieved from the Lexis-Nexis database in the political transcript category.

41. This statement by al-Qaeda's spokesman Sulaiman Abu Ghaith was aired by al-Jazeera TV and U.S. networks. The quote was taken from the Associated Press's version as publicized on http://dailynews.yahoo and retrieved on October 10, 2001 [accessed 1 April 2002].

42. See the Pew Research Center for the People & the Press, http://www.people-press.org/terrorist01rpt.htm [accessed 1 April 2002], which states: "Overwhelming support for Bush, military response, but. . . ."

43. See http://www.people-press.org/terrorist01rpt.htm.

44. Walter's revealed her "no flag" decision on *The View*, a talk show she co-hosts. See Rita Ciolli, "Flags raise among media," *Newsday*, 23 September 2001, A39.

45. The station was Long Island Cablevision. See Warren Strugatch, "Patriotism vs. Journalistic Ethics," *New York Times*, 7 October 2001, section 14, p. 1.

46. "Comment: Broadcast news," *Wall Street Journal*, 8 October 2001, A25.

47. Marvin Kitman, "The Nation's painful video vigil," *Newsday*, 23 September 2001, D27.

48. Howard Kurtz, "Media hype may no longer be necessary," *Washington Post*, 16 September 2001.

49. Kitman, D27.

50. The *New York Times*, for example, mentioned the Palestinian celebrations in nine articles following the 9–11 terrorism; the anti-American incident in Athens received twenty lines of an Associated Press dispatch on its sports pages. See "Fans in Athens try to burn U.S. flag," *New York Times*, 23 September 2001, sports section, p. 9.

51. Quoted here from John F. Burns, "A nation challenged: The wanted Man," *New York Times*, 8 October 2001, A1.

52. Quoted in Susan Sachs and Bill Carter, "A nation challenged: al Qaeda. Bin Laden spokesman threatens Westerners at home and in the Gulf," *New York Times*, 14 October 2001, section 1B, p. 1.

53. Bill Carter and Felicity Barringer, "A nation challenged: The coverage," *New York Times*, 11 October 2001, A1.

54. Robert Samuelson, "Unwitting accomplices?" *Washington Post*, 7 November 2001, A29.

55. Samuelson, A29.

56. Alex Kuczynski, "A very different Laura Bush," *New York Times*, 30 September 2001, sect. 9, pp. 1 and 7.

57. Kuczynski, 1 and 7.

58. Deborah Orin and Brian Blomquist, "Anthrax plays to empty House," *New York Post*, 18 October 2001, 5.

59. John Schwartz, "Efforts to calm the nation's fears spin out of control," *New York Times*, 28 October 2001, section 4, pp. 1 and 2.

60. Schwartz, 1 and 2.

# 3

# Political Violence as Media Event

IN THE MIDST of a big snowstorm that paralyzed the New York region during the last hours of the year 2000, crude incendiary devices went off in several luxury houses under construction in a development in Long Island's Suffolk county. When contractors and officers surveyed the damage later on, they discovered spray painted messages that revealed the arsonists' cause—a campaign of violence in the service of environmental protection. One of the slogans—"If you build it, we will burn it!"—was reminiscent of the 1989 Hollywood film *Field of Dreams*, in which Kevin Costner, in the lead role, stands in his cornfield listening to the assurances of a supernatural voice: "If you build it, they will come." In a press release, faxed to the Associated Press, the Earth Liberation Front (or ELF) claimed responsibility and issued a warning: "We will not tolerate the destruction of our island." Calling the fire bombing "an early New Year's gift to Long Island's environment destroyers," the radical environmentalists expressed confidence that their actions would cost "the rich sprawl corporations" enough to stop their appetite to build. Craig S. Rosebraugh of Portland, Oregon, acting as the official press officer for the elusive eco-terrorists, elaborated on the goals of the green extremists. Insisting that he was only passing on the messages he received from ELF activists (activists he did not know and had never met), Rosebraugh described their cause as noble nevertheless. "I hope it [eco-terrorist activity] increases and continues," he said in one of more than seventy telephone conversations with reporters in the United States and abroad.[1]

Earlier ELF attacks on what the perpetrators characterized as symbols of environmental destruction by greedy interests had concentrated on targets in the American West and caused far greater damage—for example, a devastating twelve million dollar fire set at a ski resort in Vail, Colorado, in 1998 and a $930,000 arson attack at a timber company in Sweet Home, Oregon, in 1999. For years, the ELF movement and its equally violent ally, the Animal Liberation Front (ALF), encouraged like-minded extremists at home and abroad to report their terrorist activities for postings on their Internet sites, fed their official spokesperson with information about their illegal activities, and left their signatures in graffiti on symbolic targets. In short, these and similar acts were cases of media-terrorism in that an overriding goal of the violence was publicity in the form of news coverage.

Eco-extremists—whether they called themselves ELF, ALF, Earth RightAction Group, Earth First, Vegan Revolution, or several other names—always chose symbolic targets for their attacks. Typically, they hit logging companies, biomedical laboratories, farms, genetic engineering facilities, and projects that they considered to be expanding urban sprawl or destroying the natural habitat of rare animals. Certainly poised to inflict damage on and unsettle particular "offenders," eco-extremists understood their acts of political violence as messages that the mass media of communication would carry to the most important targets of their propaganda by deed: the immediate targets of their wrath, the public, decision makers, and fellow environmentalists and possible new recruits.

On that score, they were quite successful. Up to the described fire bombing on Long Island and several similar ones in the weeks leading up to that arson, violent actions by the ELF and their allies were mostly covered by the local and regional press in the western United States. Print and broadcast media in the region published in-depth articles and editorials that condemned the terror methods of the eco-underground. In September 1999, for example, the Portland *Oregonian* published two lengthy articles by Bryan Denson and James Long about the alarming spread of eco-terrorism in the American West. Sticking to the FBI's definition of domestic terrorism as "violence intended to coerce, intimidate, or change public policy," they found that within a four-year period the western United States had been "rocked by 33 substantial incidents with damages reaching $28.8 million" (Denson and Long 1999a).

In spite of media attention in the West, it was hardly surprising that the ELF eventually expanded its operations into other regions of the country—first the Midwest, then the Northeast. In January 2000, the organization claimed responsibility for burning down a luxury home under construction in Bloomington, Indiana, to protest residential development near a watershed. But following several scarcely reported incidents in the Long Island area, a relatively small act of violence, the December 30th arson bombing described above, triggered more media attention than the far more devastating attacks that had plagued the western states for years. Indeed, when the *Oregonian* counted nine *major* acts of violence by the Earth Liberation Front throughout the year 2000, the paper included only those incidents that caused damages of at least fifty thousand dollars (Denson 2001), and thus not the Long Island fire bombing with damage in the thirty to forty thousand dollar range. In other words, not a major but a minor act of eco-terrorism resulted in heightened media attention.

Perhaps the lack of breaking news at the end of the holiday season made eco-terrorism an attractive story, when the media hype about major acts of millennium terrorism on American soil, thankfully, did not occur. Moreover, by striking an area just a stone's throw away from the New York headquarters of the major national media organizations, the eco-underground reaped not only a great deal of local but generous national and even international news coverage as well. Thus, in January 2001, the *New York Times* published seven articles that mentioned the Earth Liberation Front. Six of the rather lengthy pieces covered ELF attacks on Long Island; one reported that the group had claimed responsibility for burning the office of a logging company in Oregon. Literally all articles described eco-terrorism in the New York area and in general, the causes and grievances of the perpetrators, the angry reactions of the immediate targets, the sentiments of nonviolent environmentalists, and the frustrations of local police officers and FBI agents in the hunt for the elusive extremists. In stark contrast to this intensive coverage in the weeks following the arson incidents on Long Island, the *New York Times* had published only four articles mentioning the ELF in 2000 (the most active year of the ELF so far), three in 1999, and five in 1998. During January of 2001, the selection of domestic and English language publications available in the Lexis-Nexis computer archives contained twenty-eight articles about the activities of the Earth Liberation Front (mostly in the New York area) and the causes of such actions, compared to only nineteen articles in 2000 and forty-four items in 1998, the year of the devastating fire in Vail. Following the Long Island fire bombing, the ELF was the topic of a CBS News segment on *60 Minutes*, as a "media release" by the Animal Liberation Frontline Information Service noted with obvious satisfaction. *Newsweek* and *TIME* carried stories that were accompanied by photographs depicting ELF-inflicted damage, and National Public Radio's program *All Things Considered* broadcast two segments about the ELF. The wire services in the Lexis-Nexis archives (such as the Associated Press and United Press International) that reach news organizations in the United States and all over the globe carried a total of thirty-one dispatches about ELF activities in January 2001 versus fifty-four in 2000, thirty-four in 1999, and sixty-one in 1998. The four young Long Islanders who eventually were arrested for the arson got all the attention they could hope for—and probably more than they expected.

When asked by Wyatt Andrews of CBS News in early 2000 whether eco-violence would help to "win over the public debate in this country," ELF spokesperson Craig Rosebraugh answered, "That's not the immediate goal, I don't believe. The immediate goal is to cause economic damage."[2] But this was not a plausible answer for the official press representative of extremists who never missed a chance to exploit their violent deeds and to spread their propaganda, nor was it consistent with what Rosebraugh had told the *Oregonian* earlier. The newspaper's investigative team reported, "Rosebraugh wishes there were more high-profile arsons such as the Vail blaze. It drew worldwide attention and, he says, showed that a radical environmental movement in the American West was gaining momentum and impact" (Denson and Long 1999b). In fact, three of the four persons arrested for the arson attacks on Long Island told investigators during plea-bargaining negotiations that they resorted to violence after earlier, quite harmless actions (for example, putting glue into the locks of a furrier's store and the "liberation" of a dozen ducks from an "abusive" farm) had not resulted in the hoped-for publicity. According to one account, encouragement to resort to violent means came from the Internet: "In chat rooms linked to the ELF site, anonymous people counseled them *to escalate their tactics to gain publicity for their environmental messages* [emphasis added]."[3]

With the media success of the Long Island operation under its belt, the ELF warned of "an escalation in tactics against capitalism and industry" for the year 2001 in a communiqué to and distributed by Rosebraugh who runs the North American Earth Liberation Front Press office. Not surprisingly, there was more violence in the name of the ELF and its political goals in the following months. In February 2001, for example, the ELF claimed responsibility for a fire at the Delta & Pine Land Company Research cotton gin in Visalia, California, and explained its motive in a statement:

> We chose this warehouse because it contained massive quantities of transgenic cotton seed in storage. But now, this seed will no longer exist to contaminate the environment, enrich sick corporations, or contribute to its warped research programs."[4]

At least some citizens took exception to the media's tendency to cover and interview representatives or members of terrorist groups the same way that they treat legitimate political actors—perhaps even less critically. After National Public Radio aired an interview with ELF spokesperson Rosebraugh in the program *All Things Considered*, some listeners protested that the interviewer had not been tough enough in questioning her guest. To their credit, the anchors of the well-regarded show took note of these reactions as the following excerpts from the broadcast of January 4, 2001 demonstrate:

*Linda Wertheimer, host:* It's Thursday, the day we read from your letters. We had a number of letters from listeners upset with my interview with a representative of the Earth Liberation Front on that group's use of arson in the name of environmentalism. This is David Phillips of Asheville, North Carolina. "I was appalled to hear a representative of the Earth Liberation Front justify arson in an attempt to prevent urban sprawl. Their foolish strategy puts them on the same level as the KKK and does more harm to their cause than good. Terrorist tactics such as these will turn the public against them."

*Noah Adams, host:* Also, this from Claude Nicely of Clarkston, Washington. "The respect you accorded that man is appalling. The man is a terrorist, representing a terrorist organization. Would you have accorded the same level of softball interview in respect to Theodore Kaczynsky had you talked with him before he was apprehended?"

The letter writers cited in the program, and probably others who were not mentioned or did not bother to write, were unhappy about the way National Public Radio had reacted to the amateurish fire bombings in the New York region. Indeed, from the perspective of the ELF, their media-centered goals worked perfectly in that their deeds were generously covered in the mass media and their spokesperson was interviewed without facing hard and critical questions.

How this kind of attention by the mass media in the United States and abroad put eco-terrorism on the map was easily recognized in the spring of 2001, when the United Kingdom suffered tremendous economic losses as the result of a major outbreak of foot-and-mouth disease among its cattle and when the president of the National Farmers Union (NFU), Ben Gill, suggested that eco-terrorists deliberately triggered the outbreak. Gill said, "There's no doubt foot-and-mouth spread to the UK illegally, and, unfortunately, we cannot rule out eco-terrorism."[5] While the Friends of the Earth (FoE) group's executive director Charles Secrett condemned Gill's comments, the very idea of connecting environmental radicals to the devastating livestock disease suggested how serious the movement was taken after years of eco-violence. A few months later, cattle farmers in the Midwest were fearful and outraged after learning that a leader of another radical animal rights group, People for the Ethical Treatment of Animals (PETA), said "she hoped foot-and-mouth disease found its way to America because it could turn more people into vegetarians."[6] It was also reported that PETA sent a letter to the World Dairy Expo scheduled for the fall of 2001 in Madison, Wisconsin, demanding the cancellation of the event. While the Expo organizers stood firm, a number of other animal events were canceled for fear that "agri-terrorists" could deliberately infect the state's livestock with the dreaded disease. As the media reported on these incidents and developments, the fear of a new kind of terrorism spread among farmers in the United States. When lawmakers in Wisconsin and several other states drafted legislation that aimed to make the infection of animals with a disease a crime, as well as the mere threat to do so, the wide range of possible terrorist acts became more transparent to more people.

Animal rights and environmental protection extremists did not rest after the events of September 11th. On the contrary, in the eight weeks following the attacks on the World Trade Center and the Pentagon at least six terror acts were claimed by the Animal Liberation Front and the Earth Liberation Front—among them an arson fire at a primate research center in New Mexico and a break-in at an Iowa fur farm releasing more than one thousand mink. Indeed, on the day international terrorists killed more than three thousand people in New York, Washington, and near Pittsburgh, the Animal Liberation Front took credit for the burning of a McDonald's in Tucson, Arizona. And although the news media were preoccupied with the kamikaze attacks on New York and Washington and the counterstrikes against targets in Afghanistan, they reported nevertheless on these cases of domestic terrorism as well.[7]

## Mass-Mediated, Antiglobalization Terror

Extremists in the environmentalist movement and their amateurish recruits were not the only adherents of political violence who exploited the mass media at the end of the twentieth and the beginning of the twenty-first centuries. Indeed, extremists in the multifaceted antiglobalization, anticapitalist movement took the most successful page out of the playbook of political violence. It began in Seattle, Washington, in late 1999, where the World Trade Organization (WTO) convened for a summit. Even before the world delegates assembled for their first session, violence broke out in the streets of the inner city. While some forty thousand men and women representing labor unions, environmental groups, and various other organizations, expressed their opposition to the globalization policies of the WTO peacefully, a relatively small number of protesters (about 150) in fatigues and black jackets retrieved hammers, M-80 firecrackers, and spray paint from their knapsacks and vandalized brand name stores such as Starbucks, Nike, FAO Schwarz, and Old Navy. The rampage by self-described anarchists and the subsequent battle between protesters and police wouldn't have been more than a nuisance without the massive media coverage it received in the United States and abroad. Instead, it was not the WTO meeting but the violence of a few extremists and the overzealous reactions of the security forces that became the major news story. This was precisely what the anarchist clique had in mind because, as sympathizers explained, they had not committed "mindless and adolescent vandalism—it was done for political reasons."[8]

To simply state that the news of the violence in Seattle was massive and excessive does not convey the breathtaking scope of the media attention. *Newsweek*'s coverage of "The Battle of Seattle" was an instructive example of how the media reported on the protests that turned violent. From the cover photograph that depicted riot police manhandling a young protester on the ground and two full-page pictures inside the newsmagazine that documented what *Newsweek* called a "spasm of violent rage," to the eight additional pages of text and visual images that described the street violence and what the coalition of violent and peaceful antiglobalization activists "really want[ed]," the news magazine elevated the street events in Seattle and their roots to primary importance.[9] The coverage elsewhere—whether in newsmagazines, newspapers, or the electronic media—was also heavily tilted in favor of the violence surrounding the WTO summit. More than one hundred segments by ABC News, NBC News, and CNN News were devoted to the Seattle summit, and the vast majority dealt either exclusively or partially with the violence outside the meeting hall. While similar in its attention to what many media organizations dubbed as the "Battle of Seattle," CBS News broadcast less segments (eighty-one) than its competition about the WTO meeting but was equally focused on the violent aspects of the Seattle events.

Moreover, the tiny minority of violators who planned and carried out the brutal actions received a great deal of news coverage, introducing their rationale to the public. In the ten days following the disturbances in Seattle, the English language wire services available in the Lexis-Nexis database carried twenty-three dispatches that dealt specifically with "anarchists" who initiated the disturbances and the aims of these protesters. Thus, an Associated Press dispatch from December 3, 1999, explained why a group of anarchists was occupying a Seattle warehouse: "The occupation is a protest against the WTO because big business world-wide is a major cause of rising housing costs and homelessness" (Geranios 1999). Newspapers represented in the Lexis-Nexis archive published altogether eighty articles about the role of these "anarchists," their ideology, and their opposition to the globalization stance of the WTO. Some of the articles described the antiglobalization extremists in quite sympathetic terms. And although linking their violent actions to their political motives, none of these publications called the anarchists "terrorists" or their acts of violence "terrorism."

A lengthy article in the *New York Times*, for example, describing young anarchists in the context of the Seattle incidents, contained the following passages:

> While they accepted the term anarchist, some suggested that "antiauthoritarian" or "humanist" better expressed their basic belief that all governments and corporations are bad and should be drastically curtailed or abolished. Many are articulate and evidently well read, but few said they wished to discuss much of their upbringing. . . .

A few, in fact, said they might have smashed a window or two, but carefully noted that any destruction they might have committed was against stores representing what they said were "multinational corporations" like Starbucks, Nike or the Gap. "We didn't hurt any person or any living thing," said a young bandanna-wearing man who would not give his name (Verhovek and Kahn 1999).

In the *Financial Times* of London, Gerard Baker characterized the violence in Seattle as "America's first post-modern riot," argued that the "Seattle riots demonstrate the failure of mainstream US politics to provide an outlet for protest," and predicted that "226 years after the Boston Tea Party, the Seattle coffee shop riot will leave its mark" (Baker 1999).

Newspapers were not the only media organizations that paid attention to the small group of antiglobalization terrorists among the more than forty thousand peaceful protesters in Seattle. ABC News reported in four TV broadcasts, NBC News in two, CBS News and CNN on one TV program each, and National Public Radio covered this particular group once.

The following is an excerpt from a report by Kelly O'Donnell on the NBC *Nightly News* broadcast of December 2, 1999:

> *Unidentified Protester:* We feel it's necessary, sometimes, to break the law and be rebellious.
> *O'Donnell:* Their strategy: open advocacy of violence. A member calling himself "Sanchyo Koyen" on that same show.
> *Sanchyo Koyen:* Because the bottle leaving your hand hits into a cop who's dead. Because the sound of breaking glass is music.
> *O'Donnell:* In Seattle store fronts tonight marred by their symbol: an "A" for "anarchy."

O'Donnell closed the segment with the following evaluation, "Experts believe this group has been around only a year, but, in just three days, their mark left on Seattle and watched around the world."[10]

Given this level of media attention to the deeds and motives of a small faction of protesters, who provided the mass media with dramatic images of seemingly young idealists clashing with brutal riot police, one can't help but conclude that the publicity rationale undergirding political violence had worked superbly. This point was not lost on the anarchists themselves, who, like the ELF and other eco-terrorists, cultivated their media image. Some reporters who tried to interview the anarchists occupying a Seattle warehouse were advised to contact the group's "publicist." Although chiding the "corporate media" for biased reporting, these anarchists (said to share unabomber Theodore Kaczynski's antitechnology, anticonsumerism views) recognized the value of nonstop media attention. "The WTO protests are a watershed," they proclaimed on one Web site and predicted that "after the Battle of Seattle the anarchists will no longer be ignored."[11] If this seemed an overly optimistic assessment, it was not. The actions, staged by a few anarchists, surrounding the WTO meeting ignited a chain reaction in the triangle of political communication described in the previous chapter: Almost always in these cases, the political violence in Seattle resulted in news reporting that put the perpetrators' causes and grievances in front of the general public and decision makers alike. When he arrived in Seattle to attend the WTO meeting, President Bill Clinton denounced the political violence that had occurred, but he also expressed sympathies for the sentiments of the protesters and suggested that, in the future, nongovernmental organizations, such as environmental groups and labor unions, should have a place at the negotiating table when global issues are discussed. One wonders whether the President would have made this point without the much publicized violence by a bunch of anarchists.

This is not to suggest that the news media should have ignored the violent part of the Seattle protests; if they had done so, they would have failed in their basic mission and responsibility—to inform the public. But understanding the fundamental role of the press does not mean that one should ignore the disproportionate volume of media attention devoted to the disturbances and the faction that caused them. The news coverage magnified the violence at the expense of thousands of peaceful protests and the proceedings at the WTO summit itself. There is no doubt that the dramatic visuals of violent deeds in the streets and the catchy sound bites ("Hey, hey. Ho, ho. The WTO has to go!") manipulated the media to report about a minor case of political violence as if it constituted a "riot" or "riots," as many reports labeled the disturbances. This kind of exaggeration attested to the tendency of the contemporary news media to magnify violence, whether of the political or purely criminal variety, in the ever increasing temptation to cross the once distinct line between news-as-information and news-as-infotainment—with infotainment winning hands down.

The imbalance in the news was not lost on attentive citizens who noticed that the few violent protesters received the bulk of media coverage, while the message of nonviolent critics of the WTO and its policies was lost. One reader of the *St. Louis Post-Dispatch* wrote in a letter to the editor,

> I, my family and my neighbors were severely disappointed by the coverage of the World Trade Organization protests in Seattle. The events described to me by people who were there bear little resemblance to what I was told by the media. The articles and pictures in the Post-Dispatch focused on the few people who wore costumes, not on the Christian groups, unions, and human rights groups— 50,000 citizens making their voices heard in a democracy. Articles focused on a few hundred people who fought back when attacked and gassed, not on the 49,700 whose behavior was impeccably non-violent. Little space was devoted to the WTO itself, or to its efforts to reverse the labor, human rights and environmental standards that Americans have worked to achieve.[12]

Another reader complained,

> Much has been made of the violence done to Seattle's downtown shops by black-clad "anarchists." The irony is that a few shattered shop windows are receiving more media attention than the large-scale violence visited on people all over the globe by the World Trade Organization.[13]

One reader noted in a letter to the Boston Globe that "a few protesters in Seattle engaged in vandalism, but the vast majority were completely non-violent."[14]

With the huge success of Seattle under their belts, antiglobalization extremists upstaged their far more numerous nonviolent brethren at subsequent international forums with antiglobalization terrorism that resulted each instance in a great deal of media attention. During a meeting of the International Monetary Fund and the World Bank in Prague in late September 2000, some hundred extremists stood out from the crowd of ten to twelve thousand peaceful demonstrators and orchestrated two days of violence that, unlike the incident in Seattle, deserved the riot label. On day one, the protesters threw chunks of pavement and Molotov cocktails toward a police cordon that protected the Prague Congress Center, where the delegates met. When the police responded with tear gas, water canons, and swinging batons, the activists who wore masks and protective padding backed off temporarily, only to attack shops and restaurants in the Czech capital. Several dozen persons, among them two delegates, were injured. Steve Schifferes of BBC News, who witnessed the protests in Prague, reported:

> Things soon turned violent as anarchists began to tear down barriers near a rail line that runs under the road bridge [that leads to the convention site]. There was the repeated sound of tear gas being fired, and black smoke as riot police raced to the spot. Soon there was also black smoke rising, as BBC camera crews filmed what appeared to be petrol bombs thrown by the demonstrators.

The following day, a smaller group of extremists attacked police officers guarding the Hilton hotel, where many of the delegates stayed. "Whether the IMF and the World Bank exist or do not exist is a matter which will be decided by the will of the 182 countries who are represented here, not by a handful of hoodlums in the streets of Prague," said India's Finance Minister Vashwant Sinha.[15] But the mass-mediated violence of protesters, who accused these organizations of doing more harm than good to poor nations on account of their lending practices, had certainly caught the attention of the delegates. Before the disturbances forced organizers to end the event a day earlier than planned, James Wolfensohn (World Bank) and Horst Koehler (International Monetary Fund) assured protesters outside that they were mindful of their demands, such as canceling the debt of very poor countries, and were willing to engage in a dialogue with their critics.

By the time the European Union convened at the French Riviera in early December 2000, antiglobalization protests and antiglobalization terror had become part of international summits. In Nice, the actions of peaceful protesters were lost in a wave of violence committed by anarchists and members of well-established terrorist organizations from the region—specifically Basque and Corsican separatists. As several thousand militant protesters (many of them masked, clad in black, and out-of-control) hurled flares, garbage cans, and gasoline bombs at riot police, smashed windows with sledgehammers and baseball bats, set fire to a bank building, and sprayed their slogans onto storefronts, they also injured two dozen police officers and caused significant property damage. Many of the peaceful protesters were angry and disgusted that political violence by a minority had once again received all of the media attention. Members of labor unions and other nonviolent organizations, who demonstrated for a more socialist rather than capitalist Europe, were overshadowed by the perpetrators of violence. "We are peaceful protesters. We do not want any violence," said one frustrated student. "These people are terrorists."[16]

Several weeks later, when Swiss police used what was widely criticized as excessive force to stop antiglobalization protesters from entering the Alpine community of Davos and demonstrate against the World Economic Forum, angry protesters went on a rampage in Zurich, overturning cars and smashing windows. The fact that the organizers of the Davos meeting had invited and listened to globalization critics had not pacified the militants of the movement. But, then, giving a speech to influential corporate and political leaders is not the material that should be highlighted in the news. Whether in Prague, Nice, or Zurich, when antiglobalization violence broke out, reporters reminded their readers, viewers, and listeners often that the "Battle of Seattle" was the model for this new wave of antiglobalization riots. Yet, the problems plaguing international events in the post-Seattle period were far more serious; the extremist elements flocking to them seemed certain that raising the level of violence would assure continued media attention. After thousands of antiglobalization protesters and riot police clashed violently during a meeting of the Global Forum of political, finance, and technology leaders in Naples, Italy, in the spring of 2001, one Neapolitan said what he witnessed was "like guerrilla warfare."[17]

In April 2001, black-clad anarchists with ski masks or handkerchiefs over their mouths also led the charge against the Summit of the Americas in Quebec City and Canadian riot police protecting the perimeters of the conference site, where President Bush and the heads of thirty-three other countries met to discuss a hemispheric trade zone or FTAA (Free Trade Area of the Americas). Once again, more than twenty thousand peaceful protesters from North, Central, and South America demonstrated peacefully against the proposed trade initiative, with many demonstrators charging that large corporations would benefit from the new solution at the expense of working people everywhere. Once again, the violence that injured dozens of protesters and dozens of policemen was the work of modern anarchists. While most anarchists known as "black blocs" tried to hide their personal identity, some displayed the letters CLAC for the Quebec-based anarchist organization La Convergence des luttes anti-capitalistes (the Anti-Capitalist Convergence). There was no doubt that the much-publicized violence in Seattle was the fuse that ignited this sort of political violence. The radical organizers mentioned the Seattle model on their Web sites; violent and nonviolent protesters in Quebec City talked about the success of the Seattle initiatives. One young demonstrator in a ski mask, who was mindful that people remembered Seattle, told a reporter, "If we can pass our message, we have gone in a good direction."[18]

Their message did get out. Just as in Seattle, Prague, Nice, Davos, and Naples, the mass media, especially television, devoted most headlines, visuals, and text overwhelmingly to the politically motivated violence rather than to the peaceful protests and the summit procedures. All news stations, such as CNN and MSNBC, reported nonstop about the clashes between protesters and riot police in Quebec City, repeatedly replaying the most stunning scenes in which violent protesters tore down part of a fence that had been especially built to keep them away from the Summit site. A number of Summit participants referred in their speeches to the protesters' concerns. President Bush, for example, promised to listen to those "inside this hall and to those outside this hall who want to join us in constructive dialogue." Brazil's President Fernando Henrique Cardoso said that he sympathized with the protesters' "fear of a free trade agreement or globalization without a human face."[19] While Cardoso and others were critical of the violence outside, neither the media nor the Summit leaders would have paid this degree of attention to the protesters had there only been peaceful demonstrations. Following the events in Quebec City, Fareed Zakaria concluded in his "World View" column in *Newsweek*, "By taunting the police, beating drums and throwing rocks, the rioters make it pretty clear that they want not rational dialogue but the world's attention—and they have succeeded again." Zakaria also noted that the "success" of these sort of violent protests had "begun to persuade some left-of-center politicians in the West to start speaking the new language of anti-globalization."[20]

But during a European Union summit in Götheburg, Sweden, in June of 2001, when hundreds of anarchists devastated the center of Sweden's second largest city by smashing windows, looting stores, setting fire to makeshift barricades, and battling the police, Britain's Prime Minister Tony Blair, the leader of the Labor Party, and Germany's Chancellor Gerhard Schroeder, a Social Democrat, were particularly critical of those responsible for the violence that left several dozen persons severely injured. Blaming the "anarchist traveling circus" for the riots, Blair called on other heads of government "not to concede an inch" to the violent protesters, while Schroeder said that "no country should tolerate these criminals."[21] Yet, several days of massive street violence had once again gained far more attention from the news media and the public than had the substantive discussions during the EU meetings. As the German Press Agency reported, "television networks all over Europe were showing the horrifying pictures" of the riots in Sweden.[22]

A few weeks later, violent antiglobalization activists (an estimated several thousand) and a massive police force (about twenty thousand) clashed during the Group of Eight economic summit in Genoa, Italy, in the most violent encounter of this kind. One protester, a twenty-three-year-old Italian, was killed by police bullets; many others—on both sides—were injured. As was the case at all antiglobalization protests since Seattle, the legitimate concerns of the vast majority of demonstrators were lost in news reports that focused mostly, in many cases exclusively, on the violence in the streets. More than similar incidents from Seattle to Götheburg, the brutality of the Italian police, filmed by TV crews and viewed by audiences around the globe, became a major issue. Ramon de Miguel, Spain's European Affairs Minister, called the street scenes during the Genoa summit "a replay of fascism."[23] And Herman Lutz, the leader of the European Police Union, who watched the riot scenes on TV, thought that it must be "in some kind of dictatorship or in Eastern Europe or in Cuba, but not among us in the middle of Europe."[24] While such criticism was justified—even the chief of the Italian police Gianni De Gennaro acknowledged that some police units used excessive force—this widely publicized finger pointing was precisely what the violent anarchist core hoped to accomplish: to bare the flaws and inhumanity of and to stir wider radical opposition against the institutions they fought.

### Hostage Drama as "Reality" Television Show

"Every day Renate Wallert dies a little bit more," the female anchor on one of Germany's TV channels said with feeling in her voice. Dispirited hostages and their armed captors appeared on the television screen. The human drama that German audiences watched day after day in the summer of 2000 unfolded far away on another continent in a remote jungle on the island of Jolo in the southern part of the Philippines. On this occasion, the camera focused on the

fifty-seven-year-old-German teacher, Renate Wallert, who suffered from a se-
vere case of hypertension. Lying in a hammock, she was shivering and crying.
Her husband Werner tried to get her to drink some water. Nearby, the couple's
son Marc (twenty-seven) looked on—helpless and resigned. In another scene,
the sick woman was pondering suicide. And then there was the moment, when
her husband, after using a knife to open a nasty infection on his hand, collapsed suddenly. Galib Andang, one leader of the hostage-holders who went
by the nickname Commander Robot, was not moved. Some time earlier, he
had told the hostages rather triumphantly that international journalists were
on their way. "Soon the whole world will see how you suffer," he had said with
the confidence of a television executive who has landed a hit show.[25]

And what a hit show it became, fitting right into the then quite new "reality" genre of television. Providing far more drama, suspense, and human interest than *Survivor* or *Big Brother*, this reality show was offered, in one version or another, on literally all of Germany's television and radio channels and
in the print media as well. The international cast of twenty-one hostages—the
German family along with French, Finnish, South African, Lebanese, and
Malaysian citizens—quickly formed several cliques that did not always see
eye-to-eye. This conflict and the ever changing captors-captives relationship
provided the stuff that reality television thrives on. However, there was one
crucial difference here: The hostage drama on Jolo was not reality television
of the *Survivor* variety, but brutal real life drama. A mix between terrorists and
bandits, the Abu Sayyaf group, who demanded a separate Muslim state in the
southern Philippines and the release of two prominent terrorists from U.S.
prisons (Ramzi Yousef found guilty in the World Trade Center bombing and
Sheik Omar Abdel-Rahman in jail for conspiring to blow up landmarks in
New York), had beheaded two Filipino hostages earlier that year and now
threatened the lives of their new captives. But as audiences in Germany (and
in France and Finland as well) were able to follow the hostage saga close up on
their television and computer screens and in the rest of the mass media as
well, the lines between news and entertainment were often blurred. Whether
it was the exotic setting on a far away island in the Pacific or the immediacy of
the hostage situation brought right into living rooms, or perhaps both, audiences watched as if they were following reality entertainment shows which are,
after all, also covered as news events. At the height of the drama, one of Germany's most respected journalists and TV anchors, Ulrich Wickert, said that
he could not remember having ever seen anything like this in television. He
suggested that people who watched the hostage drama "must be told that this
is not infotainment, that here real peoples' lives are in danger." Although recognizing the problems of live TV transmissions that the hostage-holders ac-
commodated, and, in fact, wanted, Wickert nevertheless supported the con-

tinued broadcast of these visuals and interviews under duress because of their "news value."[26] When Marc Wallert, the last of the German hostages, was finally freed, his first words to waiting journalists were: "It is incredible, it is like in the movie, I can't believe it."[27] Even for the hostages, who had been forced to play starring roles in the terrorism show and had sometimes courted and sometimes cursed the intrusive media, real life seemed, in the end, like fiction—a movie or infotainment. This confusion also befell the mother of the Oklahoma City bomber, Timothy McVeigh: when she called McVeigh's father after learning of their son's arrest, she did not cry out that Tim was held for an unspeakable act of violence, instead she screamed, "Timmy is all over CNN" (Michel and Herbeck 2001, 264).

Not surprisingly, for those Europeans who watched the Philippine jungle reality show for months, the German, French, and Finnish hostages became instant celebrities in their respective homelands. And just like movie stars, the hostages were admired by their fans and put down by their detractors. Renate Wallert became the object of a passionate public debate after her release, when she traveled home to Germany after leaving her husband and son behind in captivity. Part of this debate took place in letter to the editor sections of newsprint.

In Germany's largest daily newspaper, *Bild Zeitung*, for example, Renate Wallert's supporters wrote,

> Everyone who condemns Mrs. Wallert now, because she left her husband and son behind, should go for twelve weeks to Jolo to the rebels.
> Whoever sits in the safety of Germany should not judge Mrs. Wallert. I am sure it was with a heavy heart that she left husband and son behind.

But her detractors criticized her and her family harshly:

> A masterful acting job! An "Oscar" for Renate Wallert.
> For me Mrs. Wallert was never credible. Her moaning in television was awful and miserable. And how can one leave one's son and husband.

Fellow citizens were especially caustic because one of the Wallerts' sons, who had not been kidnapped, had taken steps to market and sell the hostage story to the highest bidder while his parents and brother were held hostage in a distant jungle. In a letter to *Bild Zeitung*, a reader complained,

> While the family was still in captivity the enterprising son in Goettingen [the Wallerts' home town] signed exclusive marketing contracts. This gentleman should be asked to pay back the public funds [spent for efforts to free the hostages].[28]

In the 1970s and 1980s, when hostage-taking for political purposes was popular among many groups in many parts of the world, especially in Europe, the Middle East, and Latin America, those captors, too, vied for media coverage to get their messages across. But whether the so-called students in the U.S. Embassy in Teheran during the Iran hostage crisis (1979–1981) or the Muslim Fundamentalists in Lebanon during the long-lasting hostage situations of the 1980s, these terrorists allowed only sporadic media access to their captives and, whenever it fit their plans, made videotapes or other forms of communication available to the press (Nacos 1996b). The Abu Sayyaf wrote a new chapter in the annals of hostage-holders' media management. At times the terror gang asked western journalists for "fees" in exchange for access to their jungle camps, and, when this method did not yield enough hard cash, they took whole groups and individual media representatives hostage, stripped them of their belongings, and extorted ransom. Even after the Abu Sayyaf's tactics had scared western reporters away, the captors and their hostages remained a prominent story in Europe, especially France, Germany, and Finland, thanks to the feeds by a Philippine TV station with obviously good terrorist connections. In spite of their shrewd news management, the Abu Sayyaf must have been surprised by the massive attention they received abroad. Kidnappings had been their trademark all along as a means to collect ransom money for arms and support from their comrades in the fight for a separate Muslim state. They struck gold when they abducted twenty-one persons from a nearby Malaysian island on Easter Sunday 2000: the German, French, and Finnish citizens proved especially valuable because the European governments asked officials in Manila for a peaceful, not military, resolution of the hostage crises. After the Abu Sayyaf compelled the media to cover the hostages and transmit their demands and grievances to the world, the abductors also upped the ante with respect to their ransom demands: one million dollars per European hostage—far more than what they asked for the Asians they held. At this point, it must have been clear to the captors that the people in France, Finland, and Germany, after witnessing the fears and hopes of their captive brethren, wanted a happy, not a bloody, ending of the hostage story—a sentiment that was not lost on leaders in those countries.

Whether the kidnappers had staged the hostage situation and, from their perspective, mass-mediated terrorism at its best with the input and assurances from sympathetic quarters abroad, such as longtime friends in Libya's highest circle (as rumors had it), remains unclear. But while France, Germany, and Finland did not to agree to pay ransom, they were in contact with Libya's leader Muammar Gadhafi and embraced his offer to negotiate the hostages' release. Sending a Libyan emissary who was acquainted with the Abu Sayyaf to negotiate a deal, Gadhafi eventually paid the demanded ransom or, as Libyan officials called it, "development aid" to the hostage-holders. When the terrorists released the Europeans in batches, the hostages, who had been held for more than four or five months, did not fly straight home but made Tripoli, Libya, their first stop as they had agreed to in exchange for their freedom. Wearing t-shirts with a picture of Gadhafi and the name of the International Gadhafi Foundation, the ex-hostages were content to play a part in Gadhafi's shrewd propaganda game. The onetime sponsor of international terrorism was now hailed for saving hostages' lives and negotiating their freedom. And the media was there to report the love-in Gadhafi style and transmit the visuals of the happy occasion straight into European living rooms. As the *Washington Post* commented,

> Actually, Mr. Gadhafi is not a born-again humanitarian but a calculating benefi-
> ciary of the kidnapings [sic]. His ransom-paying was conditional on European
> kowtowing. Indeed, with the European's acquiescence, he prolonged the
> hostages' agony, requiring the six let go this week to make a stop in Tripoli,
> Libya's capital, after their release. As relatives and friends waited back in the
> hostages' home countries, he used them as props in a "welcoming ceremony,"
> whose major themes were the greatness of Moammar Gadhafi and the perfidy of
> the United States. By the way, officials of France and Germany were present dur-
> ing this propaganda assault on the NATO ally.[29]

Regardless of some media voices in the United States and in Europe that were critical of Gadhafi and the European governments involved, the Abu Sayyaf group and Gadhafi, the onetime (and perhaps still) sponsor of terrorism, demonstrated how to milk the mass media for their propaganda purposes.

Before the Abu Sayyaf took the Europeans hostage, the group was hardly known outside the Philippines. This changed once the media reported on the identity of the hostage-holders, their grievances, demands, and ultimate political goals. While the human drama with the hostages at center stage received the lion's share of the coverage, there were numerous and often sympathetic reports about the plight of the Muslims in the Southern part of the Philippines. Just as citizens in France, Finland, or Germany during the hostage ordeal came to recognize the faces of their respective countries' hostages, the public also became aware of the Abu Sayyaf and his objectives. From the beginning of the hostage situation on the island of Jolo in late April 2000 through the end of that year, the group was mentioned by name in 153 stories in the leading German newspaper *Die Welt* and there were sixty-five in the leading French newspaper *Le Monde*. The rather limited number of German news sources in the Lexis-Nexis database (not including the mass tabloids, regional presses, or the transcripts of TV and radio channels), produced 2,200 documents containing the term "Abu Sayyaf" for the period beginning April 23, 2000, the day of the hostage taking, and ending December 31, 2000. The still more limited selection of French news sources available in the Lexis-Nexis archives lists a total of 1,445 documents for search word and time period.

In sharp contrast, the far more comprehensive selection of the U.S. print press in the Lexis-Nexis database carried only 373 stories mentioning the Abu Sayyaf during the time, when a U.S. citizen, twenty-five-year-old Jeffrey Schilling, was held hostage and repeatedly threatened to be killed by the group. This modest interest in the American hostage on the part of the U.S. press was partially caused by the captors: By the time they grabbed Schilling, they had scared the foreign media away and no longer granted media access to their hideaways and hostages. Moreover, the young American had become a hostage under rather bizarre circumstances: He visited the Abu Sayyaf jungle camp with his Filipino wife, a cousin of one of the terrorists, when he was kidnapped. While not granting Schilling direct contact with the media, like their European hostages earlier, the captors allowed and even encouraged Schilling repeatedly to contact radio stations via cellular phone to beg the U.S. government for his freedom and to demand ten million dollars. Commander Robot had told the European press all along that he was after an American hostage because, in his calculation, one American was worth ten times as much as a non-American. But given the circumstances of Schilling's abduction, the inability of the media to investigate his claims and his situation, and the lack of powerful visuals, this hostage made the news in his homeland far less often than the Europeans did in their respective countries.

But there was probably another reason why the U.S. media showed little interest in Schilling's captivity: The U.S. government, first during Clinton's and later during George W. Bush's presidency, refrained from public comments aside from occasional low-key and low-level statements that Washington would not pay ransom or otherwise get involved. The media's reaction was markedly different after Abu Sayyaf kidnapped three Americans along with seventeen Asians on April 27, 2001, and eventually beheaded one of the U.S. citizens. Soon after this new hostage drama began, the U.S. State Department, as well as spokespersons at the U.S. Embassy in Manila, referred frequently to the situation. In the four months following the kidnapping—before the confirmed death of Guillermo Sobero, a forty-year-old American from Corona, California—the U.S. print media available in the Lexis-Nexis archives published a total of 466 articles mentioning the "Abu Sayyaf"—more than they did during the seven-and-a-half months of Jeffrey Schilling's captivity. In both cases, the American media had no direct access to the hostage-holders or the American hostages. But whereas U.S. State Department officials kept a very low profile during Schilling's captivity, they were far less hesitant to speak out against the Abu Sayyaf after Sobero and two other Americans were kidnapped. In both instances, the media seemed to take their cue from Washington: When U.S. officials were mostly silent (in the Schilling case), news reports were scarce; when officials spoke out (in the case of the three other American hostages), news reports were far more frequent.

Following the events of September 11, 2001, the Abu Sayyaf became a target in the American "war against terrorism" in that a U.S. military contingent was flown to the Philippines to advise the Filipino army in its battle against the Islamic extremists after it was revealed that the Abu Sayyaf group had ties to al-Qaeda and groups affiliated with the bin Laden-led terror organization.

## The Terrorist Scheme and the News

These three cases of political violence and the news coverage they received speak to terrorism's considerable success in exploiting the mass media for publicity purposes. The American media over-covered the eco-terrorist incidents near New York and reacted with saturation coverage and overdramatization to the antiglobalization violence in Seattle; the German and French media did both in an even more extreme fashion with respect to the hostage drama in the Philippines. The exposure in the news assured the particular perpetrators of the attention they craved. In addition, news reports described and discussed the grievances and causes that motivated the respective groups to resort to violence in each of these incidents. While such propaganda may not enlist outright support and new recruits for a particular cause, it comes to the attention of the public, especially the interested public, and may even enlist sympathies. After reading about the fire bombings committed by the Earth Liberation Front, a reader of the *Baltimore Sun* wrote,

> It seems that eco-terrorists are those who perpetuate terror on the ecosystem. To give that designation to the ELF misses the point entirely. Those who develop forests, wetlands, and open space for the sole purpose of making a buck are the real eco-terrorists and should be stopped. The ELF presents one method among many to protect the environment.[30]

Similarly, there were more expressions of support for the causes of the protesters in Seattle—the violent faction included—than for the targets of the protests: the World Trade Organization and proglobalization corporate interests. In a letter to the editor, one reader, representative of others, wrote in the *Los Angeles Times,*

> When idealistic youth and organized labor are in agreement on such powerful issues, the press should at least air their position. The WTO is an organization that is stacking the deck against a hard-working middle class—not just in America but worldwide. The American Dream—an ideal that transcends borders—is not a handout, it is an opportunity, and the WTO destroys opportunity for millions by linking big business with big government.[31]

While most people in Europe who followed the hostage drama in the Philippines did not express sympathies for the hostage-holders, many were troubled by the willingness of their governments to deal with the captors if only with Muammar Gadhafi as go-between. These sentiments were especially strong because many citizens suspected that they were not fully informed about the transactions that eventually led to the release of the hostages. In a lengthy and thoughtful letter to the publisher of the newspaper *Frankfurter Allgemeine Zeitung*, one reader took issue with the German government's soft stand in the hostage saga, arguing that an earlier government had faced similar problems and had been tougher. The reader argued, "Then the unpopular but the only right decision was made: no deals with terrorists in order to prevent greater evil either in the particular case or in future copy cat deeds. To go onto one's knees for perpetrators is the wrong signal."[32] While none of the three cases examined here came even close to the terrorist spectaculars of the 1980s, 1990s, or the anti-American terrorism in the new century, those responsible for the political violence in these three instances were very successful in invading the triangle of political communication that was described in the introductory chapter (or, to put it from the perspectives of the perpetrators, the calculus of mass-mediated political violence or terrorism worked beautifully).

This conclusion seems at odds with the widely held view that only truly spectacular incidents of political violence result in massive news reporting and have a chance to rise to the level of media events. Based on detailed content analyses of news coverage, students of terrorism have assumed for a long time that when more blood is spilled in instances of political violence, more printer's ink and air time are devoted to those events by the mass media. While not discarding this conventional wisdom, one needs to recognize that even relatively minor cases of political violence, if committed during particular events, in particular locations, and against particular targets, are likely to attract a great deal of media reporting even if there is no loss of life, no major injuries, no significant damage to property. I chose the three cases analyzed in this chapter precisely to demonstrate terrorism's considerable publicity success, regardless of whether the acts of political violence rise to the level of terrorist spectaculars. Major terrorist incidents, such as the suicide attack on the USS Cole in 2000 and the simultaneous bombings of the U.S. embassies in Kenya and Tanzania in 1998, as well as the investigations, arrests, and trials that followed those lethal attacks, were more massively covered over a period of months and years than the three cases analyzed in this chapter. Thus, from August 12, 1998, when the embassies in Kenya and Tanzania were bombed, to December 31, 2000, the *New York Times* devoted 304 news stories to the bombings and their aftermath, CBS News dedicated 186 stories, NBC News

**TABLE 3.1**
**News Coverage 1/1/1999 through 12/31/1999**

|                  | ABC News | CBS News | NBC News | NPR | N.Y. Times |
|------------------|----------|----------|----------|-----|------------|
|                  | (N)      | (N)      | (N)      | (N) | (N)        |
| Terrorism        | 216      | 434      | 191      | 85  | 948        |
| Health Insurance | 176      | 389      | 274      | 269 | 2,177      |
| Medicare         | 94       | 285      | 157      | 134 | 756        |
| Poverty          | 45       | 76       | 39       | 79  | 1,256      |
| Social Security  | 100      | 310      | 119      | 145 | 1,551      |

N = Number of news segments/stories
*Source*: Compiled from Lexis-Nexis data and *New York Times* on-line archive.

developed 73 reports, ABC News 65, and NPR 34. In less than three months, from October 12, 2000, when suicide bombers struck the USS Cole, to December 31, 2000, CBS News devoted 252 segments to the incident, ABC News 163, NBC News 109, the *New York Times* 79, and NPR 24.

One does not need to ignore or minimize the consequences of mass-mediated political violence and the ever present threat of terrorism to recognize that other problems deserve the same and even greater attention. This point was not lost on Shanto Iyengar and Donald Kinder, who found that during a six-year period in the 1980s, the Evening News of the three major TV networks (ABC News, CBS News, and NBC News) broadcast more stories about terrorism than about poverty, unemployment, racial equality, and crime (Iyengar and Kinder 1991, 27). While not quite as drastic as in the 1980s, this imbalance in the news continued in the 1990s and into the new millennium. Table 3.1 shows that throughout 1999, CBS News and ABC News addressed terrorism far more frequently than poverty, Medicare, health insurance, and Social Security. NBC News mentioned health insurance issues more often than terrorism, but poverty, Medicare, and Social Security were referred to less often. While paying a great deal of attention to this kind of political violence, National Public Radio and the *New York Times* were less slanted in favor of terrorism. During the 2000 presidential election campaign, the major candidates discussed terrorism occasionally, but their focus was on domestic policy issues, such as Medicare and Social Security. Not surprisingly, the media agenda reflected the candidates' major themes and issues to some extent. Still, as table 3.2 shows, terrorism was more frequently discussed on TV and radio news broadcasts than all or some of four important domestic policy issues. The sole exception was the coverage in the *New York Times* where terrorism was less often addressed than Medicare, Social Security, poverty, and health insurance. What is particularly striking for 1999 and 2000 is the lack of attention paid to

**TABLE 3.2**
**News Coverage 1/1/2000 through 12/31/2000**

|                  | ABC News | CBS News | NBC News | NPR | N.Y. Times |
|------------------|----------|----------|----------|-----|------------|
|                  | (N)      | (N)      | (N)      | (N) | (N)        |
| Terrorism        | 179      | 336      | 136      | 67  | 889        |
|                  |          |          |          |     |            |
| Health Insurance | 69       | 315      | 211      | 223 | 2,051      |
| Medicare         | 258      | 280      | 130      | 120 | 1,059      |
| Poverty          | 22       | 40       | 19       | 60  | 1,522      |
| Social Security  | 157      | 256      | 107      | 90  | 1,831      |

N = Number of news segments/stories
Source: Compiled from Lexis-Nexis data and New York Times on-line archive.

poverty compared to terrorism by both TV and radio news media. The *New York Times* was a notable exception in this respect.

### Suicide Bombers in the News

When suicide bombers strike, they are condemned as terrorist killers by one side and celebrated as martyrs and heroes by the other. This became obvious amidst a wave of Palestinian suicide bombings inside Israel during the second Intifada. Seen from abroad, as Bueno de Mesquita has observed, "the initial impact [of suicide bombs targeting civilians] is revulsion, but the long-term impact is that it makes people aware of the desperate plight of those doing it."[33] However, this long-term effect is not automatic but the result of news reporting. As the number and the severity of lethal suicide terrorism against Israelis increased in the fall of 2000 and, even more so, in 2001, the U.S. media reported at length about the tragedies surrounding civilian victims of such attacks, especially if American citizens were among them. But there were also stories about the young bombers, their mentors in the Hamas and Islamic Jihad organization, and their own parents willing to let their children die "if that's what it takes to get our homeland back."[34] In a strange way, these lethal attacks on civilians, however strongly condemned abroad, emerged as Palestinians' most valuable public relations tool. The western mass media (including American print, radio, and television), simply by covering the phenomenon of suicide bombers, seemed to highlight the image of the Palestinians as an oppressed and weak people unable to fight Israel on an equal military scale. In the words of David Plotz, these images suggested "to the outside world that this is an unfair fight—the plucky poor Palestinians doing the only thing they can to resist the Zionist oppressors. . . . This image of the unfair fight is critical to the Palestinians. . . . The longer the bombing campaign goes on, the more enraged Israelis will become and the more likely they will be to counterstrike too forcefully."[35]

Within a three-week period in the summer of 2001, when a series of deadly suicide bombings occurred in Israel, the major American TV networks aired several reports on the young Palestinians willing to die and help "to liberate Palestine." The print media, too, reported on the background of Palestinian children and youth in the growing ranks of suicide bombers: In a segment on ABC's *World News This Morning*, for example, a thirteen-year-old boy named Muhammed was shown as he drew a picture of himself with explosives strapped around his body—ready to blow himself up, if that meant killing Jews and "liberat[ing] Palestine."[36] On CBS's *60 Minutes*, Bob Simon interviewed Hassan Salameh, the mastermind of an earlier Palestinian suicide wave, and told the story of nineteen-year-old Majdi, who was recruited in the Al Fawar refugee camp for a suicide mission by his cousin, Abu Wardeh, a twenty-year-old psychology student. Abu told Simon that Majdi had made his decision "to meet God as a martyr" within half an hour and recalled, "I described to him how God would compensate the martyr for sacrificing his life for his land. If you become a martyr, God will give you 70 virgins, 70 wives and everlasting happiness."[37] Following the suicide bombing of a crowded pizzeria in downtown Jerusalem that killed fifteen civilians, including six children, NBC's *Nightly News* reported on the funerals of thirty-one-year-old Judith Shoshana Greenbaum, a pregnant teacher from New Jersey, and that of twenty-three-year-old Izzedin Masri, a suicide bomber. Correspondent Jim Maceda concluded his broadcast by saying, "Two funerals: Judith Shoshana Greenbaum mourned today an innocent Jewish victim. Izzedine-al-Masri [sic] as a new Palestinian hero."[38] This was the lead paragraph in a *Washington Post* article headlined "Where Palestinian 'martyrs' are groomed": "Two young men described as volunteer suicide bombers stood silently as their Islamic mentor bid them a tranquil good evening. 'And don't forget to say your prayers,' he reminded them as they left his home."[39]

In describing the human faces behind the young suicide bombers and those recruiting and sending them to kill innocent victims and themselves, these and similar reports seemed at times equally as sympathetic to these Palestinians as to their Israeli victims. Moreover, words alone did not tell the whole story. In late 2000 and throughout 2001, Palestinians seemed to win the publicity war between competing visual images of human suffering on both sides. This was not lost on Israelis and their friends in the West. Indeed, Colonel Raanan Grissin of the Israeli Army suggested, "You've got to lose on the battlefield in order to win with the media. In other words, the more casualties you have, the more you're presented as the underdog, as the weak side, the greater is the likelihood that you will be able to draw the sympathy or attention of the public."[40] At the same time, media analyst Daoud Kuttab concluded that "the whole revolution of the information [with the instant transmission of visual images] is really, in a way, helping the Palestinians in the media campaign."[41] Aware of losing the public relations war, the Israeli Army gave its soldiers small digital cameras to document "Palestinian gunfire directed at them and themselves not as aggressors but as besieged."[42] Digital cameras in the hands of Israeli soldiers or not, the news coverage abroad did not change in fundamental ways. Since the Palestinian side provided more visuals of victims than the Israelis, they and their cause seemed at times to receive more compelling attention in the media abroad.

This advantage was even more pronounced in the spring of 2002, when an unprecedented number of Israeli civilians were victims of Palestinian suicide bombers and Palestinian civilians were harmed during the military response by Israeli Defense Forces. While both the supporters of the Israelis and the Palestinians criticized the western media, and particular American news organizations, for showing bias in favor of the other side, there was evidence of far more visuals (and spoken and written reports) of Palestinians as victims of Israeli military actions in TV news, newspapers, and news magazines than of Israeli victims of Palestinian suicide bombings. At least in part this was caused by the nature of the conflict: After each of the devastating suicide attacks Israel's response professionals quickly transported the injured to hospitals and removed the dead, leaving less terrifying scenes for camera teams and reporters than were found by the media in the ongoing fighting in the West Bank. Moreover, many news organizations seemed more inclined to publicize touching human interest stories about suicide bombers—especially female ones—than of the victims of suicide attacks.

### Terrorists, the Media, and the Celebrity Culture

Just in time for his execution, MSNBC presented a special program about Oklahoma City bomber Timothy McVeigh as part of the series "Headliners and Legends" that is typically devoted to Hollywood and Broadway stars. For Caryn James, a TV critic for the *New York Times*, the program "said everything about the transformation of Mr. McVeigh into a celebrity, however vilified."[43] This was hardly surprising at a time, when "life itself is an entertainment medium" (Gabler 1998, 6). As Neil Gabler reminds us, early movie producers discovered that

> audiences need some point of identification if the show is really to engross them. For the movies the solution was stars. For the life movie it is celebrity. Though

stardom in any form automatically confers celebrity, it is just as likely now to be granted to diet gurus, fashion designers and their so-called super-models, lawyers, political pundits, hairdressers, intellectuals, businessmen, journalists, criminals—anyone who happens to appear, however fleetingly, on the radar of the traditional media (Gabler 1998, 7).

While not listing "terrorists," Gabler is well aware that the saturation coverage of terrorist spectaculars makes the perpetrators of mass-mediated political violence excellent candidates for celebrity status, just like O.J. Simpson or Princess Diana. Using one example, Gabler critiqued the glamour treatment that McVeigh received from *Newsweek* magazine this way:

> The cover photo of McVeigh staring off dreamily into space, his lips resolute but also soft, was pure Hurrell, the romantic photographer of Hollywood's golden age. (McVeigh had joked with the photographer Eddie Adams not to let any of the trashy magazines get the photos.) Meanwhile, the interview inside was pure *Photoplay*: gushy, reverent, excited. McVeigh looked, wrote *Newsweek*, "a lot more like a typical Gen-Xer than a deranged loner, much less a terrorist (Gabler 1998, 181).

Certainly, the ever stronger shift from hard news to infotainment—even in serious news organs such as *Newsweek*—figures prominently into this obsession with celebrities on the part of the news media and their audiences. McVeigh's celebrity status was never more obvious than in the days and hours before and after his execution, when news anchors and reporters of all television networks gave "blow-by-blow" accounts of his last hours and minutes—without having access to the actual execution, he was a celebrity for his fans at home and abroad for years—because of his media exposure. According to Michel and Herbeck,

> Some women sent nude pictures of themselves. A young woman from Germany sent perfumed letters with lipstick kiss marks and erotic, extremely detailed stories of her sexual fantasies about McVeigh. From a woman in Ann Arbor, Michigan, came the first of several marriage proposals. . . . And a woman in Baltimore sent a one-hundred-dollar check, telling McVeigh, "Don't give up, fight back" (Michel and Herbeck 2001, 299).[44]

Some of the families that lost loved ones in the Oklahoma City bombing were not happy about the massive news coverage of McVeigh's execution. The daughter of one victim complained bitterly to NBC's Katie Couric that McVeigh "made himself a name" through this kind of television exposure.[45] But she and other family members of victims as well as survivors of the terror had been enlisted shrewdly to take part in this last media circus surrounding McVeigh's final hours. Especially repugnant was the way the TV networks exploited those who survived the Oklahoma blast or lost loved ones in that nightmare by pressing them to articulate their innermost feelings about McVeigh's demise and relive the horror and grief of the past. Jane Clayson, co-host of *The Early Show* on CBS, interviewed Kay Fulton, whose brother was killed in the Oklahoma City bombing, and Tony Brown, whose father-in-law had died in the blast, shortly after they had witnessed McVeigh's execution. The following excerpt from that interview is a good example of the line of questioning:

> *Clayson*: You were hoping to make eye contact with Timothy McVeigh today. Did you?
> *Fulton*. I—I was hoping that he would some-somehow acknowledge our presence, and—and he did. However briefly, he did turn and—and look at each of the witness rooms.
> *Clayson*: And what was that like when he turned his head to your witness room to acknowledge you?
> *Brown*: I took a deep breath, a very deep breath, but knowing that just within a few minutes it would be over.
> *Clayson*: Mm-hmm. When you saw that needle inserted, with McVeigh laying there on the gurney, what was going through your mind? Were you thinking of your father-in-law? Were you thinking of the victims? Were you just happy that he was dying?
> *Brown*: All the above. All the above . . .
> *Clayson*: And when he did die, when he was gone, what was it?

In her discussion of the mass media's role in presenting violence as public entertainment, Sissela Bok quotes a TV reporter who was guided by the belief that "one has to show very strongly emotional images of victims of violence in order to arouse an indifferent public. A wall of indifference has to be overcome" (Bok 1998, 115). The television networks certainly labored hard to exploit and magnify every possible emotional image as they reported the McVeigh execution—whether those images highlighted the grief for the victims, flashbacks to the horrors of the bombing, or pleas of McVeigh's lawyers to explain him as a veteran, a son, and a brother. While many people were relieved that efforts to televise the implementation of the death penalty were rebuffed by the Justice Department and were thus spared of the unthinkable spectacle of a public execution via modern communication technology, Frank Rich took a different stance when he wrote:

> True, the actual images of our government taking McVeigh's life weren't on the air, but their absence made the show more grotesque. Left to the audience's imagination, a death by lethal injection may be more disturbing than its depiction—especially when the four minute act itself is padded out with flashbacks to the greatest (i.e., goriest) video hits from the murderer's crime and promoted

with logos like "Date with Death." Anchors across the TV spectrum talked incessantly about how "somber" the day was, but not so somber that their bosses forsook selling commercials. Wal-Mart, which banned the sales of a journalistic book about McVeigh in its stores, did not refrain from hawking household wares to those tuning in for his execution. When Home Depot's ads for Father's Day presents and snappy trailers for Eddie Murphy's summer yukfest blurred with interviews with Oklahomans whose loved ones had been slaughtered in the Murrah Building, death not only lost its sting, but became merely another sales tool.[46]

While most flagrant in its self-serving and excessive coverage, television was not the only medium that helped McVeigh to achieve fame. Table 3.3 shows that in the last five-and-a-half months of his life, the frequency of news about McVeigh was very generous in television, radio, and print. In all major outlets except the *New York Times*, McVeigh received almost a third as many mentions as the President-elect and then President George W. Bush, and stories about him far exceeded the volume of coverage devoted to Vice-President Richard Cheney, who was widely seen as equally influential and important as the new President. McVeigh's death did not end the media's fascination with the Oklahoma City bomber: Three days after his execution it was revealed that CBS purchased the rights to *American Terrorist: Timothy McVeigh and the Oklahoma City Bombing* by two reporters of the *Buffalo News*, Lou Michel and Dan Herbeck, as the basis for a miniseries about McVeigh and the most deadly act of terrorism on American soil.

Just as the mass media was essential in McVeigh's celebrity status, they were instrumental in making Osama bin Laden a household name even before the attacks on New York and Washington on September 11, 2001. Bin Laden was indicted in New York for masterminding the bombings of U.S. embassies in Kenya and Tanzania in 1998, he regularly issued terrorist threats against the United States and the West, and he was listed on the FBI's "Most Wanted List"—certainly enough reasons for the news media to report on him, his organization,

**TABLE 3.3**
**People in the News (1/1/1001 to 6/30/2001)**

|  | ABC News | CBS News | NBC News | NPR | N.Y. Times |
|---|---|---|---|---|---|
|  | (N) | (N) | (N) | (N) | (N) |
| T. McVeigh | 348 | 250 | 215 | 178 | 212 |
| Pres. Bush | 891 | 923 | 513 | 767 | 3,511 |
| V.P. Cheney | 28 | 19 | 14 | 14 | 372 |

N = Number of news segments/stories
*Source*: Compiled from Lexis-Nexis data and the *New York Times* on-line archive.

**TABLE 3.4**
**People in the News (1/1/2000 through 12/31/2000)**

|              | ABC News | CBS News | NBC News | NPR | N.Y. Times |
|--------------|----------|----------|----------|-----|------------|
|              | (N)      | (N)      | (N)      | (N) | (N)        |
| bin Laden    | 27       | 66       | 8        | 7   | 176        |
| Tony Blair   | 27       | 46       | 1        | 20  | 371        |
| G. Schroeder | 2        | 8        | 1        | 7   | 137        |

N = Number of news segments/stories
*Source*: Compiled from Lexis-Nexis data and the *New York Times* on-line archive.

and their deeds and causes. But one wonders whether bin Laden deserved nearly as much, equally as much, or more attention than the legitimate leaders of important allies or adversaries of the United States. In 2000, for example, CBS News and NBC News broadcast significantly more stories mentioning bin Laden than segments referring to Great Britain's Prime Minister Tony Blair and Germany's Chancellor Gerhard Schroeder. ABC News presented the same number of stories mentioning bin Laden and Blair, far less referring to Schroeder. Both National Public Radio and the *New York Times* devoted more stories to Blair than to bin Laden, but the *New York Times* devoted far more to the terrorist than to Germany's head of government, Schroeder (see table 3.4). Whereas Blair, Schroeder, and other legitimate leaders had a hard time appearing in the news in America, especially in television, Osama bin Laden had no such difficulty. Whether it was another general threat against the United States, the West, and Israel or a more specific threat against a U.S. president or a U.S. embassy, whenever bin Laden sneezed, or was said to have sneezed, the news media took notice.

As Simon Reeve observed, in Osama bin Laden the "world's media had found a new hate-figure to occupy their attention"(Reeve 1999, 2). While bin Laden plotted his fight against the United States and trained his followers in the art of terror from the rugged terrain of Afghanistan, where he was under the protection of the Taliban, he was masterful in exploiting the mass media for his purposes by giving occasional interviews (even to western journalists), issuing *fatawa* or religious edicts to rally fellow Muslims and to frighten his declared enemies, and making his videotaped messages and films available to the press. Thus, in the summer of 2001, a daily newspaper in Kuwait, *al-Rai al-Aam*, received the copy of a one-hundred-minute videotape in which bin Laden took responsibility for and expressed pride in the bombing of the USS Cole in the port of Aden, Yemen. According to the newspaper, the film also showed members of the bin Laden terrorist group, al-Qaeda, training in Afghanistan for the "new holy war on Israeli and American targets" that bin Laden declared on this occasion.[47]

There is no doubt that bin Laden resorted to violence to further his goal to inflict as much pain and damage as possible on his declared enemies and even threatened to "annihilate the West" (Reeve 1999, 265). But although he did not claim responsibility for major acts of terror immediately after the incidents, he praised those deeds eventually and let it be known that he was behind them. Like other terrorists, bin Laden had short-term goals, such as eradicating the U.S. presence in Saudi Arabia and elsewhere in the region, and long-term objectives, such as defeating America and the West and spreading the message and influence of his brand of Islam. Yet, just like others who use and promote political violence as a means to their ends, he, too, recognized that an act of terror alone, even if it is an act of catastrophic dimensions, does not communicate the intended message or messages sufficiently. Thus, he chose all kinds of methods to go public and reportedly even prepared a book manuscript. According to Reeve,

> By mid-June 1999, Osama bin Laden was touting around draft copies of a book he has written in flowery Arabic, setting out his vision of the future. Sources in Pakistan who claim to have seen copies report that it bears the title America and the Third World War, and consists of a lengthy exhortation to Muslims to rise up and destroy the United States (Reeve 1999, 265).

After the events of September 11, 2001, bin Laden didn't have to say or write anything to dominate the news.

While casting McVeigh and bin Laden (even before 9–11) as celebrities, the mass media in the United States and other western countries had long provided other terrorist figures opportunities to make their case in the public sphere. Thus, when Unabomber Ted Kaczynski, whose sixteen letter bombs killed three persons and injured twenty-three others, was willing to talk, he was interviewed by Stephen J. Dubner of *TIME* magazine. Dubner's long story explained Kaczynski's background, focused especially on his relationship with his brother, who had turned on him, and gave the Unabomber the opportunity to vent his antitechnology attitude. There was even a plug for the Unabomber's political goal and dream, when Dubner wrote,

> What Kaczynski wants is a true movement, "people who are reasonably rational and self-controlled and are seriously dedicated to getting rid of the technological system. And if I could be a catalyst for the formation of such a movement, I would like to do that."[48]

In fact, had Kazcynski chosen to, he could have had far more publicity for his grievances and objectives than the sole interview with *TIME*. From *20/20, 60 Minutes II, Good Morning America,* and the *Today Show* to *Larry King Live* and the *Roseanne* show, from the *New Yorker* to the *Denver Post,* many well-known media organizations and figures asked the Unabomber to use their platform to explain himself to fellow Americans. Letters that Kaczynski donated to the University of Michigan's Special Collection Library reveal how members of the fourth estate tried very hard to convince the terrorist to talk to them. Here are excerpts from some of the interview requests sent to this inmate in the Florence Correctional Institute in Colorado who had lived as a hermit in a primitive cabin when he assembled and sent his deadly bombs:

> I've been a journalist most of my life, but also a wildlife film maker and writer. I'm as intrigued by your comments on the morality of your actions as I am by your strong feelings about the environmental ravages of technology.
> —Don Dahler, ABC's *Good Morning America*
>
> I wanted to let you know personally that I would obviously be very interested in also sitting down with you for an interview. It would give you a chance to explain your experiences to our huge audience and also the opportunity to share your views and concerns, which I know you've long wanted to.
> —Katie Couric, NBC's *Today Show*
>
> Your case is particularly fascinating since you reject the findings, and no one can dispute that you are an extremely smart man.
> —Greta Van Susteren, CNN
>
> Several doctors and some of your lawyers have claimed you suffer from schizophrenia. I want to give you the opportunity to respond point-by-point to their allegations and to show the American people that you are, in fact, rational, clearheaded, and sane.
> —Shawn Efron, CBS's *60 Minutes II*[49]

Media figures bent over backwards to curry favors with a man who killed and injured people for his political agenda—all for the sake of getting an interview that probably would not tell us anything new about the Unabomber but would offer him opportunities to publicize his agenda. Or take another case: When Sheik Hassan Nasrallah, the leader of the Lebanon-based Hizbollah or "Party of God," one of the most notorious anti-Israeli and anti-American terrorist groups, felt the urge to address the American public, Ted Koppel of ABC's *Nightline* granted him the television stage. While the Unabomber was behind bars and unable to wage his campaign of terror, when showcased by *TIME* magazine and courted by its scooped rivals, Sheik Nasrallah was still leading the organization that continued to engage in mass-mediated political violence.[50]

### To Use or Not to Use the T-word

"Yes, I am a terrorist, and I'm proud of it."[51] When Ramzi Yousef made this statement in a New York courtroom before being sentenced to 240 years in prison for masterminding the World Trade Center bombing, he embraced the t-word that most contemporary perpetrators of mass-mediated political violence vehemently rejected. During the months in which the members of the antigovernment Tupac Amaru occupied the Japanese embassy in Lima, Peru, and held scores of people hostage, the Peruvian president at the time, Alberto Fujimori, repeatedly called the hostage-holders "terrorists" and their actions "terrorism," while the captors inside the embassy insisted that they were commandos of a revolutionary movement and characterized their action as a military occupation. Although some anarchists in the second half of the nineteenth century called themselves terrorists, modern-day perpetrators of mass-mediated violence abhor the label because of its negative connotations. Richard E. Rubenstein put his finger on the negativity of the term, when he concluded that "nobody wants to be called a terrorist; terrorism is what the *other* side is up to" (Rubenstein 1987, 18).[52] In chapter 1, I discussed the difficulty of defining the meaning of the term *terrorism*, suggesting a definitional solution that focuses on the link between this particular kind of political violence and the desire for publicity. In the same way that students of terrorism have wrestled with defining various types of political violence, the news media have as well. Indeed, it seems that the press's choice of terms is most inconsistent in its reporting about political violence perpetrated by groups or individuals. Research has revealed, for example, that the U.S. media is more prone to label violent acts as "terrorism" when U.S. citizens are involved than in cases without American involvement. A content analysis of three leading American news magazines from March of 1980 to March of 1988 showed that the t-word was used in 79% of the cases when American citizens were victims, but in only 51% of the cases when no U.S. citizens were involved (Alali and Eke 1991, 30). In this respect, the American media are not different than news organizations abroad. Thus, the German press readily called political violence at home or in Europe "Terrorismus" and its practitioners "Terroristen," whether committed by successors of the Baader-Meinhoff group that remained active during most of the 1990s or the Basque separatist ETA that unleashed a new round of terror at the beginning of the millennium. But at the same time, the Abu Sayyaf in the faraway Philippines were typically characterized as "militante Moslem-rebellen" (radical Muslim rebels) or "Rebellengruppe" (rebel group)—even during the time when they held three Germans hostages. The British news media were more likely to call acts of violence by the IRA or splinter groups thereof "terrorism" while reporting on politically motivated "bombings" or "hostage-takings" or "hijackings" abroad without using the t-word.

Following the terrorist attacks on the World Trade Center and the Pentagon, Reuters was reported to have banned the use of the term *terrorism* in the context of the 9–11 incidents, and CNN was said to have discouraged its correspondents from using the t-word although the network used *terrorism* or *terrorist* all the time in its on-screen banner slogans.[53] The wire services who serve many different members and clients had practiced this kind of strange political correctness long before 9–11. The most plausible reason for banning or discouraging the t-word was probably these, and perhaps other, news organizations' concern that their correspondents would lose access to terrorists and their supporters, who rejected the terrorist label.

When terrorists strike inside the United States, the American centrist bias of the media does not explain why the news tends to characterize some acts of political violence as "terrorism" and similar deeds as "crimes." In the fall of 1998, the media watchdog FAIR criticized the news media for rarely describing the cold-blooded murder of Dr. Barnett Slepian by anti-abortion extremists as an act of terrorism, while readily attaching this label to the burning down of a ski lodge in Vail, Colorado, by extreme environmentalists. A content analysis of more than five hundred print and broadcast stories conducted by the FAIR organization found that "reporters labeled Dr. Slepian's killing as 'terrorist' or 'terrorism' only six times (exclusive of quotes from sources). In contrast, reporters themselves labeled the arson attack at Vail ski resort 'terrorist' or 'terrorism' 55 times in 300 articles and newscasts."[54] The conventional wisdom that the news media take their cue from government officials was once again affirmed in the aftermath of the deadly attack on Dr. Slepian: President Bill Clinton declared "I am outraged by the murder of Dr. Barnett Slepian in his home last night in Amherst, N.Y. . . . No matter where we stand on the issue of abortion, all Americans must stand together in condemning this tragic and brutal act."[55] In fact, almost all news reports that followed called Dr. Slepian's demise "murder" and not "terrorism." The CBS *Evening News* was typical for this pattern, when it opened its broadcast with anchor Russ Mitchell stating, "President Clinton says he is outraged by the murder of a Buffalo, New York, area doctor who performs abortions."[56] One wonders about the news media's choice of terminology, if the President, in his statement only hours after the attack, had spoken about a brutal act of terrorism instead of murder. One of the few exceptions in this particular case was an editorial in the *New York Times* published after James Kopp was arrested abroad for the killing, many months later. Obviously thinking of Kopp's accomplices in the United States, the *Times* wrote that the "case could shed light on whether there is a widespread network of anti-abortion terrorists intent on depriving citizens of their constitutionally protected right to have access to reproductive health services, including abortion."[57] Besides presidents' and other opinion leaders' influence on many aspects of the news—including the linguistic choices—there may be other reasons that explain why the fourth estate was and is far more inclined to call the violent actions by the Earth Liberation Front or the Animal Liberation Front "terrorism" or "eco-terrorism" and the far more lethal acts of anti-abortion militants "murders" or "bombings." Here, the vastly different resources and the lobbying muscles of interest groups come into play. The fur industry, for example, has made a point of exposing and attacking "terrorist" actions by animal rights and other environmental extremists in their lobbying campaigns, as have other business sectors on the target lists of the Earth Liberation Front and Animal Liberation Front. While pro-choice advocates, too, characterize the attacks on abortion providers and clinics as terrorist acts, their organizations and lobbying efforts have not been successful in changing the terminology used by public officials and by the news media. It is ironic that members of FBI counterterrorism task forces frequently investigate the deeds of violent environmentalists and violent pro-life activists. Thus, FBI agents and police officers assigned to a joint counterterrorism task force in Washington were involved in the hunt for fugitive James Kopp after the assassination of Dr. Slepian, just as special agents trained in counterterrorism investigated cases of eco-terrorism in various parts of the United States. Strangely, though, law enforcement officials spoke frequently of "eco-terrorism," but rarely, if ever, of "anti-abortion terrorism."

In the Cold War era, the mainstream news media in the United States and elsewhere in the West did not hesitate to choose the t-word for the self-proclaimed Marxists of the Red Army Faction/Red Brigade variety in Europe, Latin America, and Asia with suspected (and by now proved) backing east of the Iron Curtain. Also, the terrorist label was readily attached by the American media to militant secular organizations in the Middle East (such as the Palestine Liberation Front or the Popular Front for the Liberation of Palestine), and religious groups (such as the Hizbollah in Lebanon or the Egyptian Islamic Jihad). All of these groups were fiercely anti-American (besides being declared enemies of Israel and of the capitalist West in general).

While "Arab" or "Islamic" or "Muslim" groups—or individuals, as the news often identified them—remained most prone to be characterized by the t-word, the old left/right divide no longer guided the choice of words as clearly in the post–Cold War era as it did when the old world order was still in place. To be sure, some Marxist groups that survived the fall of the Soviet Union and the Communist bloc, for example the Greek 17 November Organization, which committed political violence for more than twenty-five years, was still labeled "terrorist." But the mainstream media were just as reluctant to describe as "terrorists" the violent anarchists who turned antiglobalization protests into riots and street fights with police as they were to attach the t-word to the violent anti-abortion faction. Thus, the suggestion that the media describe violence by left-extremists as terrorist, but withhold the word from violence by right-extremists, is not justified today. Rather than the result of systematic and conscientious bias and stereotypical labeling on the part of the media, the linguistic choices seem to be based on two predominant patterns: (1) a tradition of thoughtless and stereotypical reporting patterns, and (2) a follow-the-leader syndrome in the news production that persists in other areas of reporting as well.

Here is an example of the unwitting biases in established linguistic patterns in the news with respect to mass-mediated political violence: The media in the United States and in other western countries report on "Islamic" or "Muslim" terrorists and terrorism, but not on "Christian" terrorists and terrorism, for instance in the context of Northern Ireland or anti-abortion violence in the United States committed under the banner of the Christian "Army of God." The same is true for "Jewish" terrorism expressed in violent acts by individual Israelis affiliated with or affected by extremist Jewish groups. A good example is the reporting on the Brooklyn-born Jewish fundamentalist Dr. Baruch Goldstein, who killed twenty-nine Palestinians in early 1994 as they prayed in a Hebron mosque and who was eventually killed by survivors of his attack. In reporting the incident, members of the American media characterized Goldstein's deed as massacre, shooting rampage, murder, or mass murder, but not as an act of terrorism. Ironically, even in the face of the lethal attack by this Jewish fundamentalist, some reports demonstrated in an utterly overt fashion the linguistic media biases with respect to the t-word. In the following excerpt from the CBS *Evening News*, the anchor called Goldstein "gunman," and the correspondent characterized Goldstein as "mass murderer," but the correspondent referred to a Palestinian who had killed two Israelis several months earlier as "Palestinian terrorist:"

> *Richard Threlkeld*: He [Dr. Baruch Goldstein] went to college and medical school here at Yeshiva University in New York. Eleven years ago, he emigrated to Israel. We may never know what turned Baruch Goldstein, a doctor, a healer, into a mass murderer, but there are some clues. . . .
> *Mrs. Barbara Ginsberg [Goldstein's friend]*: He was always there for anybody who was sick. OK, he refused to treat Arabs. He didn't hurt them, but he didn't want to treat them because he said, "I didn't come to Israel to treat my enemies."
> *Threlkeld:* Most likely it was this incident: A Palestinian terrorist machine-gunned a bus hear Hebron last December, killing a settler and his son. They were close friends of Goldstein's. And after that, a friend said he became convinced the only answer to terror is more terror.[58]

The remark of Goldstein's friend revealed that Goldstein seemed to consider his deed an act of terrorism, if only in response to terrorist acts by Palestinians. Except for a few citations of nonmedia sources, reporters, editors, and anchors did not use the t-word and did not refer to an "Israeli terrorist" or to "Jewish terrorism." However, the latter term was thrown into the public debate by some Israelis and Jewish Americans who were quoted in some news reports. Thus, Dean Reynolds reported from Jerusalem that "Israeli commanders [who were blamed by critics for not stopping Goldstein from entering the Moslem house of worship] said they had never even discussed the possibility of Jewish terrorism at the mosque."[59] And in a report by Aaron Brown, a man in a Jewish neighborhood of New York said, "Nine of 10 will condemn it [the attack on worshipers in the Hebron mosque] and say that it is a terrible act of violence, it's an act of terrorism. And Jewish people are not terrorists."[60]

The follow-the-leader syndrome, or, more specifically, the tendency of the news media to adopt the language of leading government officials, may have affected the linguistic characterization of the Hebron incident as well. President Clinton, in a special appearance in the White House briefing room, called Goldstein's act in the Mosque of Ibrahim "this crime" and "a gross act of murder." He equated this sort of violence by both Palestinians and Israelis, when he said, "Extremists on both sides are determined to drag Arabs and Israelis back into the darkness of unending conflict and bloodshed."[61] But he never mentioned the t-word.

All told, the mainstream media and terrorists are not bedfellows, they are more like partners in a marriage of convenience. While not without biases on the part of the media, the main feature of this symbiotic relationship is this: By accommodating terrorists and their propaganda scheme in the many ways described in this chapter, news organizations and their members serve the needs and purposes of their corporate bosses and stockholders. In their perennial hunt for larger audiences, advertising dollars, and ultimately profits, corporate media institutions dictate that special attention is paid to those events and developments that are most prone to fit the infotainment genre and believed to attract large audiences. There is no doubt that extraordinary crimes and sensational acts of terrorism as well as mere threats of terrorist spectaculars, such as the Y2K scare, fit the bill. The flip side of the coin is, of course, that other events and developments, often more important than terrorism, are under-covered or not covered at all. While this media agenda is contrary to the traditional press ideal of reporting for the public by providing citizens with the information they need to be well educated in matters of government and politics, it serves the self-interest of the corporate media and, unwittingly, the very scheme of mass-mediated terrorism.

### Notes

1. For more information about the media reporting on eco-terrorism on Long Island, see, for example, Al Baker, "Police say an anti-sprawl group burned new Long Island

homes," *New York Times*, 3 January 2001, B1; Al Baker, "Eco-Terrorism, and nary a red-wood in sight: Is suburbean sprawl debate so fevered that it encourages tourching of homes?" *New York Times*, 14 January 2001, section 14, pp. 1, 14; Andrew Murr and Tom Morganthau, "Burning suburbia," *Newsweek* (15 January 2001): 32; and David S. Jackson, "When ELF comes calling," *TIME* (15 January 2001): 35.

2. The interview that Wyatt Andrews conducted with Craig Rosebaugh was broadcast on the CBS Morning News, April 12, 2000.

3. Robert E. Kessler, "Sources: ELF acts grew more violent: Bid for publicity drove to escalation," *Newsday*, 14 February 2001, A4, A25.

4. The information was published on the ELF's Web site http://www.earthliberationfront.com/main.shtml [accessed 1 April 2002].

5. Ben Gill was quoted by the BBC. See "'Eco-terrorists' blamed for farms crisis," http://news.bbc.co.uk/ [accessed 14 May 2001].

6. The PETA leader's remarks were reported by Jessica Hansen and Meg Jones, "Lawmakers work to head off 'agri-terrorism' in state," *Milwaukee Journal Sentinel*, 3 June 2001, 1B.

7. See, for example, Richard Berman, "Enemies here threaten food," *USA Today*, 1 November 2001, 19A; Sam Howe Verhovek, "Radical animal rights groups step up protests," *New York Times*, 11 November 2001, A24.

8. "Black blocs for dummies," http://www.infoshop.org/blackbloc.html [accessed 1 April 2002].

9. See *Newsweek*, 13 November 2000.

10. Unless otherwise noted, the excerpts of radio and TV news broadcasts are taken from transcripts in the Lexis-Nexis archives.

11. The statement was posted at http://www.chumba.com/_gospel.htm [accessed 1 April 2002].

12. The letter was written by Brian Murphy, with the headline "Poor WTO coverage," and published in the Letters to the Editor section of the *St. Louis Post-Dispatch*, 17 December 1999, C20.

13. The letter was written by Jesse Cohn and published under the headline "Trade anarchy" in the Letter to the Editor section of the *St. Louis Post-Dispatch*, 3 December 1999, C20.

14. The letter was written by Debbie Phillips and published in the Letters to the Editor section of the *Boston Globe*, 13 December 1999, A17.

15. "Periscope," *Newsweek* (9 October 2000): 25.

16. The Spanish student was quoted in Robert Wieland, "Protests turn nasty at EU summit," Associated Press, 7 December 2000.

17. Mario Laporta, "Italy police crush globalization protest." http://www.dailynews.yahoo.com/ [accessed 16 March 2001].

18. Quoted here from Robin Wright, "Bush says free trade is key to meeting needs of the poor," *Los Angeles Times*, 22 April 2001, http://www.latimes.com/cgi-bin/print.cgi [accessed 1 April 2002].

19. Robin Wright, http://www.latimes.com/cgi-bin/print.cgi.

20. Zakaria drew these conclusions in "The new face of the left," *Newsweek*, 30 April 2001, 32.

21. Blair was quoted by the BBC in "Thousands march on EU summit," http://news.bbc.co.uk/hi/english/world/europe/newsid_1391000/1391980.stm [accessed 16 June 2001]; Schroeder was quoted by the Associated Press in Paul Ames, "Dozens Injured in Anti-EU Clashes," http://dailynews.yahoo.com/ [accessed 15 June 2001].

22. See "Schwedens 'Dialog-Linie' scheitert im Pflastersteinhagel," http://de.news.yahoo.com/010615/3/lozj8.html [accessed 15 June 2001].

23. Melinda Henneberger, "Outcry grows over police use of force in Genoa," *New York Times*, 8 August 2001, A1, A8.

24. Henneberger, A1, A8.

25. This section is based on author's watching of German TV news and on reports published in a variety of German newspapers.

26. Wickert is quoted here from Jakob Menge, "Die Medienhoheit der Entfuehrer," *Welt*, 29 July 2000.

27. "Marc Wallert ist am Montag wieder in Deutschland," http://www.welt.de/daten/2000/09/09/0909au190087.htx [accessed 1 April 2002].

28. All quotes in this paragraph from letters to the editor were published in "Briefe an die Redaktion—fuer und gegen Frau Wallert," *Bild*, 21 July 2000, http://www.bild.de/service/archiv/2000/jul/21/aktuell/wallert/wallert1.html [accessed 1 April 2002].

29. The quote is from an editorial, "Freedom for sale," *Washington Post*, 31 August 2000, A30.

30. The letter was written by Myles Hoenig and published in the Letters to the Editor section of the *Baltimore Sun*, 11 January 2001, 16A.

31. This letter by Rebekah Jorgensen was published under the headline "WTO protests in Seattle" in the *Los Angeles Times*, 2 December 1999, B10.

32. The letter was written by Reinhold Plemper and published in "Auf Jolo das falsche Signal," *Frankfurter Allgemeine Zeitung*, 24 July 2000, Feuilleton, 51.

33. Quoted in David Plotz, "The logic of assassination," http://www.slate.msn.com/HeyWait/01-08-17/HeyWait.asp [accessed 1 April 2002].

34. A Palestinian mother, quoted here from Michael Finkel, "The child martyrs of Karni Crossing," *New York Times Magazine* (24 December 2000).

35. Plotz, "The logic of assassination."

36. From ABC's *World News This Morning*, 31 July 2001.

37. CBS, *60 Minutes*, 19 August 2001.

38. NBC, *Nightly News*, 10 August 2001.

39. Daniel Williams, "Where Palestinian 'martyrs' are groomed," *Washington Post*, 15 August 2001.

40. The Colonel was quoted on *All Things Considered*, National Public Radio, 17 October 2000.

41. *All Things Considered*, 17 October 2000.

42. *All Things Considered*, 17 October 2000.

43. Quoted here from Caryn James, "The Oklahoma City bomber's final hours are hardly television news's finest," *New York Times*, 12 June 2001, A26.

44. It is noteworthy that McVeigh was not the only terrorist who received sympathetic letters from his admirers. Ted Kaczynski, for example, who is also known as Unabomber,

receives "mail from sympathizers and admirers." This according to Stephen J. Dubner, " 'I do not want to live long. I would rather get the death penalty than spend the rest of my life in prison.'" *TIME*, (18 October 2000). See http://www.time.com [accessed 1 April 2002].

45. James, A26.

46. Quoted here from Frank Rich, "Death with commercials," *New York Times*, 23 June 2001, A13.

47. The existence of the videotape was widely reported by selected news organizations. See, for example, the Reuter dispatch, "Paper says bin Laden group boasts of Cole bombing," http://dailynews.yahoo.com/ [accessed 19 June 2001].

48. Stephen J. Dubner, "'I do not want to live long. I would rather get the death penalty than spend the rest of my life in prison,'" *TIME* (18 October 1999). See also http://www.time.com [accessed 18 October 1999].

49. These and other letters are available on the Smoking Gun Web site, http://www.thesmokinggun.com/unabomber2/unabomber.shtml [accessed 1 April 2002].

50. The interview with Sheik Nasrallah was aired on the ABC News *Nightline* program on 19 October 2000.

51. The words were part of Yousef's statement before he was sentenced by Judge Kevin Thomas Duffy of the Federal District Court in Manhattan on 8 January 1998. See "Excerpts from statements in court," *New York Times*, 8 January 1998, B4.

52. For an excellent discussion of the definitional difficulties surrounding political violence, see chapter 2 of Rubenstein's book.

53. See, for example, Michael Kinsley, "Defining terrorism," *Washington Post*, October 2001, A37.

54. See FAIR's Web site at http://www.fair.org/extra/9812/buffalo-vaul.html [accessed 1 April 2002].

55. From *The Public Papers of the Presidents [William J. Clinton–1998, vol. 2]*, Printing Office via GPO access, p. 1860.

56. See the CBS *Evening News* transcript of 24 October 1998, as retrieved from the Lexis-Nexis database.

57. "Defending abortion rights," *New York Times*, 31 March 2001, A14.

58. CBS *Evening News*, 25 February 1994.

59. Reynold's report aired on ABC *World News Tonight*, 8 March 1994.

60. Brown's report aired on ABC *World News Tonight*, 25 February 1995.

61. Clinton's news briefing was broadcast in a CBS News Special Report on 25 February 1994.

# 4

# E-Terrorism and the Web of Hate

I CAN'T SAY GOODBYE TO YOU—I already miss you," Ofir Rahum, a sixteen-year-old Israeli from Ashkelon, told twenty-five-year-old Sali, whom he met in an Internet chat room and corresponded with via e-mail. Sali, who had introduced herself months ago as an Israeli woman of Moroccan background, answered passionately: "You don't know how much I am waiting for Wednesday." Wednesday, January 18th, 2001, was the Internet lovebirds' first rendezvous in Jerusalem. When Ofir arrived by bus, Sali met him with intense anticipation. As they drove north, the teenager did not notice that they turned into Palestinian territory and toward the town of Ramallah. Suddenly, Sali stopped her car. A man appeared and pointed a Kalashnikov at Ofir's head. When Ofir's bullet-ridden and stabbed body was found later and transferred to Israeli authorities by their Palestinian counterparts, Ofir's grief-stricken parents warned fellow Israelis: "Keep your children off the Internet. The Internet kills." At the time, Israeli investigators were not certain what they had on their hands—a crime or an act of terrorism.

In the following weeks, it became clear that Ofir Rahum was the victim of a new and particularly appalling terrorist deed. His Internet pal and love interest, Sali, was really Amneh Muna, a Palestinian woman from Ramallah, who worked as a journalist and was active in Yassir Arafat's Fatah organization. After covering the funerals of many Palestinians who were killed in the conflict with Israel, she decided to strike back and inflict pain on an Israeli family. According to her mother, "Seeing mothers crying all the time gave her the idea."[1] Muna struck up several chat room "friendships" with Israeli men. But none of her pals was more vulnerable than young Ofir, who was blinded by his first taste of a sweet romance. When the boy was harshly brought back to reality, it was too late. As Amneh revealed to Israeli investigators, Ofir fought fiercely but in vain when attacked by her Fatah friend. After her arrest and first appearance in a Jerusalem court, *Newsweek* wrote that this young woman from a middle-class family in the West Bank "hardly fits the profile of a terrorist."[2]

The fact, however, is that many terrorists do not fit carefully constructed profiles and commonly held stereotypes, nor do they limit themselves to the traditional means of communication. Instead, they increasingly utilize the opportunities of new media for their purposes. Modern-day terrorists, like their predecessors, are eager to exploit the traditional mass media while also recognizing the value of direct communication channels; terrorists can send their unadulterated messages to their target societies and to their comrades and prospective recruits. In the nineteenth century, anarchists recommended the use of simple posters to spread their propaganda. Thus, the self-proclaimed anarchist John Most wrote his advice to terrorists in the anarchist newspaper *Freiheit* (first published in London and later in New York):

> Once such an action [of terrorism] has been carried out, the important thing is that the world learns of it *from the revolutionaries*, so that everybody knows what the position is.
>
> In order to achieve the desired success in the fullest measure, immediately after the [terrorist] action has been carried out, especially in the town where it took place, posters should be put up setting out the reasons for the action in such a way as to draw from them the best possible benefit.
>
> And in cases where this was not done, the reason was simply that it proved inadvisable to involve the number of participants that would have been required; or that there was a lack of money. It was all the more natural in these cases for the anarchist press to glorify and explicate the deeds at every opportunity.[3]

With each new advancement in communication technology, terrorists gain more opportunities to publicize their own propaganda. When Marxist revolutionaries, such as Brazil's Carlos Marighela, told their terrorist comrades in the post-World War II era how to communicate with the public at large, they recommended technologies that did not exist during John Most's time. For example, Marighela used copying machines to produce large numbers of pamphlets and manifestoes. But like the anarchists of the nineteenth century, the self-proclaimed guerrillas, such as Marighela, also recognized the value of setting up their own printing presses. As broadcasting transmitters became more accessible in the latter twentieth and the early twenty-first centuries, organizations with direct or indirect involvement in terrorism established their own radio and television stations. The

Lebanon-based Hizbollah organization, known for its involvement in terrorism against Israel and Israel's friends, established its own television station in the early 1990s. Al-Manar expanded the reach of its satellite TV channels into Palestinian homes on the West Bank and Gaza during the second intifada while pursuing ambitious plans for massive expansion into other parts of the Arab world. Elsewhere, terrorist movements set up radio transmitters to broadcast pop music that was frequently interrupted by self-serving propaganda. More recently, Colombia, for example, possessed about 1,500 licensed radio stations and just as many pirate transmitters utilized by left- and right-wing terrorist groups. For example, the Revolutionary Armed Forces of Colombia (FARC), a durable Marxist guerilla movement, broadcast over an increasing number of channels. Disc jockeys played popular songs, such as "Guerilla Girls" or "Ambush Rap," with lyrics that were adapted to the FARC cause. This light diet was served with frequent doses of direct propaganda. As one disc jockey explained, "We're doing the shooting from the radio."[4]

But it was the tragedy of Ofir Rahum and his loved ones, and the tribulations of Amneh Muna and her family as well, that highlighted in a shocking way the growing role of the Internet in the terrorist calculus. Luring an innocent teenager, simply because he was an Israeli, into a prearranged ambush under the pretence of a romance that began in an Internet chat room and blossomed via e-mail correspondence, qualifies as an act of terrorism—the first case of this kind. In chapter 1, I defined terrorism as mass-mediated political violence. Surely, an intelligent woman like Amneh Muna acted in the belief that her terror scheme would leave footprints on the Net and in time be recognized and publicized fully.

While the fate of Ofir Rahum was a unique case—for the time being—the use of the Internet by terrorists and their sympathizers was not new, nor was cyber-terrorism, designed to paralyze, conquer, and/or burglarize the Internet sites of enemy targets, or terrorists' measures to protect their own sites against unwelcome "visitors" from the counterintelligence and law enforcement communities. In certain instances, the World Wide Web proved an ideal vehicle for terrorists to send their messages to the world during and after their violent actions. In this respect, the possibilities of the Internet were first realized in late 1996, after members of the leftist Tupac Amaru guerrilla group infiltrated and took over the Japanese ambassador's compound in Lima, Peru, during a reception for some six hundred guests. Terrorism experts abroad knew little or nothing about the Tupac Amaru Revolutionary Movement, but information on the group was quickly posted on Web sites established and updated by the group's supporters in North America and Europe during the four-month ordeal.[5]

## From Cyber-War to E-Terrorism

The 1999 Kosovo military conflict between the Belgrade regime and NATO was, on one level, the first Internet war. Unable to cut off all telephone lines in Kosovo and the rest of Yugoslavia, President Slobodan Milosevic could not stop the flow of uncensored information to the outside world. Instead, e-mail reports and Web site information from Yugoslav territory competed with and disputed Milosevic's propaganda, in the same way that opponents of NATO's air raids succeeded in shutting down the official NATO Web site and its propaganda for a while. The same year, after Taiwan's President Lee Tenghui declared that his country was a separate state and should be treated as such, a cyber-war broke out between the People's Republic of China and Taiwan. According to Ian Buruma, "The soldiers in this war are invisible figures buried deep inside government offices, 'hacking' their way into computers in enemy territory."[6] At one point, Beijing's cyberspace warriors planted a picture of their country's flag on the Web site of Taiwan's intelligence agency as if they had conquered enemy territory. The following year, Israeli hackers and their Palestinian counterparts followed the Chinese example: Israelis and their sympathizers abroad launched electronic attacks against Islamic militants' sites, while Palestinians and their supporters in the Mideast, the United States, and elsewhere, targeted sites in Israel and the United States. For twelve hours, a picture of the Israeli flag occupied the Web site of Hizbollah's television station al-Manar while Israel's national anthem was played. This seemed to be a major coup in the ongoing struggle for propaganda supremacy, but an attack on the site of the American Israeli Public Affairs Committee, a lobbying organization based in the United States, had more harmful consequences: Besides plastering the site with anti-Israeli slogans, a Pakistani hacker, who claimed responsibility for this act of e-terrorism, accessed thousands of e-mail addresses and credit card numbers stored in the organization's computers and sent anti-Israeli messages to the addresses while publishing the stolen credit card data on the Internet.

Nobody knows whether Israeli or Arab individuals threw the first cyber bomb in this electronic exchange. One way or the other, both sides used basically the same methods in that they invaded hostile Web sites and/or swamped them with so much e-mail that the targeted sites became hopelessly overloaded and completely incapacitated. While Israeli hackers put the sites of the Palestinian National Authority, Hizbollah, and the Palestinian Hamas temporarily out of commission, Arab militants hit Israeli sites just as hard, taking down those of the foreign ministry, the Israeli Defense Forces, the Prime Minister, the Knesset, the Bank of Israel, and the Tel Aviv Exchange Market. Indeed, well-orchestrated Internet appeals on both sides allowed large numbers of supporters to participate in the repeated outbursts of cyber-terror. By simply clicking on the listed sites of hostile organizations, visitors triggered an automated e-mail system that sent out messages on their behalf. Hizbollah attributed the crashing of its site, which normally got between one and three hundred thousand hits a day, to "nine million hits per day, mainly from Israel, the United States and to a lesser degree from Canada and South Africa."[7]

What the Palestinians came to call the Internet intifada and what Islamic extremists in general considered an Internet version of their holy war against Israel—an e-jihad—bolstered their belief that the World Wide Web offered them a level playing field. "Arab people all over the world feel they want to contribute, each according to his own capacity and expertise, in the resistance and this [e-jihad] provided a gateway to that," Hizbollah's Deputy Secretary General Sheik Naim Qassem told a Lebanese newspaper. And Hizbollah's webmaster, Ali Ayoub, quoted the late Ayatollah Ruhollah Khomeini of Iran, who once said that if every Arab threw a bucket of water on Israel, the Jewish state would drown. According to Ayoub, "This is exactly what happened, supporters of the resistance from all over the world, both Arabs and foreigners, are contributing."[8]

In reality, however, neither side gained or lost ground in the actual Mideast conflict by fighting on the Internet front—with one exception: The virtual political violence directed against hostile Web sites rewarded both sides with generous coverage in the conventional news media as well as in news sources on the Internet. In this sense, the electronic attacks and counterattacks represented another dimension of mass-mediated political violence with the advantage that no human life was lost, no human being was injured, and the material and psychological damage was relatively minor. Although these kinds of cyber-bombs are certainly preferable by far to real bombs, terrorists are likely to fight increasingly on both fronts. In the real world, only a limited number of extremists commit and actively promote mass-mediated political violence; in cyberspace, far more sympathizers seem willing to click the mouse and thereby partake in these sorts of actions.

While the actual impact of the Internet exchange between pro-Israeli and pro-Palestinian hackers was not much more than an irritant for the targeted organizations on both sides, cyber-terrorism looms large as a future threat. Without kidnapping or assassinating people, without toppling skyscrapers, bombing planes or public places, terrorists can hit and harm target societies severely via high-tech sabotage. Already, there have been some efforts in this direction. In early 1995, for example, antitechnology extremists cut the cables of Germany's public telecommunications agency at three major underground crossroads in Frankfurt, disrupting all computer, telephone, and fax traffic at the international airport and in hospitals and office buildings (Nacos 1996a, 21). In this case, the communication blackout did not cause planes to crash or patients to die on the operating tables. But the mysterious "Keine Verbindung" (No Connection) group that claimed responsibility exposed the vulnerability of the communication systems. It seems only a matter of time before terrorists will follow the Frankfurt example on a large and more harmful scale and disrupt the communication links and data flows that are vital to the functioning of the public and private sector. Some areas are especially vulnerable in this respect. A blackout of the New York Stock Exchange, for example, would paralyze both the domestic and global financial markets. In the summer of 1995, a bomb threat against the air traffic control center responsible for two New York airports (Kennedy and La Guardia) and one in New Jersey (Newark) interrupted landings and takeoffs for hours and, consequently, air traffic throughout the United States as well as international flights to and from the affected airports. One can only imagine the consequences of an act of cyber-terrorism that managed to disable simultaneously many air traffic control centers at peak landing hours.

Warning that cyber-terrorists represent a far more serious threat to the United States than rogue states firing missiles, Thomas Friedman wrote:

> In five years, with the Internet being used to run more and more systems, if someone is able to knock out the handful of key Internet switching and addressing centers in the U.S. (until recently, a quarter of all Internet traffic passed through one building in Tyson's Corner, Va., next to Morton's steak house), here's what happens: many trains will stop running, much air traffic will grind to a halt, power supplies will not be able to be shifted from one region to another, there will be no e-mail, your doctor's CAT scanner, which is now monitored over the Internet by its manufacturer, won't work if it breaks.[9]

All of this is well known to groups that promote and commit terrorism. They are fully aware of the Internet's potential for both terrorism and counterterrorism and have, therefore, high tech specialists in their midst. As a result, these groups have become skilled in using the World Wide Web for their purposes and in protecting their own Internet activities from intelligence and law enforcement agencies in the countries they target.

### Even Enemies of Modernity Utilize the Internet

Terrorists who fight modernity and its perceived evils in the name of defending traditional values and religious principles do not shy away from enlisting advanced technology for their holy wars or secular fights to enforce their agendas. The same is true for governments and movements that encourage and support terrorism. Osama bin Laden and his soul mates in the al-Qaeda organization, for example, appear traditional in the way they dress, speak, live, and preach. But like similarly inspired groups, they rely heavily on members in their midst and networks of compatible groups and individuals that are trained in and familiar with the predominant communication technologies of our time. Thus, operatives in al-Qaeda and other terrorist organizations are known to be computer-literate; they compose training manuals on their word processors, distribute them on CD-ROMs, or transmit their files via e-mail to trusted comrades.[10] Bin Laden and his people were in the habit of plotting and discussing acts of terror by e-mail as well, but they learned eventually that the FBI was utilizing its sophisticated Carnivore Internet Wiretap System in its investigations of terrorism, and they concluded that the FBI was tracking their communications as well. In this respect, bin Laden and his associates learned that e-mail exchanges can be as susceptible to intercepts as are satellite telephone transmissions, which are also popular in their circles and in other terrorist groups.[11]

But al-Qaeda and other terrorist movements have found a way around the most advanced electronic surveillance techniques: encryption in the form of software technology that locks computerized information so that it cannot be accessed by unauthorized persons and organizations. In principle, the purpose of these encryption programs—the protection of people's privacy—was and still is laudable. But the same technology has made it also very difficult for intelligence and law enforcement agencies to pick the electronic locks of information flows circulating among terrorists. When he was still leading the Federal Bureau of Investigation, Louis J. Freeh told the Citizens Crime Commission of New York that court-sanctioned electronic surveillance was an important tool in fighting crime and terrorism. In particular, Freeh said:

> Take, for example, the conspiracy in this city to blow up the Holland Tunnel, the Empire State Building, etc., that was worked on by the police department, the Bureau, all other federal agencies in town and successfully prosecuted, Mary Jo [White], by your office. We succeeded because of the ability of court-ordered electronic surveillance. . . .
>
> When Ramzi Yousef [the mastermind of the World Trade Center bombing] was being tracked in the Philippines, he left behind a laptop computer that itemized plans to blow up [eleven] U.S. airliners in the Western Pacific on a particular day. All of the details and planning were set forth in that laptop computer. There were also two encrypted files in that computer—and they took months and months, in some cases more than a year, to break down and understand. That's the kind of situation we're going to find ourselves in.[12]

The situation has rapidly worsened from the perspective of agencies concerned with preventing terrorism. Groups that favor mass-mediated political violence get ever more sophisticated in using commercially available encryption software to safeguard their communications with each other. They have learned to hide their sinister messages on Web sites and message boards that have nothing to do with terrorism or terrorists. As investigative reporter Jack Kelley revealed in early 2001,

> Hidden in the X-rated pictures of several pornographic Web sites and the posted comments on sports chat rooms may lie the encrypted blueprints of the next terrorist attack against the United States or its allies. It sounds farfetched, but U.S. officials and experts say it's the latest method of communication being used by Osama bin Laden and his associates to outfox law enforcement.[13]

Citing U.S. officials, Kelly disclosed that bin Laden and others were "hiding maps and photographs of terrorist activities on sports chat rooms, pornographic bulletin boards and other Web sites."[14] While it is increasingly difficult to unlock the encrypted messages and images, it has become even harder to find them in the first place among the many millions of sites, boards, and chat rooms on the World Wide Web.

Al-Qaeda and affiliated organizations are not the only groups that use the many aspects of the Internet for their communication needs. Like mainstream individuals and groups in all parts of the world, individual extremists and extremist groups everywhere have come to appreciate the opportunities offered by the World Wide Web. The fundamental Islamic Afghan Taliban, which supports terrorists and their activities in the Middle East, Asia, Europe, and North America (if only by allowing bin Laden and his organization to live and train in Afghanistan and by supporting other Islamic extremists in their violent acts abroad—for example, in the former Soviet republics), seemed an unlikely candidate for going on-line. But the Taliban's Web site was never directed at the mass of the people in Afghanistan or neighboring countries. As Peter Chroust pointed out,

> Up to now, the main purpose of "Taliban On-line" seems to be external communication with the new political and information elites of the Islamic "freedom-fighters" in Afghanistan, communications within the Islamic world and worldwide propaganda for the ideas of the Taliban movement.[15]

In this context, Chroust has suggested that, thanks to the Internet, "the former technological 'have-nots' appear for the first time as equal communication partners in the electronic agora."[16] While this seems to be increasingly the case, one must question whether the "example of the Taliban shows that even a society with the lowest economic resources is not condemned to remain an electronic 'have-not' [and that to] a certain extent the virtual community emancipates many of its users from many of the real limitations outside the net."[17] After all, few average Afghans own computers and, if they did, would have been prohibited from freely browsing the Internet by strict and enforced Taliban teachings.

Less traditional circles with terrorist tendencies have embraced the possibilities of the World Wide Web early on. For example, German extremists used Internet sites, discussion boards, and e-mail correspondence for years—even under restrictions invoked by governmental authorities not known to Internet hate-mongers in the United States or Canada, who are free to exploit their almost unlimited free speech rights in all media. Extremists in the Federal Republic of Germany circumvent their country's tough laws against neo-Nazi hate speeches and against undermining the Federal Republic's democratic constitution by using Internet Service Providers abroad. Principals on German left- and right-wing sites operate anonymously and hide behind the firewalls of encrypted messages, electronic boards, and mail boxes that are accessible only to trusted comrades with confidential passwords; such measures protect German extremists from being discovered, identified, and prosecuted. The neo-Nazi Thule-Netz (written in English: Thule-Net) is one of the sites that advises its e-visitors on the benefits of encryption and recommend software—in the case of Thule, it is PGP (Pretty Good Privacy).

Over the years, German authorities threatened and in some cases took legal actions against Internet Service Providers that allowed Germans to access neo-Nazi Web sites. In France, two interest groups won a court judgment against Internet portal Yahoo! that ordered the U.S. company to deny French Web surfers access to e-auctions of Nazi memorabilia. Threatened by a fine of thirteen thousand dollars for each day that exceeded the court-ordered deadline, Yahoo! obeyed the order by filtering out these sites for their customers in France.

A number of Internet Service Providers have denied service to the most offensive among the many hundreds of hate sites originating in the United States and Canada. Thus, one U.S.-based neo-Nazi voice on the Internet complained that Geocities, and other free Web hosting services as well as America Online, "adopted policies censoring pro-White pages as soon as they can find them."[18] Kahane.org, the U.S.-based Web site of the extremist Jewish Kahane movement, whose political organizations Kach and Kahane Chai were outlawed in Israel as terrorist groups and designated by the U.S. State Department as foreign terrorist organizations, was dropped by its site's American server as well.[19]

But the rejects can and do find alternative servers. In the past several years, many of these sites disappeared, when their content happened to catch the eyes of law enforcement and/or hate site sentinels, and reappeared with new domain names. But in most cases, the driving forces behind offensive hate sites are clever enough to refrain from direct calls for political violence against the targets of their hate and, in their public statements, seem to stay just within the wide parameters of their constitutional right to free expression. Yet, one can easily imagine what damage these tirades against particular groups might cause in confused minds.

Here are just a few sentences from some of the Internet sites that speak to these individuals' and groups' deep-seated resentment and hate openly directed against different racial, ethnic, or religious groups and/or people who support particular policies.

From the Web site of the Vanguard News Network:

> Spitting rocks, dogs and empty cases of Corona: the mestizo "culture" that's driving out ours. Until Whites unite and shit on Mexicans and Puerto Ricans the way they do on us, nothing changes.

> And the Jewish media are holding our hands back to prevent our doing what needs to be done. . . . Jews are nation-killers. It doesn't matter if they present themselves as conservatives or liberals, they are bent on destroying our race to further theirs. Whites must unite and treat the Jew justly before he destroys us.[20]

From the National Alliance material posted on the Web:

> We must have White schools, White residential neighborhoods and recreational areas, White workplaces, White farms and countryside. We must have no non-Whites in our living space, and we must have open space around us for expansion. We will do whatever is necessary to achieve this White living space and to keep it White. We will not be deterred by the difficulty or temporary unpleasantness involved because we realize that it is absolutely necessary for our racial survival. The long-term demographic trend toward a darker world which the disastrous policies of the last century have caused must not only be halted, it must be reversed.

> With the growth of the mass democracy (the abolition of poll taxes and other qualifications for voters, the enfranchisement of women and non-Whites), the rise in the influence of the mass media on public opinion, and the insinuation of the Jews into a position of control over the media, the U.S. government was gradually transformed into the malignant monster it is today: the single most dangerous enemy our [White] race has ever known.

> Education which concerns itself with the development of the whole person and focuses as strongly on forming character as on imparting knowledge . . . enjoyed an all-to-brief revival earlier this century in [Hitler's] National Socialist Germany, before being outlawed by the advocates of permissiveness. . . . We see the products of this system all around us: too many weak, indecisive men and too many unfeminine women.[21]

From one of the extreme anti-abortion Web sites that celebrated the second anniversary of Dr. Barnett Slepian's murder, for which James C. Kopp, a leading anti-abortion activist, was charged:

> On this second anniversary we remember that abortionist Barnett Slepian reaped what he sowed. . . . Abortionist Slepian was told he was murdering children, but he did not care that he was taking the lives of innocent babies. Someone stopped serial murderer Slepian from murdering any more children. A cause to celebrate.
>
> We as Christians have a responsibility to protect the innocent the same way we would want someone to protect us if we were about to be killed.[22]

From the Web site of the Militia of Florida:

> Earn $3,600+ per month to defend the Constitution of the United States of America. An ongoing insurrection has been officially identified coming from within the District of Columbia. All those who join "The Counter Insurgency Army of the United States of America" will accrue the above amount per month plus any other bounties that may apply until such time as the insurrection is put down.
>
> For those of you who have the urge to be up close and personal a good blade or garrote is fine. Close Quarter Battle (CQB) ambush, the weapon selection would depend largely on what the intended target is, as the hardness of the target goes up so must the caliber of the weapon, too big is better than too small here.
>
> Identifying enemies or potential enemies is a must, if at all possible learn where they make home, school they or their children attend, their place of business or employment, where they have their lunch, get to know their routine. . . . when the hammer drops then look at your efforts as a field training exercise. Knowledge is power, and you can never know too much about an enemy or potential enemy. Remember, "Death to Tyrants and their Cohorts."[23]

From the Web site of the so-called "World Church of the Creator," after a member (Benjamin Smith) had killed an African American and a Korean man and injured six orthodox Jewish men and after the execution of Oklahoma City bomber Timothy McVeigh:

> With mongrel monstrosities walking the streets, soaring "hate" crime against White people everywhere, a government in the hands of the most bestial gang in history—the Jews, and the White masses largely in stupor, it is actually surprising that more of our White Racial comrades have not yet acted as August [Benjamin Smith] acted.[24]
>
> Timothy McVeigh [was] a man who until the very end stood for what he believed in without fear, with[out] compromise, and without regret. It is not difficult to

understand why many, including me, have respect for this man, for in an age when the vast majority of men are cowards and prostrate themselves before tyranny, Tim McVeigh essentially sacrificed himself for the greater good as he saw it.[25]

It is not difficult to find these sites. Accessing one means, in many instances, that you are provided with numerous links to like-minded sites at home and abroad, both in English and in other languages. Take, for example, the site Stormfront.org, founded in 1995 by Don Black, formerly a leader of the Knights of the Ku Klux Klan, as "the first White Nationalist site on the Web."[26] The comprehensive and frequently updated site provides the addresses of Internet mailing lists, links to "newsgroups of interest to White Nationalists," dial-up bulletin board systems, four pages of alphabetically listed "White Nationalism/White Patriotism" sites, adding up to a cyberspace Who's Who, with the world's most extreme and most hateful white supremacy, neo-Nazi, and Christian identity groups, plus a list of those sites that Stormfront itself is hosting. These include White Singles (described as, "Formerly known as the Aryan Dating Page, this is a Free service available to single White women and men. Arrange dates for friendship or love. Heterosexual, White Gentiles only"), Our Legacy of Truth (described as including Adolf Hitler's "*Mein Kampf* online and '900 Quotes about Jews,' along with other articles on Race, Eugenics, Christian Identity, National Socialism and Communism"), and *The Truth At Last Newspaper* (described as being edited "by Dr. Edward R. Fields, this is America's oldest White patriot newspaper [formerly known as The Thunderbolt]. Ed has remained a prominent leader of the White racialist movement for forty years").[27]

It is ironic that the most blatant racist views of the neo-Nazi/white supremacy sites are mirrored in the material publicized on the Web pages of extreme Zionist groups and/or on the discussion boards of these sites. The perhaps most instructive case is the Web site of the Jewish Task Force (JTF), located in New York, that describes itself as "torchbearer of the magnificent legacy of the spiritual giant of our generation, HaRav (The Rabbi) Meir Kahane" and as fighting "to save America's whites and Israel's Jews from the Third World hordes."[28] Unlike Christian Identity groups and like-minded organizations in the neo-Nazi, White Supremacy/Patriot movement, the JTF lumps Jews and Christian European whites together and otherwise unleashes the same hate tirades against the same targets as do the most extreme Jew-bashing white supremacy groups on their Internet sites. Here are just a few sentences from material publicized on the site of the Jewish Task Force:

To compare the European immigrants of the last century—the Italians, Irish, Dutch, Scandinavians, Greeks, Jews and others—to the scum and refuse coming to America is preposterous. There's no comparison between the immigration that made America great versus the horrendous flood of sewage that we've witnessed since the 1960s and that's bringing America and Western civilization to their knees.

To use the threadbare argument—to say we're a "nation of immigrants' and can't reject the America-hating vermin of the Third World's Arab and African hell holes, or equally verminous Hispanic imports of Latin America—defies all logic and common sense.

The Statue of Liberty is a white woman. Can you imagine if she were a schvartze with a big nose and kinky hair? Or an Arab with a veil over her ugly face and a full length dress covering her body and what was left of her clitoris that her father chopped off when she was six years old?[29]

Just as the anti-Jewish white supremacy sites, the JTC pages contain attacks on the alleged "New World Order" conspiracy and on the "traitor media." Other extremist Jewish sites, such as those of the new Kach Movement and other groups devoted to the causes of the late Rabbi Kahane, contain message boards and/or chat rooms. The following posts are from Kahane.org message boards:

I can't stand Arabic people they make me sick, I wish they would all drop dead. I can't stand the fucking Russians, they can take their forgery Protocols of Zion and shove it up their ass, they deserve no mercy, eliminate them.

Israel learn from your mistakes! Overthrow the traitor government and tell the US to stick it. Destroy the Arab dogs in the land of Israel and then return to democracy. The Arabs only want blood! Give them their own. They US wants a Jewish whore. Do you want to be that whore?

I cannot hate Arabs as I cannot hate pigs.[30]

Just like some of the anti-Jewish white supremacy sites praised the Oklahoma City bomber Timothy McVeigh and racist killer Benjamin Smith, and Hamas and Hizbollah devoted web pages to passionate tributes to Palestinian suicide bombers for killing Israelis, some of the extreme Jewish sites celebrated Dr. Baruch Goldstein, a fundamentalist Jew, who, in 1994, massacred twenty-nine Palestinians as they prayed in a Hebron mosque before he was killed by survivors of the attack.

Actually, anyone who looks for hate-mongers on the web will find them, even without knowing the name of a single hate group and/or its URL. Just typing a racist slur into an Internet search engine will do the trick, and a list of web pages and message boards—many of them with unspeakably hateful verbal outbursts against members of particular groups—will appear.

## Web of Hate and Terrorism

July 2, 1999, was a joyful day for most Americans as they prepared for July Fourth picnics and firework celebrations. But as the sun set in the Chicago area, this peaceful Friday evening was shattered by a young gunman who stepped out of a blue Taurus on the North Side, aimed his semiautomatic handgun at a group of orthodox Jews on their way to synagogue, and opened fire. Without saying a word, he got back into his car, drove off, and fired at several other groups of orthodox men who wore the traditional long black coats and black hats. When he left the area for good, he had injured six Jews.

The gunman's next stop was Skokie, where he shot and killed African American Ricky Birdsong, Northwestern University's former basketball coach, who was walking with his children near his home. The next day, the man in the blue Taurus continued to shoot African Americans who happened to be walking down the street in Springfield and Decatur. He injured two of them.

An Asian American graduate student was the next victim. He was shot in the leg near the campus of the University of Illinois. Finally, on July Fourth, the gunman cruised near the Korean United Methodist Church in Bloomington, Indiana, obviously searching for another victim of Asian origin. When he spotted Won-Joon Yoon, a Ph.D. candidate, he pulled the trigger, killing the twenty-six-year-old Korean.

Chased by police officers, twenty-one-year-old Benjamin Nathaniel Smith, who had killed two men and injured nine others during his three-day killing-spree, shot himself. As it turned out, Smith had nourished his hate of minorities as a member of the so-called World Church of the Creator, a white supremacist organization headquartered in Illinois and led by Matthew Hale, who calls himself Supreme Leader of the Creativity Creed. The organization that is neither a church nor a religion maintains a Web site with prominent displays of the motto RaHoWa—racial holy war—and ample material about Jews, African Americans, and other inferior races representing the enemies of the supreme white race. The mass media rewarded Smith's killing spree by offering his idol, Matthew Hale, ample opportunity to preach his gospel of hate to large national audiences. Hale thanked Smith for his actions, which brought his ideas to the attention of the world and provided him with the chance to "ride the wave of publicity which his [Smith's] actions either intentionally or unintentionally created for us."[31] NBC's *Nightly News*, the CBS *Evening News*, CNN's *The World Today*, and National Public Radio's *All Things Considered* were among the prominent news programs that interviewed Hale. In the NPR program, Hale readily revealed that he referred to nonwhites as subhuman "mud people" and specified that for him "mud people" meant Asians, Blacks, Hispanics—"people that aren't white."[32] Prodded by Noah Adams as to whether he felt sorry for the victims of Smith's shooting spree, Hale said that he did not and added,

> We can have compassion for animals, but animals aren't a threat to us. The blacks and the non-whites are taking this country right from under us. We are becoming a niggerfied, Jewified, Mongolfied country, and it's disgusting. We have to stop it.[33]

In these four, short sentences, Hale, who has a law degree but was denied admittance to the Illinois bar because of his racist views, summarized the essence of his and other extremists' pseudoreligious, white supremacist propaganda. Benjamin Smith expressed the same prejudices and hateful sentiments. For example, during an interview with a PBS station in Indiana, Smith said, "The Jews and the blacks and all the mud races are trying to destroy our people, and that is why we hate them."[34] These were the same ideas and words used by Hale. The "Supreme Leader" Hale and "Brother" Smith, as Hale called his younger follower, knew each other personally, and it is entirely possible that the Internet did not bring the two men together and was not the sole or major source of racist hate material for Smith. But it is telling that FBI investigators found Smith's computer in Hale's storage unit after the killing spree and that Hale told Fred Frances of NBC News a few days after the deadly events that a "lot of our best members have come through the Internet."[35]

It is not clear whether Benjamin Smith came the Internet route, but, for sure, others did find the World Church of the Creator and its gospel of hate via the World Wide Web. After all, the Internet reportedly helped this "church" to become one of the fastest growing hate groups in the United States.[36] Like his predecessor and founder of the organization, Ben Klassen, Hale cleverly rejected any responsibility for the violence committed by his followers pointing to the "church's" commitment to "legal" actions. But in the same breath, he expressed an understanding for racist violence by repeating the group's call to a "racial holy war." Thus, in an "editorial" on the organization's Web site that was devoted to Smith and his deadly acts of terrorism, Hale wrote,

> While our Church is committed to legal resistance for many reasons per our Founder Ben Klassen's instructions, we can certainly understand his actions for our enemies have been creating the circumstances making violent resistance inevitable against their machinations for decades. . . .
> That the Church does not condone his acts does not affect the reality that when a people is kicked around like a dog, someone might indeed be bitten.[37]

A key question here, of course, is whether a connection between the content of Internet sites and terrorism exists, whether the words and the visual images publicized on many Web pages have real life ramifications and, in fact, influence people to commit violence. It is noteworthy that Benjamin Nathaniel Smith was not the only adherent of "creativity" as taught by the World Church of Creativity who resorted to racially and politically motivated mass-mediated violence or, in other words, terrorism. In the fall of 1998, four members of the World Church of the Creator were indicted for holding up a video store in Miami and allegedly acting on the organization's belief that all media-related businesses are controlled by Jews.[38] In the past, when this sort of extremist hate was dispersed exclusively in speeches, leaflets, books, and other conventional means of communication, there were also individuals and groups who acted on their aroused emotions. To stay with the example of the World Church of the Creator, one of its members was sentenced to life imprisonment for killing a black sailor near Jacksonville, Florida, shortly after his victim had returned from military service in the 1991 Persian Gulf War.[39] At the time of this racist act of terrorism, the Web of hate did not yet exist as it evolved in the second half of the 1990s and the early twenty-first century.

It is entirely logical to suspect that the proliferation of hate sites and the large number of people on-line has infected—and will continue to infect—far more people with the virus of hate than did traditional means of communication in the pre-Internet era. This was precisely the point of "Hate.com: Extremists on the Internet," a Home Box Office documentary produced in association with the Southern Poverty Law Center, a nonprofit group that tracks hate gangs in the United States. The program contained, for example, an interview with Joseph Paul Franklin, a convicted killer and follower of neo-Nazi/white supremacist leader William Pierce and his National Alliance. Pierce is the author of several best-selling books, among them *Hunter*, about a white supremacist who fights for the purity of his race. As it turns out, Franklin is the real life "Hunter," telling "Hate.com" interviewers about two female hitchhikers that he picked up and killed, after one told him about dating a black man and the other one remarked that she would do the same.

Using the pseudonym Andrew Macdonald, Pierce also authored *The Turner Diaries*, about white American supremacists' war against nonwhite minorities and the Jewish-controlled Federal Government. The best-seller was a favorite of Oklahoma City bomber Timothy McVeigh, who modeled his Murrah Federal Building attack on the bombing of the Washington FBI Headquarter described in Pierce's book. And one of the three white Texans who beat and decapitated James Byrd Jr., an African American man, as he was dragged on a chain by a pickup truck, said, according to one of his accomplices, "We're starting *The Turner Diaries* early."[40] The attraction to Pierce's second work, *Hunter*, also grew because news reports revealed that the FBI found a copy of the book in the home of McVeigh's accomplice, Terry Nichols. While both *Hunter* and *The Turner Diaries* are written as fiction in the form of a novel, they contain, in fact, most of the divisive and hateful ideas that Pierce and other right-wing extremists spread via the Internet and made accessible to increasingly larger audiences. As the founding father of America's Web of hate, Don Black of Stormfront, explained, "I am tired of the Jewish monopoly over the news media and the entertainment media, and I'm working very hard to provide an alternative to that, and the Internet is that opportunity we've been looking for."[41]

Instead of using leaflets and other old forms of communicating their ideas, groups like Stormfront, the Church of the Creator, the National Alliance, and hundreds of organizations with the same or similar agendas use their Web pages to communicate with the faithful and recruit new followers. There is no doubt that the vast majority of new recruits and sympathizers, if not all, find their way via the Internet to Don Black, Matthew Hale, William Pierce, and their equals. Reading through selected and edited "Letters from Browsers" posted on the National Alliance's Web pages affirms the effectiveness of the Internet as an ideal recruitment tool. Under the headline "Bells of Truth," one new follower wrote, "I found this website April 24, 1999. Listening to the broadcast, "New World Order", led me to listen to all on the page. Never heard these issues explained so simply and in such an easy to understand manner. Every word you spoke: Absolute truth!" An unnamed fan from Norway e-mailed that he was listening in on the National Alliance through the Internet radio and revealed that his awakening came when studying various sites on the Net. A "part-time college professor," who asked for anonymity for fear of losing his job, thanked Pierce for making his radio broadcasts accessible on the Web and added, "I tell all those that will listen to visit the site." And "a public school teacher" from California wrote, "Since I have just purchased a computer I was able to tune into to [sic] your radio program. Dr. Pierce's message, politically and philosophically, was forceful, inspiring, and honest. It should be obvious to any white American that the Jews have literally taken over the mechanisms of power in the U.S.A."[42]

One doesn't have to visit hate sites to get the idea that the hateful ideologies and blueprints for action, as contained in the fiction and nonfiction produced by William Pierce, resonate well with more than a handful of people. Since online bookstores, such as Amazon.com and Barnes&Noble.com, sell these books, they invite customers to write reviews as they do with respect to all available works. The reviews are posted on the respective online stores' Web sites. Even a cursory check of what customers wrote about the two Pierce books reveals that the majority of them evaluated the books extremely or very positively. When checked in August 2001, the average customer rating for *Hunter* at Amazon.com was better than four stars (out of the maximum five stars for the highest rating). Of the last fifteen reviews, twelve received five stars, two received four stars, and one received one star. Also in August 2001, the average customer rating for *Hunter* at the Barnes & Noble website amounted to about three-and-a-half stars.

As for *The Turner Diaries*, a sixteen-year-old high school student named Sandra awarded the reading five stars, calling it "the best book ever written" and writing "This book is so good, I have learned so much from it." Another customer, also giving five stars, wrote, "An incredible book written entirely from an unashamedly pro-European American standpoint, which in itself is unusual and openly discouraged nowadays." But a reader from Florida, who gave the book only one star, called the book "evil," "a book of the devil," and expressed sadness "that this book even exists in today's society." Rating the novel with one star, another customer called it "racist trash" and "disgusting."[43]

And for *Hunter*, one customer reviewer exemplified the fans of the book, awarding it five stars and writing: "MacDonald has done more justice to the White Revolutionary movement than any other author to date. 'Hunter' is a masterful work that is a must read for any interested American patriot. If you have any interest in learning more about the problems that this great nation is facing you must read 'Hunter,' as well as MacDonald's other work, 'The Turner Diaries.' Maybe then you will see why the government made such a deal about Terry Nichols owning a copy. Absolutely breathtaking." Another fan of the book concluded, "All in all, a brilliant book that graphically captures the inevitable race-war we'll soon face." One of the few critics who gave *Hunter* one star, seemed more disappointed that *Hunter* was "disjointed and presented the philosophies of the writer in a slip shod manner" and thus did not live up to *The Turner Diaries* in this respect.[44]

How many of the positive customer reviews came from the ranks of the right-wing extremist core, and perhaps even from members of Dr. Pierce's own group, is hard to say. It is known, however, that the leaders of some of these groups encourage their followers to carry their messages of hate—what they call the truth—to those Web sites that are not controlled by them and have not yet been exposed to the neo-Nazi/white supremacy ideology. In early 2001, for example, the World Church of the Creator called for an "Internet Blitzkrieg" on its Web site by its members because "the Internet has the potential to reach millions of White people." In particular, the call to e-arms urged "White Racial Loyalists" to "go to chat rooms and debate with 'new people,'" not those who "already know about the Jewish menace" and register their group's domain name to as many search engines as possible.[45] In a similar vein, the Jewish Task Force wrote on its hate site,

> It is imperative that Jews and righteous Gentiles who care about the future of America and Israel zealously spread the word about the JTF.ORG site. Promote it among your friends, relatives and acquaintances and convince them to do likewise. Promote it in chat rooms and user groups, on message boards, through faxes and e-mails and on radio talk shows.[46]

Racist views straight from the tenets of the most extremist hate groups are amply expressed in chat rooms and on message boards. In the wake of the bombing of the USS Cole in the port of Aden, Yemen, in the fall of 2000, the Yahoo! Message Board on this topic included many anti-Semitic posts that blamed the attack and most anti-American terrorism on a U.S. foreign policy that, according to many message board posters, is dominated by Jews. One of these writers responded angrily to a message that defended the American Jewish community:

> Manipulating that policy so that the U.S. gets dragged into the tarpit [sic] of Israel's own making while Gentile sons and daughters get killed and Israeli-American kids don't serve? That's called contributing to this nation? I call it sucking the bone marrow out, at every non-Israeli-Americans [sic] expense.
>
> You can continue to kiss the ass of America's "Modern Day Royalty," the Israeli-Americans. But not me. We were sadly mistaken when we thought we had expelled Royalty 225 years ago.

There is no doubt about the ideological background of some, perhaps many, of these message board posters because, from time to time, messages such as the following appeared: "Who rules America!!! A must Read!!! The future of America is at stake http://www.stormfront.org/jewish/whorules.html." This posting clearly points other message board participants to Stormfront and other hate groups' Web pages that contain far more detailed anti-Semitic attacks than the original post promoting the link. These, then, were precisely the shots in the battles of words, the promotion of particular hate sites, and the recruitment of new supporters and members that Matthew Hale had in mind, when he called for his Internet Blitzkrieg with a particular emphasis on invading chat rooms not yet exposed to the hateful ideas of his "Creativity" creed. Jewish extremists spread their messages in cyberspace meeting places as well as in the "Letters from our Readers" sections on the Jewish Task Force site. A message board poster from North Carolina wrote, "I have decided to devote my spare time to promoting your fabulous Web site. I have been posting the site all over the Internet on message boards. I have been promoting it daily in chat rooms, and I have been sending as many e-mails as possible every evening urging people to go to the site."[47]

In the aftermath of Benjamin Smith's racist killings, the columnist Richard Roeper pointed to the hate material posted on the Web site of the World Church of the Creator. "This is where Benjamin Nathaniel Smith found solace," Roeper wrote. "This is where he felt accepted and loved, with his own kind, fellow paranoid losers. Thanks to the Internet, I'm not so sure there are any loners any more. The pathetic misfit . . . can now go down to the basement and fire up the PC—and within a matter of seconds he'll be chatting away with like-minded hatemongers from around the world."[48] To be sure, the vast majority of people with these kinds of tendencies do not act violently on what they think and express in their Web communities. But others are tempted to and sometimes actually do follow the overt or covert calls to arms as espoused on hundreds of sites. It has not escaped the preachers of hate that young minds are especially vulnerable to indoctrination by the propaganda of hate. Some have even established special sites to brainwash children.

The "World Church of the Creator Kids" pages, for example, offer games and stories that glorify the supremacy of the white race. Thus, the short story "In love with the White People" is about a young "brother" named Robbie, "a young lad with hair of gold and eyes as emerald," who distributes white Valentine cards with the letter "W" for White to white classmates only, avoiding "all children of color." One of the recipients, a "red haired" girl "with sapphire eyes," shows her teacher the inside of her card that reads, "I really care for you, so be proud to be White." In case children do not get the moral of the story, the punch line is spelled out: "The greatest gift a White person can give another White Person is the chance at White Salvation." In the summer of 2001, the twelve-year-old son of Don Black, Stormfront's leader and web pioneer, introduced himself as the webmaster of Stormfront.org for Kids and wrote:

> White people are taught in school to be ashamed of their heritage. Teachers cram as many politically correct ideas as they can, into your head in 180 days. All the great white accomplishments throughout history are diminished. Therefore, I think that now is the time that all the white people across the globe should rise above the lies, and be proud of who we are. To take back our freedom and win for all to see our heritage in its greatest glory.[49]

These Web pages for children also offer games, music, and a lengthy "History of the White Race" that fits the neo-Nazi/white supremacy ideas.

More recently, William Pierce, the founder and leader of the white supremacy hate group National Alliance, acquired Resistance Records, the world's largest neo-Nazi music label, to sell hardcore hate rock via the Internet. Targeting skinheads and other young music fans at home and abroad, Resistance Records presents, according to its Web site, "the soundtrack for white revolution." Hardcore hate rock can be heard on Resistance Radio, which broadcasts over the Internet, and excerpts from the label's hit CDs can be heard on the label's Web site. The lyrics are essentially tirades against blacks, Asians, Jews, and homosexuals and also contain calls for violence. As the reviewer of the Angry Aryans' song, "Racially Motivated Violence," states on the label's Web site, "Some might view their [the Angry Aryans'] suggestions as hate crimes. I prefer to view them as intense motivational therapy."[50] The lyrics of "Paradise Lost" contain the following lines: "The seeds of violence sown, let my hatred be fed, / with the body count of the enemy dead Hell unleashed."[51] Words like these may be the sort of material that incites people, especially young persons, to sign on to the messages of hate and to get involved in actual violence. The Southern Poverty Law Center identified white power music as a factor behind the increase in the number of hate groups in the

United States at the beginning of the twenty-first century. In early 2001, the center identified a total of 602 U.S.-based hate groups compared to 457 a year earlier and concluded,

> Although difficult to quantify, so-called "white noise" continued to grow in popularity and availability last year, clearly helping to draw new youth in the world of organized hate. The principal purveyor of this music, Pierce's Resistance Records, has managed to get large amounts of publicity as white power rock concerts grow larger and more frequent.[52]

True enough, but the Internet sites play crucial roles in introducing young whites, especially males, to this sort of hate rock and hate literature in general.

Research has revealed an impact of the mass media's violent content on heavy media consumers and especially television viewers. According to the American Psychological Association, who reviewed research in this field,

> There is absolutely no doubt that higher levels of viewing violence on television are correlated with increased acceptance of aggressive attitudes and increased aggressive behavior.
>
> Children's exposure to violence in the mass media, particularly at young ages, can have harmful lifelong consequences. Aggressive habits learned early in life are the foundation for later behavior.[53]

While no systematic studies of possible linkages between people's exposure to hate sites on the Web and acts of political violence exist, it seems reasonable to suspect that there might be connections and that these are similar to those between heavy viewers of TV violence and aggressive behavior. For the time being, however, we are left with anecdotal evidence that links originators and/or consumers of Internet hate material to actual acts of mass-mediated political violence. In addition to the material presented in this chapter, I mentioned in the previous chapter one case in particular that demonstrated a causal relationship between Internet content and violence: the incidents concerned teenagers who committed eco-terrorism on Long Island in late 2000, after reportedly being counseled in Internet chat rooms "to escalate their tactics" and thus get the media attention that they had not reaped for their earlier and quite harmless actions.[54] The teenager may have even received assembly instruction for the crude incendiary "bombs" on the World Wide Web. The Earth Liberation Front, for example, carried a twenty-page "Arson-Around Guide with Auntie ALF" for "boys and girls . . . to help us all gain a better understanding of some of the devices used in incendiary attacks as carried out by the Animal Liberation Front." But the printable booklet was, in fact, a very detailed manual describing the materials needed to create incendiary mixtures and crude bombs.[55]

But the most damaging arson attacks by the radical environmentalists were nothing in comparison to the devastating school massacre in Littleton, Colorado, in the spring of 1999. The two high school students, Eric Harris and Dylan Klebold, who killed twelve of their fellow students and a teacher before they took their own lives, had used the Internet to fuel their obsession with neo-Nazi ideology and with Adolf Hitler (staging the well-planned assault on Hitler's birthday), to promote their racist views, and to play violent computer games.[56] Whether they could have committed the same violence without access to the Internet (by exclusively relying on books, magazines, music CDs, and movies) is not the question here. Rather, the point is that the Internet was a very convenient source to nurture hate and aggression and a very convenient medium for their own messages. Harris and Klebold left several videotapes that documented and explained their motives. The tapes were filled with tirades against blacks, Jews, women, and homosexuals—the major targets of the neo-Nazi/white supremacy hate milieu—but the videos also betrayed the two friends' hate of literally everyone else in the student body—athletes, the offspring of rich parents, and others who they perceived to be conformists. Confessing that they wanted to carry out the biggest mass murder in U.S. history, the Columbine killers left no doubt that they were shooting for publicity in the media, notoriety, and posterity. Given these circumstances, theirs was not an ordinary crime but a mass-mediated hate crime with political and ideological aspects—however twisted these turned out to be. Indeed, one can argue that the incident had aspects of a particular species of terrorism.

### Simulated Political Violence and Score Cards for Terrorist Assassinations

In 2000 and 2001, by clicking on the "Games" button on the Kahane organization's Web site, young visitors could play violent games in which they are invited to target doves among Israel's leaders as well as Palestinian leader Yassir Arafat. In "Escape of the Oslo Criminals," for example, the "insane and dangerous Oslo Architects" [Ex] Prime Minister Ehud Barak and his Labor Party colleagues, Shimon Perez and Yossi Beilin, escape their prison in the year 2010 and are running for safe houses in the territory controlled by the Palestinian Authority. Players are urged to "capture" the criminals before they reach their Palestinian friends or are lynched by fellow Israelis. But in reality, the game is the virtual assassination of the three political leaders through pop-up pictures. "Barakula" is another violent game targeting Ehud Barak, who is described as "a demented demonic beast." Players are urged to "knock this creature back to the abyss it came from." Not surprisingly, Palestinian Yassir Arafat is the enemy in another game in which players are instructed to "welcome our

friend and partner to Peace of the Brave Abu-Amar (Arafat) to Kahane Land."
Arafat's fate is not decided by a hug but by a revolver and a bullet.[57] While disturbing, these and similar games are not illegal in the United States, just as
hate speech and references to political violence are protected by the free expression guarantee of the First Amendment.

Few cases make this expansive construction of freedom of speech more difficult to understand and accept than the blatantly inciting content of the most
militant among the anti-abortion Web sites. The most controversial of them
contains the so-called Nuremberg Files—data of abortion providers and
politicians, judges, and other officials that support legalized abortion. According to the site that also condemns RU486, the so-called morning-after pill, the
Registry aims at listing "baby butchering doctors and their closest blood co-
horts in hopes that the American people will overcome the demonic forces
presently enslaving this nation and will finally prosecute the purveyors of
death listed herein."[58] Framed by drippings of animated blood, the registry
distinguishes between working "baby butchers" (names are printed in black
type), "wounded" abortion providers (names of those injured in anti-abortion
actions are grayed out), and "fatalities" (names of doctors assassinated by anti-
abortion terrorists are struck out). In essence, this is a hit list that keeps score
of physicians killed and injured by anti-abortion extremists. The site encourages visitors to "search for the office address of the baby butchers listed above"
and lists the URL of the American Medical Association as a source of such information. In addition to physicians, the site lists the names of clinic owners
and workers, judges ("their shysters"), politicians ("their mouthpieces"), law
enforcement officials ("their bloodhounds"), and "miscellaneous spouses &
other blood flunkies." If the inflamed language accompanying the lists is not
enough to stir hate and militancy in supporters of radical anti-abortion actions, the gruesome images of the picture gallery of aborted babies promises
to do so.

Other sites that have been accessible in the last several years are hardly less
shocking. For example, one anti-abortion Web site displayed a running
counter of the abortions since the Roe v. Wade Supreme Court ruling in 1973
and a selection of pictures of aborted fetuses. The text urged anti-abortion
visitors to do something against the "storefront killing centers on Main
Street," arguing, "If you had a mass murderer/child molester in your community and church, wouldn't you want to know? Join the cry for justice and
picket the communities, clubs, churches, and offices of baby killers."[59]

While the American Medical Association (AMA) was sufficiently alarmed
to establish a crisis team warning all physicians listed in the Nuremberg Files
by phone that their lives might be in danger, the ninth Circuit Court of Appeals set aside an earlier jury verdict by ruling that the publication of the

Nuremberg Files on the Internet fell within the constitutionally protected free speech. The federal appeals court held that abortion foes could not be held responsible for the possibility that their inflammatory Internet postings and leaflets might encourage some persons to commit violence against abortion providers and clinics. Circuit Judge Alex Kozinski wrote,

> If defendants threatened to commit violent acts, by working alone or with others, then their statements could properly support the [guilty] verdict. But if their statements merely encouraged unrelated terrorists, then their words are protected by the First Amendment. Political speech may not be punished just because it makes it more likely that someone will be harmed at some unknown time in the future by an unrelated third party.[60]

For the appeals court, it obviously did not matter that those in charge of the Nuremberg Files were diligent in keeping score of anti-abortion terror. Thus, one day after abortion provider Dr. Barnett Slepian was assassinated in his home, his name appeared crossed out on the Web page's registry.

While the appeal to violence against abortion providers and supporters of legalized abortion was implicit in the Nuremberg Files, the call to kill Americans was spelled out in a *fatwa* or religious verdict signed by Osama bin Laden and four other radical Islamic leaders in February 1998. The document that was posted on the Internet in several languages and on many Web sites—including American ones—contained the following call to terrorism:

> The ruling to kill the Americans and their allies—civilians and military—is an individual duty for every Muslim who can do it in any country in which it is possible to do it, in order to liberate the Aqsa Mosque and the holy mosque [Mecca] from their grip, and in order for their armies to move out of all lands of Islam, defeated and unable to threaten any Muslim. This is in accordance with the words of the Almighty God.[61]

Even when courts curb hate speech and incitement to violence, this sort of material does not vanish from the Internet but is accessible on different Web sites, through different servers that are more permissive or operate from abroad. Thus, after a jury awarded more than one hundred million dollars in actual and punitive damages against the anti-abortion activists responsible for the Nuremberg Files hit list on the Internet, and a U.S. District Court enjoined their speech, the infamous Web site disappeared for a short time only to reappear with another sponsor and domain name. Blocking Internet sites is not doing the job either because sophisticated users can find methods to bypass a server.

Establishing and maintaining an Internet site is the most inexpensive means of communicating with and influencing a potentially huge audience and recruiting members and sympathizers. Moreover, many of the extremist groups of the types mentioned in this chapter use their Web pages to enlist donations. Thus, as Jessica Stern has revealed, the Lasch-I-Taiba or Army of God in Pakistan have utilized the World Wide Web to raise funds for their radical activities. Indeed, "Laschkar and its parent organization, Markaz ad-Da'wa Irshad (Center for Islamic Invitation and Guidance) have raised so much money, mostly from sympathetic Wahhabis in Saudi Arabia, that they are reportedly planning to open their own bank" (Stern 2000, 120). The Jewish Task Force's Web site revealed that the group looked for "a wealthy Jew or a righteous Gentile with the needed millions of dollars" to push its hate agenda in a larger scale.[62] And the Internet publishers of the Nuremberg Files' hit lists promised holy rewards for donations in that "the Living God will receive your donation as a sweet smelling savor arising to His nostrils and will bless you accordingly."[63]

Considering the reach of the World Wide Web—the unfettered content of and access to its sites, and the opportunities for propaganda, recruitment, and fundraising—Internet utilities confirm that the Web of hate and terror is here to stay and is likely to play a larger role in the divisive and inciting propaganda of extremists and in the terrorist schemes of tomorrow.

## Notes

1. This quote is from Dan Ephron and Joanna Chen, "Ofir's fatal attraction," *Newsweek* (2 April 2001): 39.

2. Ephron and Chen, 39. For my account of this terrorism case, I drew from many media accounts, among them the mentioned story in *Newsweek* and Deborah Sontag, "Israelis grieve as youth who was lured to his death on the Internet is buried," *New York Times*, 20 January 2001, http://www.nytimes.com/2001/01/20/technology/20MIDE.html?pagewanted=all [accessed 1 April 2002].

3. Most is quoted here from the newspaper *Freiheit*, 27 March 1886. Most's article was reprinted in Walter Laqueur and Yonah Alexander, *The Terrorism Reader* (New York: Penguin, 1987), 100–108.

4. Karl Prenhaul, "Colombia's rebels hit the airwaves," *Newsday*, 24 December 2000, A20.

5. The hostage situation ended when Peruvian troops stormed the compound, killing the fourteen hostage-takers and freeing seventy-one of the unharmed remaining hostages. Most of the hostages had been released by the terrorists.

6. See Ian Buruma, "China in cyberspace," *New York Review of Books* (4 November 1999): 9.

7. Quoted here from a Reuter dispatch of 20 October 2000, titled "Hizbollah says pro-Israelis damaged its web site," http://www.dailynews.yahoo.com/h/nm/20001020/wr/mideast_hizbollah_dc_l.html [accessed 1 April 2002].

8. Ayoub is quoted in Ranwa Yehia, "Hizbullah: Arabs have 'tremendous power to fight' on new cyber-front," *The Daily Star On Line*, http://www.dailystar.com.lb/30_10_00/art2.htm [accessed 30 October 2000].

9. Thomas Friedman, "Digital defense," *New York Times*, 27 July 2001, A19.

10. In September 2000, the CIA obtained CD-ROM copies of a one thousand-page manual that was used to train recruits to the bin Laden cause in al-Qaeda camps in Afghanistan with methods and attack scenarios, including those used in the bombing of U.S. embassies in East Africa in 1998. This intelligence catch was widely reported in the American media. On September 18, 2000, the Associated Press, for example, carried the following story: "Terrorist manual said on CD-ROM," http://dailynews.yahoo.com/h/ap/20000918/us/terrorist_cd_1.html [accessed 1 April 2002].

11. According to *Newsweek*, the U.S. intelligence community was able to foil several of bin Laden's terrorist plans as a result of intercepted e-mails, which made the FBI's disclosure of the existence of its Internet wiretap capability all the more puzzling. See "Tracking bin Laden's e-mail," *Newsweek* (21 August 2000): 6.

12. Freeh's speech was published in *Vital Speeches of the Day* on October 1, 1999. The transcript contained a typing error in that Freeh referred to a plan to attack "1 U.S. airliners" simultaneously—the correct number was eleven airliners. See also Reeves (1999), chapter 4, for details about this foiled plan.

13. Jack Kelley, "Terror groups hide behind Web encryption," *USA Today*, 5 February 2001, http://www.usatoday.co . . . /cyber/tech/2001-02-05-binladen.htm [accessed 1 April 2002].

14. Kelley, "Terror groups hide behind Web encryption."

15. For more on the Internet and the Taliban as well as a comparison with the online practices of neo-Nazis in Germany and elsewhere in the western world, see Peter Chroust, "Neo-Nazis and Taliban On-Line: Anti-Modern Political Movements and Modern Media," in *The Internet, Democracy and Democratization*, ed. Peter Ferdinand (London: Frank Cass, 2000), 110.

16. Chroust, 111.

17. Chroust, 111.

18. See "Links to other web sites" at http://www.stormfront.org [accessed 1 April 2002].

19. While site server Scorpion Communications canceled its contract with the Kahane organization, another firm, McMurtrey/Whitaker & Associates, struggled with the decision of whether to let Kahane.org use its software to sell merchandise on its site. See Dean E. Murphy, "Ugliness online isn't terrorism," *New York Times*, 7 January 2001, Week in Review section.

20. From http://www.vanguardnewsnetwork.com [accessed 1 April 2002]. In the summer of 2001, the site carried an ad for a Visa Nextcard.

21. From http://www.natvan.com/what-is-na/na2.html [accessed 1 April 2002].

22. From http://www.freespeech.org/paulhill/PressRelease.html [accessed 1 April 2002].

23. From http://www.militia-of-florida.com [accessed 1 April 2002].

24. From "Our Fallen Brother Ben 'August' Smith" at http://www.creator.org/editorials/s-50.html [accessed 1 April 2002].

25. From the "World Church of the Creator" hotline at http://www.wcotc.com/hotline/28_24.html [accessed 1 April 2002].

26. See "Links to other web sites" at http://www.stormfront.org [accessed 1 April 2002].

27. See "Links to other web sites."

28. See http://www.jtf.org [accessed 1 April 2002].

29. The three quotes are from http://www.jtf.com [accessed 1 April 2002].

30. From http://www.Kahane.org/discus/messages/14/180.html?992195038 [accessed 1 April 2002].

31. From "Our Fallen Brother Ben 'August' Smith" at http://www.creator.org/editorials/s-50.html [accessed 1 April 2002].

32. The interview with Hale was broadcast on National Public Radio's *All Things Considered* on 6 July 1999.

33. National Public Radio, *All Things Considered,* 6 July 1999.

34. Smith is quoted here from Richard Roeper's column "Hatemongers' 'thought process' filled with irrationality JNK," *State Journal-Register,* 11 July 1999, 17.

35. The interview aired on NBC's *Nightly News* on 8 July 1999.

36. See Elizabeth Bracket of WTTW, Chicago, at http://www.pbs.org/newshour/bb/law/july-dec99/hate_8-11.html [accessed 1 April 2002].

37. From "Our Fallen Brother Ben 'August' Smith," http://www.creator.org/editorials/s-50.html.

38. This crime occurred months before Benjamin Smith's racist killing spree in Illinois and Indiana. See Pam Belluck, "Racist barred from practicing law," *New York Times,* 10 February 1999, A12.

39. Belluck, A12.

40. See Court TV, http://www.courttv.com/trials/berry/102599_ctv.html [accessed 1 April 2002]. The brutal killing occurred in June of 1998 in Jasper, Texas.

41. Quoted here from Julie Salamon, "The Web as home for racism and hate," *New York Times,* 23 October 2000, E8.

42. These excerpts are quoted here from the "Letters From Browsers" section at http://www.natall.com/letters/letters16.html [accessed 1 April 2002].

43. For customer reviews of *The Turner Diaries,* visit http://www.barnes&noble.com.

44. For customer reviews of *Hunter,* visit http://www.amazon.com

45. Quoted here from "Creativity Internet Blitzkrieg," http://www.creator.org/internet.html [accessed 1 April 2002].

46. Quoted here from http://www.jtf.org [accessed 1 April 2002].

47. Quoted here from http://www.jtf.org [accessed 1 April 2002].

48. Roeper, 17.

49. Quoted here from http://www.kids.stormfront.org [accessed 1 April 2002].

50. Quoted here from http://www.resistance.com/zine/Cdreviews/259review.html [accessed 1 April 2002].

51. Quoted here from http://www.resistance.com/zine/Cdreviews/381review.html [accessed 1 April 2002].

52. "The Year in Hate," *The Southern Poverty Law Center's Intelligence Report* (Spring 2001), 34.

53. Quoted here from American Psychological Association Commission on Youth and Violence, *Violence and Youth: Psychology's Response.* Washington, D.C.: The American Psychological Association, 1993.

54. Quoted here from Robert E. Kessler, "Sources: ELF acts grew more violent: Bid for publicity drove to escalation," *Newsday,* 14 February 2001, A4, A25.

55. "Arson-around with Auntie ALF" retrieved from http://www.earthliberationfront.com/main/shtml, [accessed 14 February 2001].

56. Many news sources reported on the two teenagers' heavy Internet use and the reactions of parents and Americans in general to the possible role of the Web in the massacre. See, for example, Amy Harmon, "Parents fear that children are one click ahead," *New York Times,* 20 April 1999; and Lawrence H. Tribe, "The Internet vs. the First Amendment," *New York Times,* 28 April 1999.

57. See http://www.kahane.net/games/ [accessed 1 April 2002].

58. This quote and further references to the Nuremberg Files and RU486 Registry are quoted here from the following sites: http://www.tcrparty.com/atrocity/aborts.html [accessed 1 April 2002] and http://www.ru486registry.com/intro.htm [accessed 1 April 2002].

59. Quoted here from http://www.operationrescue.org [accessed 1 April 2002].

60. Planned Parenthood of the Columbia/Willamette Inc. v. American Coalition of Life, No. 99-35320.

61. See, for example, http://www.emergency.com [accessed 1 April 2002]. Most sites that posted the so-called *fatwa* were neither associated with bin Laden or his allies, nor shared their views.

62. Quoted here from the Jewish Task Force Web site, http://www.jtf.org [accessed 1 April 2002].

63. Quoted here from the Nuremberg Files Web site, http://www.tcrparty.com/atrocity/aborts.html [accessed 1 April 2002].

# 5

# The Mass Media and
# U.S. Anti- and Counterterrorism

JUDGING FROM NEWS REPORTS and the portrayal of villains in our popular entertainment, Americans are bedeviled by fantasies about terrorism. They seem to believe that terrorism is the greatest threat to the United States and that it is becoming more widespread and lethal. . . . Nothing of these beliefs are based on facts" (Johnson 2001). When a former counterterrorism specialist in the U.S. Department of State made this assessment in July 2001 on the op-ed page of the *New York Times*, he cited the modest number of incidents and victims in support of his claim that the threat of international terrorism was blown out of reasonable proportion—most of all by the all-news broadcast media in their search for drama, by pundits not guided by hard data, and by politicians using the terrorism scare to appropriate money for redundant and questionable counterterrorist measures and to suggest new initiatives, such as a National Missile Defense. In response, one reader applauded the anti-hype article as "a breath of fresh air," praising the writer for offering "empirical data, not propaganda, as the basis for his assessment of international security."[1] Another reader was not persuaded by the statistics, writing that the cited numbers did not reflect the real threat by rogue states and organizations able to "target our cities and infrastructure with missiles or hand-delivered terror weapons."[2]

Two months later, when terrorists flew commercial airliners into the World Trade Center in New York and the Pentagon just outside of Washington, D.C., the most horrific terrorist incident on record ended the long-running debate about the true threat of international terrorism. Those who had minimized the danger on the basis of past experiences and data were wrong all along. In fact, in the decades preceding the 9–11 terror, significantly fewer Americans were killed in terrorist incidents than died in traffic accidents, drowned in bathtubs, or were hit by lightning bolts, but, on the other hand, more Americans died in the last two decades of the twentieth century in international terrorist incidents than in all U.S. military deployments abroad during that same time period. According to Paul Pillar,

> U.S. deaths from nonterrorist hostile action in military operations during the 1980s and 1990s (including the Iranian hostage rescue attempt, peacekeeping in Lebanon, the bombing of Libya, the escorting of Kuwaiti tankers, and Operation Fury in Grenada, Just Cause in Panama, Desert Storm in the Persian Gulf, Restore Hope in Somalia, and Uphold Democracy in Haiti) totaled 251. Even adding the 263 deaths from nonhostile causes (most of which were incurred in Desert Shield and Desert Storm) yields a total of 514, less than the number of Americans [660] killed by terrorists during the same period (Pillar 2001, 19–20).

The number of U.S. casualties during military deployments did not reveal anything about the likelihood of future situations abroad that would require U.S. military actions and could result in many more casualties. Similarly, the relatively small number of terrorism victims in the past could not predict the rise or fall of anti-American terrorism in the future. It took the events of September 11, 2001, to silence those who perceived terrorism as a minimal threat. Walter Laqueur, for example, who had once characterized terrorism as an irritant rather than a major threat, came to a different judgment in the last decade of the twentieth century, when he wrote:

> Terrorism has been with us for centuries, and it has always attracted inordinate attention because of its dramatic character and its sudden, often wholly unexpected, occurrence. It has been a tragedy for the victims, but seen in historical perspective it seldom has been more than a nuisance. . . .
> This is no longer true today, and may be even less so in the future. Yesterday's nuisance has become one of the gravest dangers facing mankind (Laqueur 1999, 3–4).

Few in the American news media seemed to notice. In 1999 the U.S. Congress appointed an expert commission to "review the laws, regulations, directives, policies, and practices for preventing and punishing terrorism directed against the United States, assess their effectiveness, and recommend changes."[3] The following year, and some fifteen months before the kamikaze attacks on the World Trade Center and the Pentagon, the National Commission on Terrorism wrote in the executive summary of its report,

> Not all terrorists are the same, but the groups most dangerous to the United States share some characteristics not seen 10 or 20 years ago: They operate in the

United States as well as abroad. Their funding and logistical networks cross borders, are less dependent on state sponsors, and are harder to disrupt with economic sanctions. They make use of widely available technologies to communicate quickly and securely. Their objectives are more deadly. This changing nature of the terrorist threat raises the stakes in getting American counterterrorist policies and practices right.[4]

Instead of reporting on the eye-opening sixty-four-page document and initiating a mass-mediated public debate about the most obvious national security threat in the post–Cold War era, most news organizations did not deem the dire predictions newsworthy. In the hundreds of U.S. newspapers that are published in all fifty states and available in the Lexis-Nexis archives, only forty-three items dealt with the Commission's report—many of them reducing it to a few lines. The *New York Daily News*, for example, devoted two sentences to the document. Of the newspapers that did take note of the report, most focused on some details identified as most likely to cause controversies, such as the recommendation for the administration to consider adding Greece and Pakistan to the list of countries not fully cooperating in the battle against terrorism, the suggested restrictions on terrorist fundraising in the United States, the monitoring of foreign students, and the use of military forces in the event of a major terrorist attack on the United States. An editorial in the *Omaha World-Herald* suggested that the National Commission on Terrorism had "envisioned a level of evil more pervasive than common sense and experience suggest actually exists."[5]

This editorial seemed to explain the media's lack of interest: Most news organizations simply did not buy the premise that international terrorism was a major threat unless there were specific alerts for explicit time periods, as was the case with the Y2K predictions.[6] Television and radio news organizations were not very interested either. The short segments broadcast on ABC's *World News Tonight* and CBS's *Evening News* (one story per network) pointed to criticism voiced against the Commission's recommendations, as did the four stories aired by CNN. NBC's *Today Show* and *Meet the Press* devoted more airtime to the report, and both programs' anchors, Katie Couric and Tim Russet, asked their guests about the likelihood of international terrorism on U.S. soil; but they, too, did not explore this most important point further, switching instead to issues raised by critics of various counterterrorist recommendations. On National Public Radio, only Daniel Schorr mentioned the report twice by name as he reported on other matters.

Finally, some columnists used the release of the report as an opportunity to attack their political foes, specifically President Clinton and his administration. Thus, Oliver North wrote that "William the Tourist was hardly down the gangway of Air Force One following his 40th 'Excellent Overseas Adventure' when the National Commission on Terrorism handed him his report card on combating terrorism. He flunked."[7] North complained that "the report details continuing Syrian and Iranian complicity in international terrorism—and makes a cogent case that the Clinton administration's ill-advised efforts to lift sanctions against Damascus and Tehran ought to be abandoned."[8] Although addressing a legitimate issue and taking a reasonable position, the idea of chiding Clinton's "ill-advised" view on sanctions appeared odd coming from a man who was a central figure in the arms-for-hostages deals between the Reagan White House and Iran.

When another blue ribbon panel, the U.S. Commission on National Security in the 21st Century, released a comprehensive report in early 2001, its warnings of a likely direct attack against Americans on U.S. soil received, as the *Financial Times* recalled later, "scant attention."[9] Nor did their urgent call for measures to prevent and counter terrorism on American soil—among them the establishment of a National Homeland Security Agency—result in media attention. Although the co-chairs of the bipartisan panel, former Senators Gary Hart (a Democrat) and Warren Rudman (a Republican), and other members of the commission went out of their way to obtain media coverage, they were all but ignored. Hart and Rudman held a news conference in Washington; members talked to the editorial boards of leading newspapers. But, as Harold Evans noted in the *Columbia Journalism Review*, "Network television news ignored the report, so did the serious news on public television. The *New York Times* and the *Wall Street Journal* did not carry a line, either of the report or the press conference."[10]

The *Washington Post, Los Angeles Times,* and *USA Today* did cover the report's warnings and recommendations, and some of the regional newspapers used wire service copy from Reuters and the Associated Press. CNN's *The Point with Greta van Susteren* was the only TV program that reported the Commission's proposals at length; host van Susteren interviewed panel members as well as other experts in the field.[11] But, as one media critic concluded, "nowhere did Hart-Rudman get the kind of discussion and amplification of the sort that tends to prompt the political machinery to operate. In short, the report passed under the radar."[12] Given this scarce coverage, the Bush White House, too, ignored the report and instead appointed its own expert commission under Vice President Richard Cheney's leadership.

It was only after the events of 9–11 that a few members of the fourth estate recognized the media's lack of vigilance. In a column titled "The Terrorism Story—And How We Blew It," Richard Cohen wrote, "We [in the media]—and I mean most of us—were asleep."[13] He acknowledged that he and his colleagues had clues and should have reported about the terrorist threat and the weaknesses in the government's counterterrorist approaches.

The media's lack of interest in credible threat assessments was also symptomatic for their reluctance to report on the state of affairs in governmental preparedness programs. In the five years from January 1996 through December 2000, the major TV networks (ABC, CBS, NBC, CNN) and National Public Radio aired a total of forty-eight stories on preparedness and twenty stories on the threat of biological terrorism. This sparse reporting would have been still more dismal without ABC's *Nightline* devoting several of its programs to bioterrorism in the fall of 1999. Most of this news was triggered by preparedness drills that simulated worst-case scenarios in order to test the readiness of emergency response specialists. Whether in television, radio, or print, the news was mostly grim. Thus, NBC News anchor Tom Brokaw said in one newscast, "There is a quiet fear among many of the nation's highest ranking law enforcement officers that this country is grossly unprepared for what could be the greatest terrorist threat of the times, that's biological warfare."[14] In the *New York Times*, Judith Miller reported, "At a time of growing fear of terrorism within America's borders, senior state and local officials say the Federal Government still has no coherent system for deterring or responding to it."[15] But with few exceptions, these mainstream media stories focused on specific drills, assessments, and warnings without exploring the underlying problems and issues in the politics of prevention and preparedness policies and, just as important, without pointing to solutions. In the spring of 2001, a small political magazine, the *Washington Monthly*, published a revealing article under the headline, "Weapons of Mass Confusion: How pork trumps preparedness in the fight against terrorism." Writer Joshua Green reported that "the billions of dollars spent to prepare for an attack has only created an expensive and uncoordinated mess."[16] He was specific in describing the politics of preparedness policy writing:

> A bidding war in Congress quickly ensued. "There was a rush on Capitol Hill," says a senior researcher in a nonpartisan national security think tank. "There were literally dozens of agencies whispering in lawmakers' ears that their organizations could do the job and, in turn, make that congressman look good for choosing them."[17]

According to Green, politics prevailed in that "Congress all but ignored the overwhelming shortcomings in the nation's readiness plan. Redundant programs are regularly funded by lawmakers who are either unaware or unwilling to address the problems."[18]

While always interested in controversy and wrongdoing, especially when they involve public officials, the mass media are far more likely to delve into questionable practices and outright missteps, when the facts—or rumors—are easily understood, shocking, and scandalous—such as the President Clinton and Monica Lewinsky scandal or the Congressman Gary Condit and Chandra Levy saga. Stories that scrutinize the cumbersome politics surrounding highly technical and specialized multi-agency programs are not attractive for news presentations that strive to entertain news consumers rather than inform and protect citizens and voters. Moreover, unlike prevention, preparedness, and counterterrorist planning, acts of political violence fit perfectly into the episodic reporting patterns that dominate the contemporary news, especially in television, at the expense of thematic or contextual presentations that transcend the details of particular cases. A cursory content analysis of leading U.S. news media reveals that, in the past, terrorism and specific threats thereof were far more often covered than counter- and antiterrorism policies and their implementation. Thus, during the five year period from January 1, 1996 through December 31, 2000, three television networks (ABC, CBS, and NBC), National Public Radio, and the *New York Times* mentioned "terrorism" in significantly more news stories than "counterterrorism" and "antiterrorism" (see table 5.1). Even if one considers that not all stories dealing with counter- and antiterrorist policies and activities mentioned the terms expressly (nor did all stories on terrorist incidents or threats contain the word "terrorism" but referred to bombings, suicide killings, hostage-takings, etc.), the lopsided advantage of "terrorism" underlined the mass media's infatuation with terrorism and their modest interest in counterterrorism. This disparity was even more extreme with respect to antiterrorism.

Even after the terror attacks on September 11, 2001, when the Bush administration pushed for and eventually got Congress to adopt several antiterrorism bills (i.e., the Antiterrorism Act of 2001, the Aviation Safety Bill), these important initiatives and eventually adopted laws did not receive a great deal of media attention nor did other anti- and counterterrorist considerations in comparison to the attention paid to terrorism and terrorist threats (see table 5.2). Television newscasts in particular dealt with antiterrorism initiatives, often by simply mentioning them in a few sentences. Longer broadcast segments and stories focused mostly on controversies between the backers and opponents of particular antiterrorist provisions rather than on the substance of the far-reaching legislation. To the extent that the news reported on anti-

**TABLE 5.1**
**Terrorism, Counterterrorism, and Antiterrorism in the News (1/1/1996 to 12/31/2000)**

|  | ABC News | CBS News | NBC News | NPR | N.Y. Times |
|---|---|---|---|---|---|
|  | (N) | (N) | (N) | (N) | (N) |
| Terrorism | 1,017 | 2,306 | 694 | 1,176 | 5,503 |
| Counterterrorism | 149 | 404 | 174 | 351 | 925 |
| Antiterrorism | 16 | 104 | 7 | 58 | 248 |

N = Number of segments/stories
*Source*: Compiled from Lexis-Nexis data.

**TABLE 5.2**
**Terrorism, Counterterrorism and Antiterrorism in the News (9/15/2001 to 12/15/2001)**

|  | ABC News | CBS News | NBC News | NPR | N.Y. Times |
|---|---|---|---|---|---|
|  | (N) | (N) | (N) | (N) | (N) |
| Terrorism | 1,395 | 1,377 | 1,374 | 1,467 | 6,527 |
| Counterterrorism | 424 | 415 | 418 | 511 | 177 |
| Antiterrorism | 50 | 16 | 14 | 39 | 61 |

N = Number of segments/stories
*Source*: Compiled from Lexis-Nexis data and the *New York Times* on-line archive.

terrorism legislation, these stories were predominantly episodic and strategic, focusing on political leaders and political parties, interest groups, and ideologies in the pro and con camps; how the various actors fought for their side; and who was ahead or behind in the battle for or against passage of a bill.

Given media organizations' inclination to over-cover acts of political violence and elevate them to the level of terrorist spectaculars, dramas, and tragedies (as described in chapter 3), the imbalance between the more than generous terrorism coverage and far less attention to anti- and counterterrorism may explain why American politicians, especially presidents from Ronald Reagan to George W. Bush, have chosen a rhetoric of aggression (i.e., war against terrorism or battle against terrorism) over an oratory of defense and reaction (i.e., antiterrorism and counterterrorism) when enlisting support for their policies.

Terrorism is at its core communication, and counterterrorism has strong communication aspects as well—at least when undertaken by leaders in democratic states who need to enlist support for their policies. Except for acts of military reprisal and preemption, counterterrorist policies and initiatives (such as law enforcement, economic sanctions, diplomatic initiatives, and readiness programs) lack most of the time the human drama that the perpetrators of mass-mediated terrorism intentionally stage. Propaganda by violent deed trumps propaganda by nonviolent deed because of the mass media's special attention to violence.

Webster's Collegiate Dictionary defines propaganda as "ideas, facts, or allegations spread deliberately to further one's cause or to damage an opposing cause" and also as "a public action having such an effect."[19] With respect to terrorist or counterterrorist violence, the violent actions constitute propaganda along the lines of the cited definition, but nonviolent anti- and counterterrorist actions, such as the creation of readiness programs, diplomatic initiatives, or tougher criminal justice measures, do not automatically qualify as propaganda because they are deeds that further a government's anti- or counterterrorist cause. Indeed, even when promoted by leaders with excellent communication skills, peaceful anti- and counterterrorist policies are far less likely to make headlines than violent measures and thus are far less likely to come to the attention of the masses.

At this point, the terms anti- and counterterrorism need clarification. Most people do not make a distinction between the terms, using them interchangeably. According to the Department of Defense *Dictionary of Military and Associated Terms*, antiterrorism means a defensive measure to reduce the vulnerability of a people to terrorist acts, while counterterrorism constitutes offensive action to prevent, deter, and respond to terrorist acts.[20]

Because military actions in response to terrorism represent the most extreme and most mass-mediated counterterrorist measures, this chapter focuses on the mass media's coverage of U.S. military responses to international terrorism and especially the news about the counterstrikes against Afghanistan in the aftermath of the destruction of the World Trade Center and part of the Pentagon. In the American context, military reprisal and preemption following international terrorist acts have been rare. There have been only four such instances thus far: the bombing of Libya in 1986 in retaliation for Libya's role in the bombing of the La Belle disco bar in Berlin that was heavily frequented by American GIs; the 1993 bombing of Iraq's intelligence headquarters as punishment for an Iraqi plot to assassinate former President George H. W. Bush during his visit in Kuwait; the 1998 missile strikes against targets in Afghanistan and Sudan following the bombing of U.S. embassies in Kenya and Tanzania; and, most recently, the extensive counterterrorist military campaign against al-Qaeda and Taliban targets in Afghanistan in response to the terrorism of September 11, 2001.

### The Bombing of Tripoli and Benghazi

A few days after being sworn in as the fortieth U.S. president, Ronald Reagan received the fifty-three Americans who spent 444 days as hostages in Iran and were released just after he was sworn in. "Let terrorists be aware that when the rules of international behavior is violated, our policy will be one of swift and effective retribution," the President warned.[21] In the following years, Reagan learned that military retaliation was easier said than done, especially when strikes against terrorists were likely to kill and injure innocent civilians. But after years of repeated anti-American terrorist acts, such as the hijacking of TWA flight 847 and the subsequent hostage situation in Beirut, the takeover of the Italian cruise ship "Achille Lauro" by terrorists who brutally killed Leon Klinghoffer (a wheelchair-bound New Yorker), and the beginning of a series of kidnappings and long hostage ordeals in Lebanon, the Reagan administration was poised to respond. In the 1980s, Libya's Muammar Gadhafi was for President Bush what Osama bin Laden has become for President George W. Bush in 2001: the world's number one terrorist and America's number one enemy. In January 1986, the United States severed the remaining economic ties with Libya, and the President threatened, in a nationally televised news conference, more drastic steps if Gadhafi did not refrain from additional terrorism. The opportunity to demonstrate Washington's determination to set an instructive counterterrorist example arose in April 1986, when a bomb went off in Berlin's La Belle disco, an establishment patronized by American GIs. Once intelligence sources abroad confirmed that Libyan agents were involved in the Berlin bombing, the Reagan administration finally obtained the smoking gun that justified the "swift retaliation" the President had promised nearly five-and-a-half years earlier.

When the rhetoric in Washington heated up amidst leaks that military strikes were imminent, American media organizations strengthened their presence in the Libyan capital. As a result, Americans learned of the bombing raids against targets in Tripoli and Benghazi from media reports immediately after the attacks began and well before the President or others in the administration informed the public. In the middle of the CBS *Evening News* on April 14th, for example, correspondents Jeffrey Fager and Allen Pizzey reported over telephone from Tripoli that the bombing raids had commenced. "Dan— Dan," Fager said with excitement in his voice, "if you can hear that in the background, there's a little bit of—a few blasts going off right now. The attack— the actual attack has been going on for ten minutes now" (Nacos 1996b, 38).

Although the media accounts of innocent victims and massive damage to civilian areas were disturbing for many viewers, readers, and listeners, the overwhelming majority of Americans supported the strikes. The *New York Times* wrote in an editorial that "even the most scrupulous citizen can only approve and applaud the American attack on Libya."[22] Most Democrats and Republicans in Congress supported the President's decision. Senator Lowell P. Weicker was an exception when he warned that the bombing of Libya was not different than what Gadhafi had done. "I don't want the United States on that level," he said.[23] Far more lawmakers expressed their disappointment over America's allies in Europe who refused to support sanctions against Libya and thereby forced the President to resort to military actions. Moreover, Republicans and Democrats in both congressional chambers used the news media to voice their opposition to the President's failure to consult with them before ordering the attack on targets abroad.

But when everything was said and done, the first retaliatory military strikes in response to terrorism rallied Washingtonians and opinion makers elsewhere in the country around President Reagan and bolstered his

already healthy public approval rating by twelve points from 60% before
the bombing raids to 72% afterwards (Nacos 1996b, 118). It is noteworthy
that this positive public reaction at home came in the face of a propaganda
battle between President Reagan and Libya's leader Muammar Gadhafi in
which Reagan, the gifted communicator, did not have the edge. In the two
weeks following the bombing of Tripoli and Benghazi, Gadhafi was mentioned more often in the *New York Times* and the *Washington Post* than was
President Reagan. In the Times, the advantage was 143 to 132 and in the
Post, 129 to 88 in favor of Gadhafi, who exploited every opportunity to tell
reporters about the innocent victims of the U.S. strikes.[24] But as far as the
American public was concerned, the U.S. President who had attacked Gadhafi for years as terrorism's sponsor-in-chief was simply more credible. The
reaction abroad, even among U.S. allies, was far less supportive of the President's counterterrorist move.

In hindsight, it is abundantly clear that many politicians and pundits in the
United States publicly questioned whether military actions against the sponsors of terrorism would prevent further political violence of this sort. Some
called on allies abroad to join the United States in tough economic sanctions;
others asked for broader Middle East solutions; still others spoke of the need
to get a better understanding of the people in the Middle East. Fifteen years
later, as the U.S. responded to the attacks of 9–11, similar questions were
raised and suggestions extended.

### Responding to the Assassination Plot against Ex-President Bush

On June 26, 1993, the U.S. military launched a missile attack on Baghdad targeting the Iraqi intelligence headquarters. Shortly after dozens of Tomahawk
missiles hit Iraq's capital in what was a surprise attack, President Bill Clinton
explained in a nationally televised address that the actions had been taken in
response to an Iraqi plot to assassinate former President George H. W. Bush
during his visit to Kuwait in April 1993. According to President Clinton, there
was "compelling evidence" that "this plot—which included the use of a powerful bomb made in Iraq—was directed and pursued by the Iraqi intelligence
service."[25] In a stern warning directed at Iraq's President Saddam Hussein,
President Clinton said:

> There should be no mistake about the message we intend these actions to con-
> vey to Saddam Hussein, to the rest of the Iraqi leadership, and to any nation,
> group, or person who would harm our leaders or our citizens. We will combat
> terrorism. We will deter aggression. We will protect our people. The world has

repeatedly made clear what Iraq must do to return to the community of nations, and Iraq has repeatedly refused. If Saddam and his regime contemplate further illegal, provocative action, they can be certain of our response.[26]

Coming soon after the first World Trade Center bombing a few months earlier, the results of an investigation into the assassination plot against his predecessor gave President Clinton an opportunity to prove to Saddam Hussein and other belligerents that he was determined to respond decisively to attacks on Americans. ABC correspondent Walter Rodgers figured that the Iraqi leader had misjudged the U.S. president by thinking that he could "strike out at a former president and then think that Bill Clinton could or would do nothing."[27] His colleague, Tom Jerrol, wondered about the political motives behind the decision to hit Baghdad, saying that President Clinton, "of course, had some frustration recently in trying to deal militarily and come up with some answers with Bosnia and also with the famine in Africa. Walter [Rodgers], should this enhance his political image here at home? That's always a consideration that we have to think of when action like this is taken."[28]

Although approving of the missile attack, the *Washington Times* did not consider the response strong enough. According to one of the newspaper's editorials, "the principle behind the choice of target was, Mr. Clinton stated, proportional. But is destroying an empty building proportionate to the attempted murder of an American leader?"[29] While recognizing the very limited effect of the missile strikes, the *Washington Post* supported Clinton in that he "did what a chief executive had to do in retaliating against Iraq's failed effort to assassinate former president Bush last spring."[30] But the same editorial also suggested that Clinton's unilateral decision countered criticism of his preference for "multilateralism" in his foreign policy approaches. Recognizing the broad support for the attack on Iraq in the Congress and from allied governments, the *New York Times* still posed the question, "Was this strike necessary?"[31] According to the editorial page, there was not enough evidence to answer in the affirmative. Instead, the editorial suggested that "the American people need more information about the reasons for and propriety of Mr. Clinton's action."[32] In an even more critical passage, the *New York Times* questioned the president's motives stating,

> Any time a chief executive who is in political difficulty at home undertakes a dramatic military action, he or she must be prepared to face questions whether that action is intended to divert public attention and bolster support for the President.[33]

Certainly, Bill Clinton was off to a shaky start during his first months in office and had not enjoyed a honeymoon period at all with political foes and pundits. This state of affairs in the political arena was reflected in Clinton's anemic public approval ratings before he ordered the missile strikes against Iraq. But unlike the *New York Times*, other authoritative voices, especially members of Congress, did not criticize Clinton's decision to punish Saddam Hussein. The public followed suit, increasing Clinton's overall approval rating by 7% (from 39% to 46%) after the missiles strikes and thus qualifying for a modest rally. The President's approval for his performance in foreign policy that was strong to begin with (48%) increased by 8%.[34]

After addressing the nation to explain the missile attack against Iraq, President Clinton justified his decision two more times and at considerable length within the next seven days—during a joint news conference with President Carlos Menem of Argentina and during an interview with foreign journalists. But in the battle for media attention, Clinton just managed a slight advantage or draw against Saddam Hussein. In the two weeks following the missile attack, Clinton was mentioned in forty-two articles and Saddam Hussein in thirty-four articles in the *New York Times*; in the *Washington Post* the ratio was 32 to 31 in favor of Clinton; ABC News mentioned Clinton and Saddam Hussein in three segments each.[35] Without compelling visuals, the strikes were not particularly interesting for television.

### Missile Strikes against Sudan and Afghanistan

On August 7, 1998, terrorists drove car bombs into the U.S. embassies in Kenya and Tanzania, killing nearly three hundred people, twelve of them Americans, and injuring several thousands. About two weeks later, on August 20, the U.S. military launched some seventy-nine tomahawk missiles against al-Qaeda training grounds in Afghanistan and against what President Clinton called a "chemical weapons-related facility."[36] The counterterrorist strikes came only three days after the President had publicly acknowledged that he had had an affair with White House intern Monica Lewinsky. Not surprisingly, some staunch Clinton critics, including reporters, editorial writers, and TV anchors, questioned whether the President had ordered the attacks for selfish political reasons. During a Pentagon press briefing following President Clinton's short announcement of the counterterrorist actions, Secretary of Defense William Cohen was asked whether he was familiar with *Wag the Dog*, a movie in which a U.S. President cooks up an imaginary war for the purpose of deflecting interest away from his sexual encounter with a teenage girl. The following is an excerpt from the transcript of the briefing:

> *Question:* Some Americans are going to say this bears a striking resemblance to "Wag the Dog." Two questions: Have you seen the movie? And second, how do you respond to people who think that.

*Cohen:* The only motivation driving this action today was our absolute obligation to protect the American people from terrorist activities.[37]

Several members of Congress, among them Republican Senator Arlen Specter, openly questioned Clinton's motives. Republican Senator Dan Coats said,

The danger here is that once a President loses credibility with the Congress, as this President has through months of lies and deceit and manipulations and deceptions, stonewalling, it raises into doubt everything he does and everything he says, and maybe even everything he doesn't do and doesn't say."[38]

While *Washington Post* staff writers faulted officials in the Clinton administration for not providing "information to substantiate their assertion that the exiled Saudi millionaire [Osama bin Laden] masterminded the recent bomb attacks on two U.S. embassies in Africa,"[39] the newspaper's editorial page did not question the soundness of the evidence nor the President's motives, concluding that "Mr. Clinton has taken the right step."[40] In stark contrast, the *New York Times* mentioned the Lewinsky case in its April 21st editorial and called on the President to "dispel any lingering doubts about his motivation by providing the House and Senate intelligence committees with a complete briefing on the bin Laden information and instructing his aides to fill out the partial accounts they have given about the raids."[41]

On NBC's *Nightly News*, anchor Brian Williams opened a segment on "How the President deals with more than one crisis at a time" by pointing to Clinton's "dual dilemmas, one a national security matter this week, one a domestic crisis that couldn't be more personal."[42] CNN's *Late Edition with Wolf Blitzer* highlighted a "look at the presidency with attention split between the sex scandal in the White House and the military strikes aimed at the terrorists responsible for the U.S. embassy bombings.[43] While most news organizations accepted the strikes against bin Laden's bases in Afghanistan, reporters expressed doubts that the struck al-Shifa plant in Sudan had, as the administration claimed, produced chemicals for use in weapons of mass destruction. Although administration officials provided reporters with some sensitive intelligence to prove their case, journalists were more inclined to believe the claims by Sudanese officials who denied any sinister purpose of the plant.

Even though reporters and pundits—especially those in the so-called liberal media—questioned the role of the Lewinsky scandal on President Clinton's decision, particularly with respect to Sudan, the beleaguered President was strongly supported by friends and foes in Washington. The Speaker of the House, Newt Gingrich, said early on, "I think based on what I know, that it was the right thing to do at the right time."[44] With the Republican leadership firmly behind the president, critics like Arlen Specter and Dan Coats went silent. In the midst of the most serious crisis of his political career, President

Clinton had resorted to his considerable political skills and kept Speaker Gingrich and other congressional leaders fully informed of the investigations into the embassy bombings. Although the War Powers Act (WPA) directs presidents to consult Congress in every possible instance before and after U.S. troops are introduced into hostilities, all presidents ignored the consultation requirement since the War Powers Act became law in 1973. This was also the case when presidents used the military during and after terrorist incidents, for example, the attempt to rescue the Iran hostages in 1980 during the Carter presidency, the bombing of Libya in 1986 during the Reagan presidency, and, in fact, the missile attacks on Iraq's intelligence headquarters in 1993 in the early phase of the Clinton presidency. But with the Lewinsky scandal and impeachment hearings looming large, Clinton followed the WPA's consultation provision to the letter so that "the interplay between the White House and the Congress was unprecedented" (Hendrickson 2000, 167). As a result, Clinton had assured himself the support of leaders in both legislative chambers.

As in other foreign crises that directly involved U.S. presidents and the national interest, this supportive stance of Washington opinion leaders and its reflection in the news affected the public's reaction (Brody 1991, 45–78), as did Bill Clinton's repeated efforts to enlist public support. Thus, on the day of the strikes, the president first made a short statement on Martha's Vineyard, where he was vacationing, and a few hours later addressed the nation from the Oval Office. After two days, he used his weekly radio address to explain the reasons for the counterterrorist strikes again.

Before U.S. missiles were launched against targets in Afghanistan and Sudan, President Clinton enjoyed a healthy public approval of over 60% in spite of the Lewinsky scandal. But just as the bombings of the U.S. embassies in Africa had not increased Clinton's public approval, there was no rally in the wake of the attacks on Sudan and Afghanistan. Indeed, from August 17, when the Gallup organization found a presidential approval of 65%, to August 21–22, Clinton's approval declined by three percentage points. This was probably more the result of Clinton publicly admitting a relationship with White House intern Lewinsky than of the counterterrorist measures, since better than three in four Americans approved of the missile attacks.[45] Just as reporters, editorial writers, anchors, and others in the media were inclined to wonder about the President's motives, pollsters, too, pushed this particular angle in questioning survey participants. But a solid majority of the public believed that the President had acted in the best interest of the public. Thus, while Princeton Survey Research Associates found that 69% of Americans thought that Clinton had ordered the attacks mainly to "fight terrorism," only 23% said that he mainly hoped to "turn attention away from the affair."[46]

Thus, even with the dark clouds of an extramarital relationship, his lies under oath about this relationship, and an impeachment procedure over his head, President Clinton found strong support for his military actions among Washington's political elite and the American public. While this support did not result in a public rally behind a President who had a healthy public approval to begin with, the majority of Americans strongly supported his military moves against terrorism. By keeping congressional leaders constantly "in the loop" with respect to the investigations into the East African bombings, Clinton had prepared the way for massive congressional support. Still, even though the President made his case repeatedly to the public while the alleged mastermind of the East African bombings, Osama bin Laden, was silent and in hiding, Bill Clinton did not win the propaganda battle in one respect: The leading media organizations paid equally as much, or more, attention to bin Laden as to the U.S. President. From August 20, 1998, the day of the strikes against Afghanistan and Sudan, to August 31, 1998, ABC News mentioned bin Laden in thirty-two segments and President Clinton in the context of terrorism and counterterrorism in only eleven segments. In the *Washington Post*, the President held a 53 to 46 advantage, in the *New York Times*, bin Laden's edge over Clinton was 73 to 68.[47]

However, while bin Laden became a household name, he did not have to fear a sustained U.S. counterterrorist campaign against himself and his comrades—not at a time when the U.S. President was in deep political trouble at home. In addition, the fact that most reporters simply did not believe administration officials' warning on the clear and present danger of the Sudanese chemical plant protected bin Laden from more drastic counterterrorist actions. As Daniel Benjamin and Steven Simon concluded,

> The [news media's] dismissal of the al-Shifa attack as a blunder had serious consequences, including the failure of the public to comprehend the nature of the al-Qaeda threat. That in turn meant there was no support for decisive measures in Afghanistan—including, possibly, the use of U.S. ground forces—to hunt down the terrorists; and thus no national leader of either party publicly suggested such action.[48]

Obviously, journalists do not like to revisit their earlier judgments as new information becomes available. Thus, when a key witness in the trial against participants in the East African bombings collaborated on the Clinton administration's claims about chemical weapons production in a Khartoun facility, a few miles away from the struck al-Shifa plant and at the time of Clinton's counterterrorist strikes, the news media all but ignored the revelation while reporting on other aspects of the testimony. Only two newspaper articles mentioned the chemical weapons point in passing.[49]

Consequently, the myth of the greatest foreign policy blunder of the Clinton administration survived and was actually revived by Clinton's foes on the cable talk show circle following the 9–11 attacks; they blamed the former President

for not fighting terrorism and the bin Laden threat in particular more decisively. They, too, conveniently forgot that the president's hands were tied in the
wake of the "wag the dog" associations.

### President George W. Bush's "War against Terrorism"

The bombing of Libya in 1983, the missile strike against Iraq's intelligence
headquarters in 1993, and the retaliation against terrorist targets in
Afghanistan and Sudan in 1998 were minor military acts of retaliation. In
stark contrast, the initial military response to the terror attacks on September
11, 2001, was not simply a quick, one-time strike situation, as were the three
earlier counterterrorist retaliations, but a major military deployment and
commitment.

On October 7th, President George W. Bush told the nation in a live broadcast from the White House that the U.S. military had "begun strikes against
al-Qaeda terrorist training camps and military installations of the Taliban
regime in Afghanistan." The President mentioned the word "war" only once
in this speech, explaining that the military action was "part of our campaign
against terrorism, another front in a war that has already been joined
through diplomacy, intelligence, the freezing of financial assets and the arrests of known terrorists by law enforcement agents in 38 countries."[50] Soon
after the President's statement, the American television networks broadcast a
lengthy response by Osama bin Laden that the al-Qaeda leader had pre-taped
in anticipation of the U.S. move and delivered to the Arab TV network al-
Jazeera. "God has blessed a group of vanguard Muslims, the forefront of
Islam, to destroy America," bin Laden said in reference to the 9–11 horror
and warned "that America will not live in peace before peace reigns in Palestine, and before all the army of infidels depart the land of Muhammad, peace
be upon him."[51]

In the nearly four weeks since the terror attacks of September 11th, the war
metaphor had been invoked so often by media organizations and by public officials that the American public was hardly surprised when President Bush revealed the start of the military phase in what cable TV networks had long described in their on-screen banners as "America's New War" or "War against
Terrorism." ABC News broadcast eighty-six stories that contained the terms
"war" and "terrorism," CBS News aired ninety-six such segments, NBC News
broadcast 133, CNN televised 316, and National Public Radio aired 166. The
U.S. print press available in the Lexis-Nexis archive published a total of 5,814
articles that mentioned the two terms.[52] Moreover, when he addressed the nation on October 7th, George W. Bush had already spoken about "war" and

"terrorism" in twenty-nine public appearances from September 11th to October 6th—more than one such association per day. In addition, there were the hundreds of statements by members of his administrations, members of Congress, and other political leaders in Washington and around the country that used the same terms, often in phrases like "war against terrorism" or "war on terrorism." Indeed, George W. Bush had used the weeks since the attacks on New York and Washington to enlist broad public and elite support at home and significant international cooperation for a multi-front war against terrorism—military measures included. In this respect, he followed the presidential playbook for handling international crises to the letter.

## Presidential Power and International Crises

While granting that modern U.S. presidents have formidable constitutional and statutory powers, Richard E. Neustadt nevertheless agrees with President Harry Truman that "presidential power is the power to persuade" (Neustadt 1980, 25). Recognizing that the constitutional arrangement is not one of separated but of shared powers, Neustadt's power model identifies a president's determination and skill to bargain with "Washingtonians" or the political elite as the key to success. In this view, then, a president's public support is only a secondary power source or "one component of the political environment and one of several factors that have an impact on how the political elite respond to political initiatives" (Kellerman 1984, 45).

Others have argued that the fragmentation of power in the Congress, changes in the presidential selection process, the decline of political parties, the expansion of the executive branch, and advances in communication technology are the most important factors that have forced recent presidents to increasingly enlist public support, and that "contemporary presidents, after carefully considering their options, will choose going public over bargaining more often than did their predecessors" (Kernell 1985, 45).

Finally, effective international leadership has been identified as an important source of presidential influence because "there are now few problems of significance to him that can be resolved by unilateral American action" (Rose 1991, 28). Thus, a contemporary American president "must also bargain with leaders of other nations, for his success in an interdependent world depends on measures taken in a number of national capitals" (Rose 1991, 28).

Richard Rose has suggested that postmodern presidents must be able to lead and persuade at one time or the other any one of these three audiences. While these imperatives are challenging enough when handled individually, they add up to a juggling act during international crises, when presidents are well advised to simultaneously go public, go Washington, and go international. These, then, were the imperatives George W. Bush was faced with when he decided to deploy military forces in the fight against terrorism.

### Presidential Leadership before the Strikes against Afghanistan

When *TIME* magazine proclaimed New York's mayor "Person of the Year" for 2001, Rudy Giuliani deserved the honor for his exemplary management of the unprecedented terrorism disaster triggered by the destruction of the World Trade Center. While the mayor immediately involved himself in the hands-on management of the crisis and appeared on television and radio to address New Yorkers, Americans, and the rest of the world repeatedly in the first hours following the attack, President Bush got off to a slow start—partly because he was in Florida when the terrorists struck, and partly because his advisers kept him away from the White House for longer than they should have. But once George W. Bush and his staff found their bearings, they did a superb job in projecting the image of a president who was a surefooted leader in this crisis. While Bush's address to the nation in the evening of the 9–11 terror was adequate at best, by the time he spoke before a joint session of Congress nine days later, he looked and sounded far more like a leader than in the previous eight months as president and during the election campaign.

Starting the day after the terror attack, the President made public appearances on a daily basis. Even when his approval rating hit an all-time record of 90% to 91%, he did not cut back his addresses to the public. Whether it was Bush's instinct or his advisers' reading of history, or both, did not matter: The forty-third U.S. President went public at a breathtaking rate. In the twenty-six days from September 11th to October 6th, President Bush made more than fifty public statements from short exchanges with the press (during what the White House called media availability) to long speeches (such as the one before the United Nations General Assembly) or joint news conferences with foreign leaders. During this short period, fifty-four of Bush's appearances fit the "going public" category—especially since they were sure to win media coverage. In comparison, George W. Bush's father, President George H. W. Bush, had managed only forty-three "going public" activities in the more than five months of the military buildup to the Persian Gulf War. Indeed, after an initial firework of public appeals, the elder Bush went silent for several weeks and lost some public support for the military buildup (Nacos 1994b, 551). In a similar situation, his son made better than two public appearances a day. On at least eleven of these occasions, Bush did not only address the American public but went Washington and/or international at the same time. Thus, when the President appeared together with the bipartisan congressional leadership or foreign leaders (i.e., French President Jacques Chirac, Canada's Prime Minister Jean Chretien, Indonesian President Mega Sukarnoputri, Japan's Prime Minister Junich Koizumi, King Abdullah of Jordan, Mexican President Vincente Fox, etc.), he appealed to the political elite in Washington and/or the international route but managed to go public at the same time.

During these weeks, Osama bin Laden was not available to the news media, gave no press conferences, granted no interviews. There were a few statements via videotape or fax and news briefings by Taliban representatives in Pakistan who acted as stand-ins for bin Laden. Yet, the American television networks mentioned Osama bin Laden more often in their stories than they referred to President Bush, while National Public Radio and leading newspapers mentioned bin Laden equally or nearly as often as Bush (see table 5.3).

Once the military actions against targets in Afghanistan began, Bush worked just as hard to appear in public in order to communicate with Americans across the country, with Washingtonian's—especially members of Congress—and with the international community. In the two months from October 7th to December 7th, the President made a total of seventy-six public statements relating to the fight against terrorism, using opportunities spanning from his weekly radio addresses to visits in an elementary school or joint appearances with Russian President Vladimir Putin. Of these seventy-six cases, twenty-five occasions also fit the "going international" imperative in that the President appeared with foreign leaders at the White House, his Texas ranch, or abroad; another ten appearances were "going Washington" appeals to support the presidential agenda, specifically antiterrorism legislation and

### TABLE 5.3
### News Stories Mentioning President Bush and
### bin Laden following the 9/11/2001 Terrorist Attacks

|  | Pres. G.W. Bush | Osama bin Laden |
|---|---|---|
|  | (N) | (N) |
| ABC News | 175 | 299 |
| CBS News | 210 | 270 |
| NBC News | 159 | 211 |
| CNN | 292 | 469 |
| NPR | 271 | 188 |
| *N.Y. Times* | 655 | 611 |
| *Wash. Post* | 684 | 490 |

N = Number of segments/stories
*Source*: Compiled from Lexis-Nexis data; TV and radio broadcasts for the period 9/11/2001 to 10/6/2001; newspaper articles 9/12/2001 to 10/7/2001.

an economic stimulus package. Once again, a comparison with the elder Bush is instructive: In the one-and-one-half months of the actual Persian Gulf War, there were only fifteen presidential "going public" activities (Nacos 1994b, 551), while there were five times as many by the younger Bush in the first two months of the war against terrorism in Afghanistan.

As a result, the public approval for George W. Bush's job performance in general and for military actions in his war on terrorism was consistently high before and after the hostilities against targets in Afghanistan began. Bush's general job approval remained consistently high and did not fluctuate in the prewar period, as was the case with his father during the build-up phase to the Persian Gulf War. Toward the end of December 2001, the Gallup Organization reported that Bush's general job approval rating stood at 86% and added,

> Bush's approval rating has remained in the high 80% range since mid-September, and the 10 readings of Bush's approval rating since that time are among the highest Gallup has ever recorded. Bush has been able to sustain his high ratings longer than any president in Gallup polling history.[53]

Also in December 2001, better than nine in ten Americans were satisfied with the progress of the war in Afghanistan.[54] Add to this the consistent bipartisan support in Congress for the military efforts in Afghanistan and significant international backing as well, and Bush's leadership style in this initial phase of his war against terrorism adhered to the threefold "going public" imperatives and proved highly successful in terms of the public, Washingtonian, and international arenas.

But in spite of George W. Bush's relentless public appearances and speeches, and in spite of the news media's attention to these events, in one respect Bush was unable to win the public relation battle with Osama bin Laden: Television newscasts in the United States continued to mention the elusive al-Qaeda leader more often than Bush, while other media organizations gave both of them about equal billing in this respect. The *Washington Post* was an exception among the leading news organizations in that the newspaper mentioned the President far more often than bin Laden (see table 5.4).

Indeed, on October 7th, the day when the bombing of Afghanistan commenced, television newscasts gave the videotaped bin Laden tirade against the United States at least the same play as President Bush's statement. The following day, October 8th, the print press followed suit: While the combined U.S. government sources dominated the crisis coverage and were quoted or mentioned in 52% of the articles in the *New York Times* and 44% in the *Los Angeles Times*, bin Laden and his sympathizers were cited in 22% of the relevant articles in the *New York Times* and 24% in the *Los Angeles Times*. Just as

**TABLE 5.4**
**News Stories Mentioning President Bush and**
**bin Laden following U.S. military Strikes against Targets in Afghanistan**

|  | Pres. G. W. Bush | Osama bin Laden |
|---|---|---|
|  | (N) | (N) |
| ABC News | 303 | 497 |
| CBS News | 201 | 434 |
| NBC News | 170 | 345 |
| CNN | 425 | 571 |
| NPR | 202 | 198 |
| *N.Y. Times* | 1,259 | 1,211 |
| *Wash. Post* | 1,201 | 881 |

N = Number of segments/stories
*Source*: Compiled from Lexis-Nexis data; TV and radio broadcasts for the period 10/07/01 to 12/07/01; newspaper articles for 10/08/01 to 12/08/01.

important, U.S. government sources were cited in four of the six crisis-related front-page stories in the *New York Times* and in all five cover stories in the *Los Angeles Times*, but bin Laden was not far behind in that he was quoted in three of the six relevant front-page stories in the *New York Times* and in four of five cover stories in the *Los Angeles Times*. On the same day, the *New York Times* devoted three and the *Los Angeles Times* two stories exclusively to bin Laden.[55]

Although President George W. Bush stopped calling bin Laden by name to deny the al-Qaeda leader the celebrity status the news had deferred on him, the media's attention to the world's most notorious terrorist did not wane in the months after the first strikes against al-Qaeda and Taliban targets. Indeed, as the massive bombings concentrated on southern Afghanistan, these actions were reported in terms of their proximity to possible bin Laden hideouts, and when the Taliban was removed from power, the mop-up actions by anti-Taliban and U.S. Special Operation teams were mostly reported as search missions to find bin Laden "dead or alive," as reporters and commentators told their audiences, repeating the phrase that President Bush used more than once. Even the TV networks' and the print press's refusal to broadcast or print bin Laden's videotaped statements in full length did not diminish his prominence in the news. Instead of replaying such tapes fully and printing the transcripts completely, as they did following the 9–11 events, news organizations' anchors, reporters, and the growing army of network consultants combed through selected facets of the visual and textual content and speculated on the air and in print endlessly about its meaning.

This was a strange way to report the news—especially on the all-news cable networks. Take, for example, the videotape that was broadcast by al-Jazeera, the Arab-language television network in a shortened version on December 26th, 2001, and a day later in its entirety. The American all-news networks announced both releases well in advance by their anchor persons and in on-screen breaking news banners; then they offered bits and pieces of the English translations in many replays and had their expert commentators analyze the spoken words as well as bin Laden's appearance without allowing viewers to see or hear the full tape. Newspapers also published detailed examinations of the material without giving their readers an opportunity to read the full transcripts. Reacting to an appeal by the Bush administration, and especially National Security adviser Condoleezza Rice in early October not to assist bin Laden in his propaganda war, the television networks and leading print organizations refrained from broadcasting or printing bin Laden's complete statements and reported selectively on their content instead. A White House spokesman characterized the bin Laden statement that was released in late December as "nothing more than the same kind of terrorist propaganda we have heard before."[56] Strangely, two weeks earlier, the Bush administration had released a "home video" (found by the U.S. military in a deserted house in Afghanistan) in which bin Laden discussed his prior knowledge of the September 11th attacks. In this case, the administration encouraged media organizations at home and abroad to fully broadcast and otherwise publicize this proof of bin Laden's involvement. Obviously, the leading American media organizations deferred to the administration's desire when it came to withholding or making available the full content of bin Laden's statements.

Broadcasting these tapes and printing their transcripts in full would have been a far better decision, just as the earlier practice of replaying bin Laden and al-Qaeda videotapes endlessly on the all-news TV channels was ill-chosen (for more on this issue, see chapter 2). But regardless of this self-censorship, bin Laden loomed large in the crisis coverage of broadcast and print organizations that devoted a disproportional amount of air time and column inches to the celebrity terrorist who was in hiding. This was a potential problem for policymakers who continued to promise that they would capture bin Laden sooner or later and win the war against terrorism. Certainly, bin Laden's propaganda and the rest of the news about him did not win "the evil one," as President George W. Bush called him, friends in the United States, but the tremendous media attention reduced the "war against terrorism" to hunting down bin Laden. Some so-called expert commentators suggested at the end of December that bin Laden was finished and that his terrorist organization had taken a devastating blow—at a time when bin Laden's fate remained uncertain and only a few of his associates were captured or killed by bombs. To their credit, the U.S. President and others in the administration warned the public repeatedly that the "war against terrorism" would be long and required patience, but the news media's tireless focus on "the world's most wanted terrorist" seemed to attribute the terror problem to one star terrorist and his group, fostering a false perception as to the scope of the threat and the prospect for its removal. Even the failed attempt to blow up an American Airlines flight from Paris to New York by a British man with ties to al-Qaeda just before Christmas 2001 was not a wake-up call for the news media to abandon their fixation with the celebrity terrorist.

As a result, in late November 2001, 55% of the public believed that the war effort in Afghanistan would not be a success without the capture of bin Laden, and three in four Americans remained optimistic that the al-Qaeda boss would be captured by the United States. However, the majority of Americans heeded the President's repeated warnings that even the complete defeat of bin Laden and the al-Qaeda leadership would not mean the end of terrorism: In mid-December nine in ten Americans considered the capturing of bin Laden as one step in the long campaign against terrorism.[57]

## The End of the "Vietnam Syndrome"?

Well before the air strikes against al-Qaeda and Taliban targets in Afghanistan commenced, President Bush, Defense Secretary Donald Rumsfeld, and other members of the administration had told the public repeatedly that the multifaceted "war against terrorism" would demand sacrifices. When the military involvement in Afghanistan began, they warned that there would be casualties. With both politicians and the public firmly behind the President's crisis management, military and political leaders seemed determined to disregard and perhaps discard the "Vietnam syndrome" that had informed U.S. policy since the end of the Vietnam war. At the heart of this enduring Vietnam war legacy among military and civilian leaders is the belief that the mass media— especially television—will turn domestic public opinion against involvement in military conflicts by dwelling on visual images of the ugly side of war. The related "body bag thesis" holds that the contemporary public cannot stomach casualties. In addition, the "CNN effect" refers to the global news network's ability to inform the public instantly and thereby pressure decision makers into quick reactions without granting them sufficient time for deliberation (Nacos, Shapiro, and Isernia 2000, 2). All of these theories add up to the conviction that elite and public support can be sustained only for rather short military deployments with clearly defined exit strategies.

If there ever was a situation that called for a fresh look at this conventional wisdom, the military move against al-Qaeda and the Taliban was it. It seemed that the "Vietnam syndrome" and the "body bag thesis" were not really tested in that only four Americans lost their lives and only a few were injured in non-combat mishaps by the end of the year 2001, when the new, provisional Afghan government took over. But what the news media either ignored or under-covered severely was the price that the United States paid for its reluctance to involve its own ground forces in hostilities and its reliance on Afghans as proxy fighters, who allowed many al-Qaeda and Taliban members to flee across the border into Pakistan or to simply blend with their homeland population and who did not capture Osama bin Laden or Taliban leader Mullah Omar. It seemed that the "body bag thesis" and the "Vietnam syndrome" had had their hands in military strategy—and the press seemed not to notice.

At a time when CNN had several competitors in the all-news television market, the "breaking news syndrome" emerged as a more potent version of the "CNN effect" in the sense that the around-the-clock news channels asked for "new developments" in the Afghanistan conflict from one "war update" to the other. Typically, news anchors would enter a commercial break by telling their audience, "We will be right back to check on the progress of the war" or something to this effect.[58] And when the bombing raids did not result in immediate and measurable gains on the ground, some inside and outside the media began to wonder whether the conflict in Afghanistan would turn into a Vietnam-like fiasco and another military quagmire for the United States. Expressing impatience, one media critic wrote,

> The bombing war against the Taliban and al Qaeda forces in Afghanistan is not moving as fast as armchair generals in the news media and in the Congress would like. We have become so accustomed to relatively quick conflicts in the past decade or so, as in the Persian Gulf War and in Belgrade, that three to four weeks of bombing and covert military ground actions—with no major military victories—has stretched the patience of the talking-head critics on television.[59]

Talking heads on television were not the only circles that displayed impatience only two or three weeks into the U.S. involvement in Afghanistan. Charles Krauthammer, for example, wrote three weeks after the first air strikes:

> The war is not going well and it is time to say why. It has been fought with half-measures. It has been fought with an eye on the wishes of our "coalition partners." It has been fought to assuage the Arab "street." It has been fought to satisfy the diplomats rather than the generals. Thirty years ago in Vietnam, we fought a war finely calibrated to win "hearts and minds." Bomb today, pause tomorrow. That strategy met with nothing but pain and defeat.[60]

Richard Cohen found another angle to the legacy of Vietnam when he criticized that the Bush administration seemed "genetically tight-lipped," and press briefings at the Pentagon resembled more and more "the ones conducted daily during the Vietnam war." He added,

> It is Vietnam that haunts the military—not only the fear of a quagmire but concurrent fear and loathing of a critical press. But it is another aspect of Vietnam that should haunt both the military and its civilian bosses—the erosion of trust. As the [Vietnam] war dragged on, little the brass said was taken at face value. . . .
>
> The war [in Afghanistan] is not off to a great start. We know that. We are not worried. We are prepared to a bitter and lengthy fight. We don't expect miracles but we do expect candor. So far, we have received neither.[61]

And R. W. Apple wrote in a news analysis,

> Like an unhappy specter from an unhappy past, the ominous word "quagmire" has begun to haunt conversations among government officials and students of foreign policy, both here and abroad. Could Afghanistan become another Vietnam? Is the United States facing another stalemate on the other side of the world? Premature questions may be, three weeks after the fighting began. Unreasonable they are not, given the scars scoured into the national psyche by defeat in Southeast Asia. For all the differences between the two conflicts, and there are many, echoes of Vietnam are unavoidable.[62]

During the month from October 15th to November 15th, 2001, the U.S. newspapers archived by Lexis-Nexis carried a total of 804 news stories, news analyses, and opinion pieces that contained the words "Afghanistan" and "Vietnam." During that same period, these newspapers published 102 articles that mentioned both "Afghanistan" and "quagmire."

When Kabul was liberated and the defeat of the Taliban in all of Afghanistan was in sight, the Vietnam analogies disappeared quickly from the mass-mediated discourse—even with respect to issues that could have profited from a few reminders—such as the mentioned problem with the use of proxy forces. But one way or another, the "breaking news syndrome" and its need for progress and quick results had been a major factor in revisiting the ghosts of Vietnam and in demonstrating that this legacy of the past would have to be dealt with during future military deployments of some duration.

### Mediated Public Deliberation and the *New York Times*

In December 2001, James Fallow, who earlier criticized the contemporary media for concentrating on scandal-and-spectacle-minded news (Fallows 1996), praised the war-related news coverage of the *New York Times*, suggesting that the newspaper deserved quite a few journalistic prizes for its reporting after the events of September 11, 2001. Fallows mentioned in particular that the newspaper published "more war-related stories each day than you can actually read. Analytical and investigative pieces that anticipate what you'd want to know."[63]

But what about the diversity of opinions on important issues stemming from anti- and counterterrorist initiatives on the opinion pages of this influential newspaper? Recognizing that public deliberation "is essential to democracy in order to ensure that the public's policy preferences—upon which democratic decisions are based—are informed, enlightened, and authentic," Benjamin I. Page assigns a central role to "professional communicators" in the mediated deliberations of modern mass societies (Page 1996, 2). Since staffers write a newspaper's editorials, one wonders whether their opinions are also reflected on the op-ed pages and in the letters to the editor or whether these contributions offer a rather wide diversity of views.

On September 12th, the day after the terror strikes, several letters to the editor in the *New York Times* took categorical positions on the two issues that would be central in the mass-mediated discourse in the days and weeks to come—whether or not to retaliate militarily against those responsible for the horror of 9–11 and whether or not to curb civil liberties at home for the sake of greater safety. A reader from Tennessee demanded, "Now America must wield the sword in defense of liberty." But a letter writer from Pittsburgh appealed for restraint, writing, "Violence does not deter the violent. . . . The only sane and civilized way to settle international disputes is by international negotiations." A reader from Bethesda worried about the protection of civil liberties in the aftermath of the terror attacks pleading, "The inevitable temptation to change fundamentally the nature of our society, by attacking the civil rights and civil liberties of any individual or group, must be resisted."[64] The pro and con viewpoints on military reprisal that were reflected in the letters to the editor section were not spelled out on the op-ed page, where William Safire wrote, "When we reasonably determine our attackers' bases and camps, we must pulverize them—minimizing but accepting collateral damage—and act overtly or covertly to destabilize terror's national hosts."[65] Anthony Lewis cautioned that "one danger must above all be avoided: taking steps that in the name of security would compromise America's greatest quality, its open society."[66] In one of its editorials, the *New York Times* touched on both reprisal and civil liberties, writing that "retaliation is warranted" once the architects of the horror are identified and warning that "Americans must rethink how to safeguard the country without bartering away the rights and privileges of the free society that we are defending."[67] The views expressed in the letters that the *Times* published the following weeks and months were more diverse than the opinions on the op-ed page and more timely than the editorial writers with respect to civil liberties issues. As table 5.5 shows, in the three months from September 12, 2001 to December 12, 2001, all editorials in the *New York Times* and eighteen of nineteen op-ed pieces expressed opposition to post-9–11 actions and antiterrorist measures at the expense of civil liberties; in the letters to the editor section letters ran 47 to 25 against curbing civil liberties but opposing views were expressed far more frequently than in editorials and op-ed page opinion pieces.

During the same time period, the *New York Times* presented its readers with opinions about the use of the U.S. military in the fight against terrorism in general and in Afghanistan in particular that ran strongly in favor of such actions, just as surveys at the time found consistently that the overwhelming majority of the public backed military responses. Except for an editorial in which the newspaper wrote that the "Bush administration would make a serious mistake by moving to wage war in Iraq,"[68] the rest of the relevant editorials were supportive of the administration's military plans and actual deployments (see table 5.6.).

To the newspaper's credit, there were no indications at all that its editorial positions on the two issues influenced the selection of viewpoints that were

TABLE 5.5
**Opinion on Civil Liberty Curbs in the Fight against Terrorism
in the *New York Times* from September 12, 2001 to December 12, 2001**

|  | Support curbs | Ambiguous | Oppose curbs |
|---|---|---|---|
|  | (N) | (N) | (N) |
| Editorials | — | — | 5 |
| Letters to the Editor | 25 | — | 47 |
| Op-ed columns | 1 | — | 18 |

N = Number of published opinion pieces
*Source*: Compiled from *New York Times* printed editions.

TABLE 5.6
**Opinion on Military Actions against Terrorism/Afghanistan
in the *New York Times* from September 12, 2001 to December 12, 2001**

|  | Support/for | Ambiguous | Opposed/against |
|---|---|---|---|
|  | (N) | (N) | (N) |
| Editorials | 10 | — | 1 (Iraq) |
| Letters to the Editor | 40 | 13 | 12 |
| Op-ed columns | 6 | — | 3 |

N = Number of published opinion pieces
*Source*: Compiled by author from *New York Times* printed editions.

expressed in the letters to the editor sections. In this case, the "professional communicators" did not shape the public discourse as presented in the letters section according to their own viewpoints and preferences. The same was true for those op-ed pieces that took stands on counterterrorism and the use of military force; the fact that the viewpoints expressed in editorials and op-ed articles on civil liberties were all or nearly all against curbs does not necessarily suggest the opposite. In this particular case, the right-leaning and left-leaning regular columnists, such as William Safire and Anthony Lewis, and outside contributors of the political right and left, were in rare agreement. Conservative columnist Saffire, for example, sharply criticized the Bush administration for considering military courts for the trial of terrorists and took aim at Attorney General John Ashcroft (whose nomination he had supported) for suggesting that "anybody that even took that point of view was on the side of terrorists, helping and abetting."[69]

### Covering Antiwar Protests Abroad and at Home

Following the first strikes against targets in Afghanistan, angry antiwar protests—some accompanied by violence—erupted in several Muslim countries. The American news media reported about these demonstrations, and they should have, except that the news conveyed the impression that much of the Muslim and Arab world was in an anti-American uproar, expressing itself in massive demonstrations everywhere and all the time. By focusing on angry protesters who burned the American flag and raised their fists against America, the media (especially television) provided their audiences with only one facet of the whole reality and conveyed an utterly wrong picture of what was really happening in this part of the world. Based on media visuals in particular, Americans were led to believe that most Arab and Muslim countries experienced massive anti-American demonstrations during this period. This was simply not the case. Martin Indyk kept track of such protests in twenty-one Arab countries from the time of the first U.S. attacks on targets in Afghanistan and found the following: In these countries combined, there were nine anti-American demonstrations in week one, three in week two, one in week three, two in week four, zero in week five, and one in week six.[70]

While these anti-American outbursts were over-covered, domestic protests against military retaliation in response to the 9–11 terror were largely ignored or harshly criticized in the mainstream media. One observer wrote that there simply was no antiwar movement to speak of:

For nearly half a century—from 1953, when the guns fell silent in Korea, until this year—the United States never went to war, whether directly or by proxy, without significant domestic opposition. . . .

This time there has been nothing of the kind. Apart from traditional pacifists, who oppose any use of force on principle, and a tiny handful of reflexive Rip Van Winkles, almost no one objects, in broad outline, to the aims and methods of the antiterrorism campaign.[71]

National Public Radio was among the few news organizations that reported at some length on a "burgeoning" or "fledgling" antiwar movement and the intolerant reaction it met inside and outside university campuses.[72]

Although American campuses were tranquil, some commentators attacked the few peace activists, pointing their fingers at the "academic al-Qaida" and "the lunatic ravings of those who hide behind the Constitution while trying to destroy it, and whose perspective is not that different from the pathological hatred and fanaticism that motivates Osama bin Laden."[73] Readers who resented antiwar activists were not quite as extreme in their comments. A reader of the *Pittsburgh Post-Gazette* wrote, for example, "I've been trying for a long time to understand the peacenik movement. It all sounds so nice, warm and fuzzy—but makes absolutely no sense, especially in this current crisis."[74]

A few newspapers published opinion pieces by opponents of military retaliation, far more newspapers simply did not pay attention to the antiwar fringe. The *New York Times* did report on several protest events, but only in short articles typically relegated to inside pages. Thus, an antiwar demonstration in Washington that drew (according to the police) about nine thousand or (according to organizers) twenty-five thousand protesters, was covered in 381 words and accompanied by a photograph that depicted antiwar protesters confronted by counterprotesters who supported military action in response to terrorism. The television networks mostly ignored domestic antiwar demonstrations, and when they did cover them, they only devoted a few sentences to such protests. From September 15, 2001 to December 15, 2001, ABC News aired one TV segment that mentioned domestic antiwar protesters, CBS News aired three, NBC News televised one, and CNN broadcast two. Those who dissented military reaction to the 9–11 terror got little access to the mainstream media.

## Mainstream Media's Patriotic Influence

While alternative periodicals reflected oppositional views, the mainstream media were in fact part of the massive rally-'round-the-flag that placed the overwhelming majority of America firmly behind the war against terrorism. This stance was enormously helpful to the crisis-managing President Bush, who simply did not have to worry about the news media at home but rather enjoyed an extraordinary degree of cooperation and consideration from these quarters—especially with respect to the military engagement abroad. Hendrick Hertzberg wrote that there was "no real antiwar movement since September 11, 2001, for the same reasons that there was none after December 7, 1941."[75] For precisely the same reasons, the mainstream media reflected and were part of the broad consensus for the President's military campaign against bin Laden, al-Qaeda, and the Taliban—a high degree of support that President Bush's predecessors did not receive in the aftermath of comparably minor military actions in response to anti-American terrorism.

Accordingly, the news reflected little or no critical questions with respect to the administration's conduct of the war on terrorism in Afghanistan, the limited access of the American press to hostilities that involved the U.S. military, and plans for future counterterrorist actions. In late February 2002, when Senate Majority Leader Tom Daschle raised questions about possible next steps in the fight against terrorist states and organizations, several Republicans questioned his patriotism. "How dare Senator Daschle criticize President Bush while we are fighting our war on terrorism, especially when we have troops in the field," Senate Minority Leader Trent Lott said. Representative Thomas Davis III argued that Daschle's "divisive remarks have the effect of giving aid and comfort to our enemies by allowing them to exploit divisions in our country."[76]

Few media commentators and editorial writers stood up forcefully in defense of freedom of speech and the need for public discourse. Among the exceptions was the *Washington Post*. In an editorial, the newspaper recalled several incidents during the Clinton presidency, when Senator Lott had questioned ongoing military actions both in Kosovo and the Persian Gulf. "Senator Lott now would have us believe that raising such questions is divisive," the *Post* wrote, "but what's divisive and dangerous is stifling debate for political gain."[77]

Veteran newsman Neil Hickey concluded that the Pentagon's war reporting rules in the case of Afghanistan were the toughest ever imposed by the U.S. military. But the lack of genuine war news did not stop news organizations, least of all cable networks, from reporting extensively on the war against the Taliban and al-Qaeda. It might well be that experienced correspondents were "frustrated and mutinous," but you did not sense that from the coverage of even the most serious newspapers, news magazines, television and radio new programs.[78]

The events of September 11, 2001, changed the mindsets of Americans—including those in the mainstream media. As a result, the news reflected and reinforced the views and policy preferences of the administration, the political elite, and the vast majority of the public. The media elite seemed sensitive to the perennial charge that the "liberal" news media were out of touch with the majority of Americans and not as patriotic as the rest of the country.

## Notes

1. This statement was contained in a letter by Arsalan Tariq Iftikhar published in the "To the Editor" column of the *New York Times*, 14 July 2001.

2. From a letter by Joseph E. Muckerman published in the "To the Editor" column of the *New York Times*, 14 July 2001.

3. Report of the National Commission on Terrorism, "Countering the Changing Threat of Terrorism," Pursuant to Public Law 277, 105th Congress, 49.

4. "Countering the Changing Threat of Terrorism," 6.

5. "Secure, yes, but also free," *Omaha World-Herald*, 12 June 2000, 6.

6. Major acts of terrorism in the United States were feared for the New Year's celebrations, marking the end of the twentieth and the beginning of the twenty-first centuries. The Y2K threats, which were believed to target the Internet and computer systems as well, were widely reported in the news.

7. Oliver North, "Tackling terrorism," *Washington Times*, 11 June 2000, B3.

8. North, B3.

9. Edward Alden, "Report warned of attack on American soil," *Financial Times*, 12 September 2001, 5.

10. Harold Evans, "What we knew: Warning given—story missed," *Columbia Journalism Review* (November/December 2001); see http://www.cjr.org/year/01/6/evans/asp [accessed 1 April 2002].

11. CNN, *The Point with Greta van Susteren*, 31 January 2001.

12. Evans, "What we knew: Warning given—story missed."

13. Richard Cohen, "The terrorism story—and how we blew it," *Washington Post*, 4 October 2001, A31.

14. NBC *Nightly News*, 8 December 1997 (transcript retrieved from the Lexis-Nexis database).

15. Judith Miller, "Nation lacks plan to deter terrorism," *New York Times*, 6 September 1998, 30.

16. Joshua Green, "Weapons of Mass Confusion: How pork trumps preparedness in the fight against terrorism," *Washington Monthly* (15–21 May 2001), 15.

17. Green, 16.

18. Green, 20.

19. *Webster's Ninth New Collegiate Dictionary* (Springfield, Mass.: Merriam-Webster, 1989).

20. Following the events of 9–11, William Saffire cited the Department of Defense *Dictionary of Military and Associated Terms'* definitions and added that with respect to September 11, "Doves prefer antiterrorism; hawks plump for counterterrorism." See William Saffire, "Nameless event: The terrorist attack lacks a universal label," *New York Times Magazine* (7 October 2001): 24–26.

21. Lee Lescaze and Lou Cannon, "Reagan warns against future terrorist acts," *Washington Post*, 28 January 1981, A26.

22. "The Terrorist and his Sentence," *New York Times*, 15 April 1986, A30.

23. Weicker is quoted here from Steven V. Roberts, "Attack on Libya: The View from Capitol Hill," *New York Times*, 15 April 1986, A17.

24. These statistics are the results of a search of the two newspapers in the Lexis-Nexis archive from 15 April 1986 to 30 April 1986. The search words used were "Reagan" and "Libya" and "Qaddafi" and "Libya."

25. President Bill Clinton, quoted here from the transcript of ABC Breaking News, "U.S. Strikes Against Iraq for Bush Attack," 26 June 1993.

26. "U.S. Strikes Against Iraq for Bush Attack," 26 June 1993.

27. Walter Rodgers, quoted here from "U.S. Strikes Against Iraq for Bush Attack," 26 June 1993.

28. Tom Jerrol, quoted here from "U.S. Strikes Against Iraq for Bush Attack," 26 June 1993.

29. "A message for Saddam," *Washington Times*, 28 June 1993, E2.

30. "Strike on Baghdad," *Washington Post*, 28 June 1993, A18.

31. "Was this strike necessary?" *New York Times*, 28 June 1993, A16.

32. "Was this strike necessary?" A16.

33. "Was this strike necessary?" A16.

34. These figures are from Gallup polls taken 18–21 June 1993 and 29–30 June 1993. A subsequent survey, taken 9–11 July 1993, resulted in a one percent decrease of Clinton's general approval and a seven percent decline in his foreign policy approval.

35. Compiled from Lexis-Nexis data using the search words "Clinton" and "Iraq" and "Saddam Hussein" and "Iraq."

36. This statement by President Bill Clinton, Federal News Service, 20 August 1998, was retrieved from the Lexis-Nexis database.

37. News briefing by William Cohen, Secretary of Defense, 20 August 1998, according to FDCH Political Transcripts.

38. Quoted here from Todd S. Purdum, "U.S. fury on 2 continents: Congress, critics of Clinton support attacks," *New York Times*, 21 August 1998, 1.

39. Vernon Loeb and Michael Grunwald, "Officials won't detail evidence on bin Laden," *Washington Post*, 21 August 1998, A19.

40. "In self-defense," *Washington Post*, 21 August 1998, A22.

41. "Striking against terrorism," *New York Times*, 21 August 1998, A22.

42. Brian Williams, NBC *Nightly News*, 21 August 1998.

43. CNN, *Late Edition with Wolf Blitzer*, 23 August 1998.

44. Todd Purdum, "U.S. fury on two continents," *New York Times*, 20 August 1998, A1.

45. The cited approval ratings come from surveys by the Gallup organizations. On August 21, 1998, the day after the counterstrikes, 75% of the respondents approved of the strikes (Gallup); on August 22, 1998, the Pew Research Center measured a 79% approval for the strikes.

46. This survey was undertaken by Princeton Survey Research Associates, 21–24 August 1998. Immediately after the counterterrorist attacks on August 20, 1998, Gallup found that 58% of respondents believed that Clinton had acted "solely in the

best interest of the country." The strong bipartisan congressional support, and perhaps the President's repeated public explanations, strengthen the public's approval of the counterterrorist measures.

47. These statistics were compiled from the Lexis-Nexis archive from 20–31 August 1998 (for ABC News) and from 21 August–1 September 1998 (for the *New York Times* and the *Washington Post*) by using the search words "President Clinton" and "Afghanistan" and "bin Laden" and "Afghanistan."

48. Daniel Benjamin and Steven Simon, "A failure of intelligence?" *New York Review of Books*, (20 December 2001): 80.

49. Benjamin and Simon, 77.

50. From a statement by President Bush on 7 October 2001, according to the Federal News Service transcript.

51. Quoted here from "Bin Laden's statement," *New York Times*, 8 October 2001, B7.

52. The Lexis-Nexis data was searched for the period from 12 September 2001 to 6 October 2001, using the search words "war" and "terrorism."

53. Quoted here from "Latest Summary: American Public Opinion and the War on Terrorism," Gallup Organization, 21 December 2001, http://www.gallucom/poll/releases/pr010926b.asp [accessed 1 April 2002].

54. This statistic is from a Gallup Organization survey conducted 14–16 December 2001, in which 92% of the respondents expressed satisfaction with the war effort, with 69% "very satisfied."

55. The cited numbers are from a content analysis of the October 8th editions of the *New York Times* and *Los Angeles Times* conducted by Alicia Colligan, "The U.S. strikes back," Unpublished term paper, 8 December 2001.

56. Scott McClellan, the White House spokesman, was quoted in James Risen, "A gaunt bin Laden on new tape," *New York Times*, 27 December 2001, A1.

57. These figures are from Gallup polls on 26–27 November 2001 and 14–16 December 2001.

58. I heard this particular sentence in newscasts of WCBS radio in New York, but similar words, such as "We will be right back with the war on terrorism," from other radio and television news anchors.

59. Donald Lambro, "Arsenal armed with patience," *Washington Times*, 1 November 2001, A20.

60. Charles Krauthammer, "Not enough might," *Washington Post*, 30 October 2001, A21.

61. Richard Cohen, "War behind schedule," *Washington Post*, 6 November 2001, A23.

62. R. W. Apple, "A military quagmire remembered: Afghanistan as Vietnam," *New York Times*, 31 October 2001, B1.

63. See James Fallows, "Howell Raines owes me an apology," *Slate* (3 December 2001), http://slate.msn.com/?id=2059201 [accessed 1 April 2002].

64. These three letters appeared under "Dispatches from a day of terror and shock," *New York Times*, 12 September 2001, A26.

65. William Saffire, "New day of infamy," *New York Times*, 12 September 2001, A27.

66. Anthony Lewis, "A different world," *New York Times*, 12 September 2001, A27.

67. "The national defense," *New York Times*, 12 September 2001, A26.

68. "The wrong time to fight Iraq," *New York Times,* 26 November 2001, A16.

69. Quoted here from Saffire on NBC News *Meet the Press* 30 December 2001. See http//www.msnbc.com/news/678851.asp [accessed 1 April 2002].

70. These numbers are mentioned by Fareed Zakaria in "Let's spread the good cheer," *Newsweek* (26 November 2001): 50.

71. See Hendrik Hertzberg, "Differences," *The New Yorker* (3 December 2001): 37.

72. Linda Wertheimer spoke of a "burgeoning" antiwar movement in the *All Things Considered* program of 14 September 2001, and her colleague Neil Cohen spoke of a "fledgling" antiwar movement on the *Talk of the Nation* program of 28 September 2001.

73. From a commentary by Mackubin Thomas Owens, "The academic al-Qida— Hypocrites hiding behind the constitution," *Providence Journal-Bulletin,* 26 October 2001, B7.

74. "Letter to the editor," *Pittsburgh Post–Gazette,* 22 October 2001, A14.

75. Hendrick Hertzberg, "Differences," *The New Yorker* (3 December 2001): 37.

76. See Todd Purdum, "Democrats starting to fault president on war's future," *New York Times,* 1 March 2002, 1. This article focuses, as the headline signals, on the statements made by Democrats, not the reactions by Republicans. Republican reactions were reported by Helen Dewar in "Lott calls Daschle divisive, GOP attacks prompted by remarks on direction of war," *Washington Post,* 1 March 2002, A6.

77. "Debating the war," *Washington Post,* 3 March 2002, p. B6.

78. For more on the way the Department of Defense invoked censorship, see Neil Hickey, "Access denied: Pentagon's war reporting rules are tougher than ever," *Columbia Journalism Review* (January/February 2002): 26–31.

# 6

# Responding to Terrorist Crises:
# Dealing with the Mass Media

W HEN TERRORISTS TARGET Americans and/or American facilities abroad, foreign response professionals and foreign governments, not U.S. authorities, are in charge of dealing with and managing these crises, whether they concern hijackings, other hostage situations, or hit-and-run incidents, such as facility attacks, bombings, or suicide missions. From the American point of view, when a terrorist incident takes place in the jurisdiction of hostile or indifferent governments, particular problems arise. Besides excluding U.S. response professionals, law enforcement specialists, and political crisis managers (or limiting their roles), these overseas cases tend to magnify the messages of foreign news sources. The reason is obvious: When anti-American terrorism occurs abroad, public officials, terrorists, supporters of terrorists, and other actors in those countries and regions are closest to what happened, why it happened, and what is done or not done in a particular situation. As a result, these foreign actors, far more than American officials, are the preferred news sources.

Detailed content analyses of news reporting during and after major anti-American incidents outside the United States have showed that the coverage of official sources in the most heavily covered "golden triangle" of Washington's foreign and national security news beats (White House, Department of State, and Department of Defense) tends to pale in terms of frequency and length of reporting and in terms of prominence of placement in comparison to foreign actors (Nacos 1996b, chapter 2). Just as important, in the domestic sphere, the traditionally most authoritative and most extensively covered foreign policy sources, e.g., American government officials, are less attractive to the media than are the U.S. victims of terrorism, whether survivors of hit-and-run attacks, hostages, or the families, friends, and neighbors of such victims. In other words, when anti-American terrorists strike abroad, the American authorities lose their media advantage over other American sources and over foreign sources, an advantage that is typical in other types of foreign crises that affect Americans and U.S. interests (Cook 1994; Nacos 1996b).

As a result, terrorists, their supporters, and government officials abroad, especially when the latter have hostile or ambivalent sentiments toward the United States, are in excellent positions to exploit the media in order to convey their self-serving messages to the American and international public and to their domestic audiences as well. The official Washington, the President and his advisers included, is often left to rely on the mass media, notably television, for news of the latest developments concerning terrorist incidents abroad. For the White House as well as the Departments of State and Defense, television news, especially that provided by all-news channels such as CNN, is, even in normal times, equally informative as, or even more revealing than, the information received by American diplomats who are stationed abroad. But television's advantage as a source of pertinent information is never more obvious than during and after anti-American terrorist incidents in foreign lands, when presidents and their highest advisers must rely on breaking news to remain informed. The reason is not that reporters are smarter and quicker than American diplomats or intelligence agencies, but rather that terrorists themselves, indigenous government officials, and other foreign sources at incident sites tend to single out the mass media to disseminate their information.

Former Pentagon official and terrorism expert Noel Koch revealed that, when faced with terrorist situations, "one of the first things we do is tune in CNN" (Martin and Walcott 1988, 191). Top officials in other departments and agencies came to similar conclusions. Even when they had open phone lines to a particular U.S. Embassy, they learned more from watching television networks than from listening to their colleagues abroad or reading the intelligence dispatches of the National Security Agency (NSA). As Oliver North, who served on the National Security Council staff during the Reagan presidency, put it, "CNN runs ten minutes ahead of NSA" (Martin and Walcott 1998, 191).

Thus, besides being unable to take the lead in responding to overseas terrorist incidents or in the management of such crises abroad, the U.S. government also loses its otherwise well-documented media advantage to foreign and domestic actors. This is not an enviable situation at times, when terrorists and other actors abroad try hard to use their media access in order to frighten and threaten Americans and when Washington's crisis managers need to communicate calmness, confidence, and an aura of control to a shell-shocked, fearful, or impatient domestic public. However, no matter how hard U.S. officials may try in such situations, media coverage will eventually reveal that American political leaders, emergency response specialists, and law enforcement agencies are not in the position to take charge and manage a particular crisis.

This is very different when terrorism, whether of the domestic or international variety, is committed on American soil. While no one would wish for terrorism inside U.S. borders rather than abroad, from the perspective of those who must respond to this sort of political violence, strikes inside the United States are at least more manageable than comparable incidents abroad: When terrorists act inside the United States, American political leaders, American response experts, and American law enforcement agencies are in charge, and, frankly, they are in a far better position to deal with the crisis at hand. One important reason for this advantage is that in any kind of emergency situation inside this country, whether natural or manmade, American response professionals are the most authoritative sources of information, and thus they are the most sought out by the media. This is an ideal position from which to convey important information to the public at large and to communicate with the victims, with the victims' families, friends, and neighbors, with the perpetrators and their supporters, and, last but not least, with political decision makers in various jurisdictions. In short, under these circumstances, those who respond to a terrorist event have the opportunity to manage information and influence the public in what they believe is the best solution for resolving an emergency situation of this kind and/or dealing with the aftermath of such an incident.

If this gives the impression that reacting to terrorism at home is little more than routine for seasoned response professionals as far as their handling of public information and news media are concerned, this is certainly not the intent and would not square with reality. It did not take the World Trade Center and Pentagon attacks on September 11, 2001, and the subsequent bioterrorism in the form of anthrax spores, to recognize the difficulties of the media-related parts in managing terrorist crises. Even in the domestic setting, political leaders and emergency response professionals deal typically with media representatives and organizations that have vastly different interests and priorities in many respects.

At this point, it is necessary to remind the reader of terrorism's fundamental publicity goals as outlined in chapter 1. Because terrorism is a means to communicate messages to the public and to governmental decision makers, terrorists, on the one hand, and crisis managers and response professionals, on the other, compete for media attention. There is probably no better example than that of Timothy McVeigh and the Oklahoma City bombing to demonstrate that news coverage is the precondition for advancing terrorists' substantive goals. Even before McVeigh finally revealed the media-centered plan behind the 1995 Oklahoma City bombing, it was perfectly clear that the news had carried his intended messages. Without Timothy McVeigh or his accomplice, Terry Nichols, saying a word in the aftermath of the devastating blow that left 168 persons dead and many more injured, the news ran with the clues he left: By igniting the bomb on the second anniversary of the FBI's raid on the Branch Davidian sect's compound in Waco, Texas, during which cult leader David Koresh and eighty of his followers died, McVeigh made sure that the mass media would dig into his and like-minded people's causes and grievances against the Federal Government. More important, as the news devoted a great deal of attention to the incident at Waco and the sentiments of right-wing extremists opposed to the Federal Government's alleged abuse of power, the public was reminded daily of the Waco nightmare that many Americans had probably forgotten. The result was a dramatic change in public attitudes toward Federal agents' actions during the Waco incident. Shortly after the Oklahoma City bombing in April 1995, nearly three in four Americans approved of the actions of the FBI in Waco, but three months later, after an intensive mass-mediated debate of Waco and Oklahoma City, two in four Americans disapproved of the way the FBI and other Federal agencies handled the Waco situation. Similarly, while two in four Americans did not support a new round of congressional hearings on Waco shortly after the Oklahoma bombing, several weeks later, three in five supported additional hearings. By triggering news coverage that revisited troublesome questions about the Waco raid, the Oklahoma City bomber achieved what legitimate political actions, such as petitions to political leaders and peaceful protests, had not accomplished: Although the Congress had held hearings into the Waco incident in 1993 and exonerated the FBI, new hearings were conducted because of the Oklahoma City bombing, the heavy news coverage of the linkage between that bombing and Waco, and the turnaround in public opinion with respect to the FBI's actions and the need for more congressional hearings.[1]

Following these developments closely, McVeigh was pleased that the FBI and Attorney General Janet Reno were treated much more harshly in the new round of congressional hearings on Waco than during the original inquiry. He was "thrilled" when the Clinton administration appointed John Danforth, former U.S. Senator from Indiana, to head up a special investigation into the Waco incident. Although McVeigh was neither happy with the Danforth report, which put the blame for the Waco inferno squarely on cult leader David Koresh, nor with the outcome of a civil trial in Texas, in which a jury exonerated the government agents involved, he was convinced that his act of terror was a success because he accomplished his goal of alerting the American public to what he called abuse of power on the part of the Federal Government and, more importantly, he initiated changes in the FBI's and other federal agencies' rules of engagement in confrontations like Waco.[2] It is ironic that McVeigh's accusations against the Federal Government and its agents were once again highlighted, when his execution was stayed by Attorney General John Ashcroft after it was revealed that thousands of pages of the FBI's investigation into the Oklahoma City bombing had not been made available to McVeigh's defense attorneys.

Terrorists know that political violence is a potent means to penetrate the strong links between the mass media, the general public, and the governmental realm—connections that I describe earlier with respect to "The Triangle of Political Communication" (see chapter 1, figure 1). The act of terrorism is a master key for unlocking the door that grants access to the mass media. This means that crisis managers and response specialists compete with the perpetrators of political violence in that each side wants to have the loudest and most persuasive voice and messages. In this competition, terrorists seem to start out with a significant advantage because their violent deeds are a powerful message that commands the mass media's attention and thus that of their target audience(s). But response specialists and crisis managers (such as members of police and fire departments, emergency medical teams, National Guard, etc.) and political leaders (such as mayors, county executives, governors, and presidents) are nevertheless in excellent positions to dominate the news because they are part of one of the cornerstones in the "Triangle of Political Communication" with formal and informal links and relationships in place before emergencies arise.

Finally, terrorism's victims, their families and friends, and the public at large may also have their own ideas about how a particular incident should be handled that are different from the response specialists' at the scene and the crisis managers' in their command centers. This is likely to be the case during hostage situations, when the authorities may not want to give in to the demands of hostage-holders, while hostages and their loved ones may press for the release of captives—at any price.

It is clear then that the interests of the mass media, terrorists, their victims, all kinds of societal groups (such as the relatives and friends of victims), as well as response specialists call for a delicate management of public information and media relations on the part of those who respond to and deal with terrorist crises. Figure 6.1 lists the various actors whom crisis managers and response specialists must keep in mind when they deal with the media-related features of their task.

| Perpetrators of Terrorism |
| Accomplices/Supporters |
| Victims of Terrorism (Hostages/Casualties/Injured) |
| Families/Friends of Victims |

| Mass Media (traditional & new)    Response Professionals/Crisis Managers |

| General Public |
| Political Leaders (in Local, State & Federal Offices) |
| [Governments & Publics Abroad] |

**FIGURE 6.1**
**Crisis Response Professionals and the News Media/Public Information**

Recognizing that the news media and terrorism response specialists have very different objectives, one student of mass-mediated political violence stated,

> The mass media aim to "scoop" their rivals with news stories that will grip and sustain the public's attention and hence increase their ratings and revenue. The police, on the other hand, are first and foremost concerned with the protection of life, the enforcement of the law and apprehending those guilty of committing crimes.... There have been many examples where the efforts of the police have been directly threatened by the behaviour [sic] of sections of the media (Wilkinson 2001, 181).

Actually, the best examples of news reports interfering with rescue efforts or other activities by the authorities did not concern simply actions by the police but by other response professionals, such as hostage rescue commandos, as well. While the idea of divergent objectives of the media and the terrorism response community is obvious, the relationship between the two sides is far more complex than one purely shaped by conflict and adversity.

For those who manage terrorist crises and are part of the emergency response teams, the most important thing to remember is this: The mass media can and do interfere with the plans and intentions of those who are in charge of handling terrorist crisis. But the same reporters and news organizations can also be very helpful and, in fact, crucial in efforts to manage such incidents.

Trying to curb the press and thus one of the most fundamental civil liberties of democracies in general and the United States of America in particular—freedom of the press, freedom of expression—is counterproductive and likely to fail. In totalitarian or authoritarian states, this will work. But in liberal democracies, moves by public officials to censor reporting on terrorism would strengthen terrorists' accusations against overbearing governments and abuse of power. Thoughtful and well-planned media liaison, on the other hand, can harness the possible excesses of reporting and, in fact, allow a degree of information management.

While each terrorist crisis has its own complex characteristics and therefore calls for particular responses, there are some basic rules of thumb, caveats, experiences, and practical examples to draw from. The following ten recommendations for terrorism response professionals and crisis managers are meant as guidelines for incidents on American soil, but many aspects can also be instructive for dealing with anti-American terrorism abroad.

*Recommendation #1: Feed the beast: Providing the media with a steady flow of information is not an option but an absolute imperative during and after terrorist incidents.*

In his book *Feeding the Beast: The White House versus the Press,* newsman Kenneth T. Walsh describes the contentious relationship between the White House and the media during Bill Clinton's presidency. According to the author,

> One of the Clintonites' biggest problems was their failure to "feed the beast," as the media are called by Washington insiders. The White House would have been well advised to listen to Jack DeVore, the longtime press secretary of former senator and Treasury secretary Lloyd Bentsen, who said that a press secretary's job was to manufacture a constant supply of doggie biscuits for the press. Reporters would gleefully lick the hand that fed them, but if you ran out of treats or news, DeVore said, the press would devour your arm and try for more (Walsh 1996, 9).

Just like public officials in the White House, Congress, and in other institutions, those who respond and manage terrorist incidents must attend to the basic information needs of the news media and thus avoid frustration and hostility on the part of reporters and their home offices that could influence the news presentation and ultimately damage crisis respondents' reputation, public image, and credibility. Whether crisis managers like it or not, unless they feed the beast, unless they respond to the necessities of the fourth estate, unless they know about and try to accommodate the deadline cycle and the logistics of news production, they will lose their advantage as the most authoritative news sources. A media beast deprived of food in form of information is likely to turn on those who are closest to the emergency, criticize the

way the crisis is handled, and look elsewhere to still its appetite for information and new angles with which to tell the story. Often the result is that rumors, not facts, are reported and attributed to anonymous sources. In this respect, the coverage of terrorist incidents and crimes can pose the same
problems for those dealing with such cases. For example, because law enforcement officials did not provide much information to the press following
the murder of two popular professors at Dartmouth College in New Hampshire, some news organizations followed whatever lead they could possibly
come up with—often forced to revise or repudiate their "exclusives."[3]

Far more damaging was the failure of officials in the George W. Bush administration to inform the American public accurately, competently, and with
one voice about the anthrax bioterrorism threat that followed the kamikaze
attacks on the World Trade Center and the Pentagon. As media observer
Howard Kurtz noted,

> After six weeks of generally sympathetic coverage, the anthrax-obsessed press is
> turning on the Bush administration. In a spate of stories and segments, top officials
> are being depicted as bumblers who failed to move aggressively against anthrax-
> tainted mail while offering shifting [public] explanations of the danger.[4]

Kurtz quoted one White House correspondent complaining that administration officials "don't know what they're talking about."[5] It did not help the relationship between the anthrax crisis managers and the press when administration sources blamed people in the media for being at fault and "on the verge
of [anthrax-related] panic."[6]

To be sure, one way or another reporters will question all kinds of sources,
but if crisis managers and emergency response professionals play ball with
media representatives and react to their need for information, they maintain
their vantage point from which to frame and shape crisis information and
construct the predominant story line. Most of all, it is important that those
who deal with the media have knowledge of the latest developments and ac-
curate information. With this in mind, how can response professionals prepare for the worst-case scenario?

First, just as those people involved in preparedness planning think of contingencies for all kinds of scenarios in terms of negotiating with hostage-holders,
rescuing hostages, or treating injured victims, it is important that they also develop plans for press and public information if terrorists strike. And just as
specialists simulate various tasks and requirements of the preparedness scenario, the response community is well advised to undergo its media planning
during such exercises. Confronting a serious disaster, the leading elected officials must deal directly with the news media and must inform the public immediately. Depending on the seriousness of the situation and the incident

site(s), this informer would be the president, governors, mayors, and/or county executives. But other top administration officials, as well as leaders in law enforcement and other parts of the emergency response community, also must be prepared to handle the public information task and media liaison duties. For this reason, it is recommended that these organizations designate persons in all emergency agencies who are to take lead roles in these areas. Although the FBI is the principal agency in the realm of domestic terrorism and the Federal Emergency Management Agency (FEMA) is assigned the major response responsibility in domestic disaster situations, local police and fire departments are probably better prepared to handle many aspects of press liaison during a crisis than are regional and federal officials. This does not mean that the FBI, FEMA, and other agencies will not deal with the media. But during and immediately after major incidents occur, the designated leaders in the community of response professionals must step up to the plate very quickly and provide information—often to the elected official who will directly interact with reporters and, through the media, with the public. Since journalists tend to cover preparedness exercises, the media/public information plan can and should be tested during such simulations.

Second, terrorist incidents often involve nongovernmental and governmental organizations, for example, the bombing of corporate headquarters or the hijacking or bombing of commercial airliners. In such cases, private corporations as well as public agencies are involved in crisis response measures—including media and public information. Is the commercial airline, whose plane has been targeted, or the bank, whose office has been struck, in charge of media and public information? Or does this role fall on public officials in the response community? These questions should be entertained and answered before actual terrorist situations occur so that the private and the public organizations and leaders are prepared to coordinate and cooperate and thus avoid confusion, miscues, and misinformation. In the wake of a terrorist strike, emergency response professionals need to work with nongovernmental organizations—especially in the area of public information.

Third, in the real world, the working press approaches and questions anyone at or near emergency sites that may possibly have some information. For this reason, it is not enough that officials in key positions are familiar with the opportunities and pitfalls of dealing with the news media. Ideally, every person in the response community should have some rudimentary understanding of what to do and what not to do when approached, interviewed, and pumped for information by reporters. The policeman who secures emergency sites, the fireman who operates equipment in rescue attempts, the emergency medical team that transports victims to hospitals, and the physician who works in the emergency room have firsthand experiences, observations, concerns, hopes, and conclusions that reporters want and should hear. All of these emergency professionals are privy to firsthand information, impressions, feelings, speculations, and rumors that could cause harm to hostages, innocent bystanders, emergency workers, and the law enforcement process if they are revealed to the press or to the general public—and thus to terrorists and their supporters as well.

Doris Graber has pointed out that reporters and public officials alike sometimes "spin their own prejudices into a web of scenarios that puts blame for the disaster on socially outcast groups (Graber 1997, 141). In the hours and days after the Oklahoma City bombing, for example, the mainstream media reported about an "Arab-looking" man as a possible suspect while so-called experts espoused a "Middle East connection" when questioned by reporters. As a result, innocent Arab Americans in Oklahoma and elsewhere became the targets of physical attacks and insults, while an equally innocent Arab American was held and questioned by the FBI as a suspect. It is not clear where this particular rumor originated. But the example should serve as a warning to response professionals not to become involved in rumor mongering because of the potentially catastrophic consequences. Indeed, when aware of rumors, officials are well advised to caution the media and the public not to spread and subscribe to unsubstantiated information.

Local response personnel in places that are otherwise far removed from the major media markets are especially vulnerable when the national media descends onto a terrorism site. This is understandable but potentially harmful, according to one expert in the field who noted two decades ago,

> The lights, the cameras, the media's competitiveness, the pressure of deadlines, and other demands of a harried press corps can overwhelm untrained police officers attempting to deal with the media and can feed easily into the unfolding situation at hand (Miller 1982, 81).

Since this observation was made, the press has become far more competitive and aggressive in a media landscape that is increasingly shaped by a large number of all-news radio and television channels that thrive on breaking news stories with live broadcasts. As a result, not only small town police personnel and other emergency respondents but their colleagues in far larger jurisdictions are challenged by an onslaught of the media during major crises.

*Recommendation #2: Crisis managers and response professionals must understand that the media, especially television and radio, are the most effective means to reassure and calm an unsettled public.*

When terrorists strike, they kill, hurt, and frighten their immediate victims in order to get the attention of and influence the general public and governmental decision makers. As they strike innocent persons and demonstrate the impotence of the targeted government to protect its citizens, terrorists spread fear and anxiety in their target audience and could even cause panic in the threatened society. While political instability is an unlikely consequence of terror in the American setting, terrorists certainly endeavor to make citizens wonder whether their government and its officials are fit to prevent terrorism in the first place, or at least effectively respond to acts of political violence.

For these reasons, crisis managers must utilize the news media in order to project the image of professional, resolute, and competent leadership, even in the most difficult of circumstances. If an event has catastrophic dimensions, crisis managers and response professionals probably have more pressing problems than appearing before microphones and cameras, but they still need to find some way to disseminate information to the news media if only to let the populace know that something is being done, that the political leaders and the response community are on top of the crisis. In this respect, terrorist crises are like other disasters—hurricanes, earthquakes, floods, or riots.

When people are affected by a crisis, or hear about a particular disaster, they turn to the news media, especially radio and television, for information. If electric power fails, many still rely on battery-powered electronic media, especially radio. Under no other circumstances are the ratings for TV and radio stations as high as during crises. As one media scholar noted,

> Information about crisis, even if it is bad news, relieves disquieting uncertainty and calms people. This mere activity of watching or listening to familiar reporters and commentators reassures people and keeps them occupied. It gives them a sense of vicarious participation, of "doing something."
>
> News stories [also] serve to reassure people that their grief and fear are shared (Graber 1997, 143).

Following the 1993 World Trade Center bombing in New York's Wall Street area, local newscasters urged people trapped inside the twin towers to remain calm and reassured them; they took phone calls from some of the people unable to leave the stricken building and thereby reassured the public as well. No doubt, the local media provided an important public service and followed the social responsibility ideal of the media in an exemplary way. The media played a similar role during a long hostage ordeal in which heavily armed members of the Hanafi Muslim sect held scores of hostages in three buildings in the center of Washington, D.C., for a prolonged period. One observer concluded that "the media benefited the police because their reporting kept citizens from becoming overly concerned, and because news reports assured citizens that the police had the situation well in hand" (Miller 1982, 82).

But while it is true that citizens feel better simply because they receive information via the news and see the faces and hear the voice of familiar news anchors and reporters, crisis managers are nevertheless counseled to use the media, not only indirectly but directly as well. By appearing in news conferences and granting interviews as soon as possible, crisis managers can best exploit the extraordinary public attention in order to get their messages across, to demonstrate their composure, and to convince citizens to keep their cool and trust that the authorities will do everything possible to protect and assist them.

By seizing the opportunity to "go public" in the early stage of a crisis, public officials are in an excellent position to frame the dimensions of the incident, the quality of their own responses, and thus the public perceptions of both. These first perceptions of how the public and private sector and the political leadership responded to the emergency will shape the public debate that is likely to follow once the most critical phase of the crisis has passed.

There is no better model for crisis managers than Rudy Giuliani, who was the shining light during New York's and America's darkest hours, days, and weeks following the terror attacks on the World Trade Center and the Pentagon. While President George W. Bush was obviously ill advised when he did not immediately head back to Washington from his visit in Florida and therefore was slow in assuming the role of national crisis manager, Mayor Giuliani impressed people in the New York metropolitan area and Americans everywhere with his cool, competent, hands-on leadership as he used the mass media skillfully to communicate with the public regularly. By showing that he and the emergency response specialists wasted no time and effort in dealing with the crisis at hand, the mayor had a calming effect on a city and country jarred by an unprecedented catastrophe. While he was actively involved in the emergency response, he knew instinctively that he had to address citizens in the metropolitan area at once. Two hours and six minutes after the first plane hit the World Trade Center's North Tower, Giuliani was live on New York 1, an all-news cable TV channel, urging calm. To this end, Giuliani said:

> The first thing I'd like to do is to take this opportunity to tell everyone to remain calm and to the extent they can, to evacuate lower Manhattan. We've been in contact with the White House and asked them to secure the space around the city. They've been doing that for at least the last hour, hour and a half. I've spoken with the governor several times and I agree that the [local primary] election today should be canceled.[7]

But while the Mayor reassured fellow citizens that everything humanly possible was done, he did not hide the incredible horror in Manhattan's downtown but described what he had seen and felt:

> I was there shortly after it happened and saw people jumping out of the World Trade Center. It's a horrible, horrible situation, and all that I can tell them is that

every resource that we have is attempting to rescue as many people as possible. And the end result is going to be some horrendous number of lives lost. I don't think we know yet, but right now we have to just focus on saving as many people as possible.[8]

Some three-and-one-half hours later, the Mayor held his first news conference that was broadcast by the local, national, and international media. "We will strive now very hard to save as many people as possible," he said, "and to send a message that the City of New York and the United States of America is much stronger than any group of barbaric terrorists."[9]

Giuliani displayed strong and tireless leadership under unthinkably grim circumstances and, at the same time, compassion and grief, not only in these initial public communications but in the many press briefings that followed in the next hours, days, weeks, and months as well. He and others on the crisis management team made exemplary use of the mass media to inform the public as fully as possible about the situation and to direct people in the metropolitan areas as to what they should and should not do. This was a momentous task given that tens of thousands of people in the New York metropolitan area were directly affected by the terror—either because they were in the hit buildings or were relatives, friends, or colleagues of these victims—and were desperate for information. In addition, most people who lived or worked in New York City looked for and received information about public and private transportation, school and business closings, etc. from the media

In short, no prewritten blueprint for this kind of emergency response could have prescribed a more perfect utilization of the mass media than the "going public" patterns that came naturally to Mayor Rudy Giuliani.

Once he was back in the White House, President George W. Bush, too, addressed the American public regularly and effectively. In less than four weeks following the events of 9–11, he made more than fifty public statements designed to convey the reassuring picture of an effective crisis manager.

*Recommendation #3: The emergency response community must utilize the mass media as vital instruments for enhancing and coordinating their actual emergency efforts—especially when telling the public what to do and what not to do.*

It has been argued that in times of major domestic emergencies, radio and television become "vital arms of government" because they offer officials literally unlimited access to communicate with the public, with emergency specialists, and with other government authorities (Graber 1997, 135). While officials can be especially effective by personally appealing to their various audiences, they also can convey their needs, concerns, and warnings indirectly through reporters and other media personnel.

In the hours and days following the Oklahoma City bombing, for example, local television, radio, and the print press were superb in serving the public interest not merely by informing their audiences of the bombing, its consequences, and the response activities, but also by functioning as conduits between emergency response specialists and the public in the affected city and beyond. In publicizing and repeating officials' appeals to citizens not to enter the disaster area and not to interfere with rescue efforts, but to donate blood for the injured in specified places, or to contribute warm clothing for rescue workers, the media assisted crisis managers a great deal. Moreover, as the national media reported on what response specialists described as difficult rescue efforts, emergency specialists around the country responded by offering to travel to the wounded city and assist exhausted rescue workers who had worked nonstop for days and nights. Following the first World Trade Center bombing in 1993, TV and radio stations repeatedly broadcast important information released by public officials and spokespersons for private companies. For example, the employees of firms affected by the explosions were told not to report to work that evening and the next day(s). Motorists learned which streets were closed for all traffic; all citizens were informed of important emergency phone numbers.

Undoubtedly, during the most serious cases of terrorism on U.S. soil so far, crisis managers and emergency specialists utilized the mass media for their purposes in various ways. But the information disseminated by the media typically comes from all kinds of sources and is easily contradictory and confusing. For this reason, it is advisable to coordinate the release of information designed to enhance response efforts and, if possible, speak with one voice to the media and the public.

Again, Mayor Guiliani and others in his crisis team were flawless in keeping the public abreast of the step-by-step rescue efforts and in telling New Yorkers how they could help or could hinder these difficult efforts. But despite of all their competence and skills in dealing with the news media, even these crisis managers could not prevent some news reports that were based on rumors. For example, several days after the collapse of the World Trade Center, the media reported that a group of missing firemen had been found alive in the rubble. As it turned out, the report, raising the hopes of many families, was erroneous.

Finally, it is important that response professionals avoid the jargon that is common and appropriate when they communicate with other specialists in their field. Unlike beat reporters who are familiar with the work and the language of law enforcement officials and others in the emergency response community, general reporters and most citizens are not. Statements in news conferences and answers to reporters' questions must be given in the plain language that everyone understands. Using abbreviations is fine, when everyone knows the full meaning, but these abbreviations can annoy people who do not know what is meant and have to ask for further explanations.

*Recommendation #4: Trained personnel in close proximity to response profes-*
*sionals must monitor the mass media around the clock for accuracy in crisis-*
*related news and, during hostage situations, for news items that could endanger*
*the lives of hostages and law enforcement officers and/or hamper efforts to end a*
*stand-off.*

The response community must prepare for reliable personnel inside emergency command centers to monitor the mass media throughout the most critical phases of a crisis in order to ensure that publicized information is correct and that appeals for assistance of one kind or another are made only when prepared and backed up by organizational moves to facilitate responding citizens (for example, a vast number of blood donors ascending on hospitals or schools or churches, or emergency workers coming from afar to assist in rescue tasks, or people massing medical facilities to receive antidotes for released biological or chemical agents). To do this job well, monitors must be close to crisis managers. If publicized information is wrong or contradictory, if rumors are elevated to the level of hard news, if appeals to help have resulted in sufficient offers, if a stricken population is misdirected with respect to treatment facilities, then the media must be contacted immediately so that mistakes are corrected or changing circumstances are reflected in the news. Given the all-out competition between news organizations, the pressure to present breaking news, the determination to report some new angle although a terrorist situation has not changed, and the tendency to sensationalize even genuinely dramatic situations, the hastily reported and often unverified news is likely to contain inaccuracies, mistakes, and problematic features.

Hostage situations are particularly prone to suffer from crisis reporting, especially live broadcasts, which lack the safeguards otherwise built into the news process with roles for editors, news directors, and even legal advisers. At worst, the press publicizes information that has the potential to interfere with efforts to resolve a crisis and that endangers the lives of hostages, rescuers, and other actors. Since terrorists seek publicity when they strike, it is not surprising that they are eager to follow the news about their particular deeds. After igniting the potent bomb at the Joseph P. Murrah Federal Building, driving away, and being arrested for driving a car without license plates, Timothy McVeigh watched television while he was processed in an office in the Noble County Sheriff's Department. After the blast, he had not bothered to return to the Murrah Building to survey the damage he had caused. Hours later, he got his chance:

> McVeigh pretended to pay little attention to the television, but he was watching
> and listening to every word. This was the first opportunity to see what his bomb
> had done to the Murrah Building. His initial reaction was disappointment.

Damn, he thought, the whole building didn't come down. But McVeigh says how that even that [sic] revelation had a silver lining for him: with part of the Murrah Building still standing, in its ruined state, the American public would be left with its carcass, standing as a symbol (Michel and Herbeck 2001, 245).

In McVeigh's case, his next stop was a county jail cell where he had no access to the news media. In other cases, terrorists follow the news continuously for clues of whether their deeds had the intended effects or, especially during hostage situations, to learn about actions and reactions of crisis response specialists and other actors in their target audience. After Corey Moore, an African American ex-Marine, took two white persons hostage in the city hall of Warrensville Heights, Ohio, to protest the treatment of black people in the United States, he eventually released one of his captives in exchange for a television set in order to monitor the news of the incident and to check whether hostage negotiators were truthful or deceiving him.[10] During the 1977 Hanafi Muslim incident in Washington, D.C., during which one person was killed, several people injured, and more than one hundred taken hostage in three different buildings, eleven people were able to hide in one part of one of the buildings and evaded capture. At one point, a basket with food was lifted by rope to a window of the room where these people were hiding. A cameraman filmed the lifting of the basket, and a local station broadcast the video. It is believed that members of the Hanafi group who were not involved in the hostage-taking, or supporters of the sect, monitored television news, notified the captors by phone, and set off a search by the heavily armed Hanafis for the missing people. By monitoring the news, the police knew of the sudden problem and prepared for a rescue effort that eventually freed the group of eleven from their hiding place—before the Hanafis got to them.

These and similar examples underline the importance of monitoring incident news around the clock by crisis command centers and reacting promptly to exploit new opportunities for crisis resolution, law enforcement, etc., or to prevent potentially harmful consequences of publicized information.

*Recommendation #5: Response specialists must keep in mind that most journalists and news organizations cooperate with the authorities faced with truly serious incidents. In this cooperative mode, the media can be instrumental in resolving these types of crises.*

While reporters are chasing exclusives in order to scoop the competition, many of them are not inclined to disregard that they could endanger the victims of terrorism, especially hostages, and the members of rescue teams by reporting indiscriminately and revealing tactical information. During the Iranian hostage crisis, for example, some reporters and their news organizations were aware that a few members of the U.S. embassy staff in Teheran had fled before the takeover and had found shelter in Canada's embassy. During the hijacking of TWA Flight 847 in 1985, some American journalists learned that another member of the U.S. military was aboard the hijacked airliner besides Navy diver Robert Stethem, who was brutally murdered by the terrorists simply because he was part of the American armed forces. In both cases, these facts were not publicized because responsible journalists did not want to jeopardize the welfare, or even the lives, of fellow Americans. In the changed media world of the twenty-first century, with heightened competition, such information is less likely to be withheld than in the past. Accordingly, when faced with terrorist incidents, leaking sensitive information to the press or disclosing this sort of intelligence confidentially are not options that response professionals should consider.

But in some situations, law enforcement officials and other response professionals may consider asking media organizations for assistance and cooperation. The most obvious cases arise when terrorists demand that the media in general, or specific news organizations, publicize their manifestos, statements, or communiqués in exchange for ending a hostage ordeal or ceasing deadly terrorist campaigns. Although the official position of the U.S. government is that its officials will not negotiate with terrorists and will not give in to their demands, in reality response professionals do negotiate and do accommodate terrorist objectives—especially in cases of domestic terrorism and with respect to terrorists' publicity requests.

In this respect, cases of mass-mediated terrorism are treated like incidents arising from criminal hostage situations. For example, in late January 2001, the last two of seven Texas prison escapees agreed to surrender peacefully to law enforcement officers in Colorado Springs, Colorado, after an opportunity to vent their grievances during a telephone interview with Eric Singer, a local television anchor. Law enforcement officers did not object to the live broadcast but in fact assisted in arranging the interview during which the escaped prisoners complained about the conditions in the Texas penitentiary system. It was far more controversial when the *Washington Post* and the *New York Times*, at the request of Attorney General Janet Reno and the FBI, published a thirty-five thousand word manifesto authored by the then still elusive "Unabomber," Theodore Kaczynski, in September 1995. By publicizing the tract against the ills of technology and consumerism five days before the author's deadline, the publishers justified their action with the desire to prevent the threatened mailing of yet another deadly letter bomb by a terrorist who had already killed three people and injured many more via explosive mailings. This was not the first time that law enforcement and other agencies asked the media to publish terrorist statements. In fact, in 1976, at the urging of the FBI and the FAA, four U.S. newspapers published the statements of Croatian nationals during a lengthy hijacking and bombing incident. Assured that their pleas for Croatia's independence had been published and had reached the American and international public, the hijackers surrendered in Paris.

While law enforcement specialists, hostages and their families, and news organizations justify their concessions to terrorists with the argument that they are trying to protect the victims, or potential victims, neither law enforcement nor media organizations should agree easily to these kinds of compromises. Obviously, resolving a terrorist crisis or removing a terrorist threat (and thereby sparing hostages' lives and suffering) must always be the primary consideration of response professionals. But response professionals must also never forget that giving in to terrorists with respect to their media-centered goals could well encourage members of the same or different groups to resort to more political violence for the sake of media and public attention.

*Recommendation #6: Although representatives of the news media will demand access to the site of a terrorist act, response professionals have the right and the responsibility to limit or deny access if the presence of media representatives threatens the safety of victims and response personnel or inhibits rescue efforts, negotiations, or other means to resolve the emergency.*

Even in instances when political leaders acting as crisis managers and response professionals cooperate with the media, members of the fourth estate are likely to insist on access to the site of terrorism and reject restrictions in the name of the First Amendment and the constitutional guarantee of freedom of the press. The fourth estate tends to construe the First Amendment as the public's assurance of the right to be informed by a press that is free of governmental interference. Thus, the media will argue, in order to fully inform the public, the working press has an access right. However, the Supreme Court and lower courts have not backed such an absolute right to access. In *Branzburg v. Hayes,*[11] the Court held that the Constitution does not guarantee the news media special access to information that is not available to the public at large. "Newsmen have no constitutional right of access to the scenes of crime or disaster when the general public is excluded," the Court ruled. Earlier, in *Zemel v. Rusk,* an unanimous Supreme Court ruled that the "right to speak and publish does not carry with it the unrestrained right to gather information." While the denial of unauthorized entry to the White House inhibits citizens' ability to gather information on the way the country is governed, the Court wrote, "that does not make entry into the White House a First Amendment right."[12] In yet another decision, *Los Angeles Free Press, Inc. v. City of Los Angeles,* the Court of Appeals of California ruled,

> Restrictions on the right of access to particular places at particular times are consistent with other reasonable restrictions on liberty based upon the police power,

and these restrictions remain valid even though the ability of the press to gather news and express views on a particular subject may be incidentally hampered."[13]

The point here is not to encourage law enforcement officials and other response professionals to automatically deny media representatives access to incident sites whenever terrorism occurs. It should be clear from the previous recommendations that such a policy and practice would backfire because it would surely create an adversarial relationship with the fourth estate, risk the response community's status as primary news source, interfere with crisis managers' need to inform the public, and diminish their chances of cooperating with media organizations.

But when the presence of the media interferes with the work of rescuers, negotiators, or other response professionals, law enforcement officers have the right to limit, or deny, media access. One way to deal with the onslaught of large numbers of newsmen and women would be to restrict access to the immediate incident site to those reporters who cover the police, fire, and emergency beats on a regular basis and possess press credentials issued by local police departments. Indeed, a Federal Appeals Court in California ruled precisely along these lines when it held that "regular coverage of police and fire news provides a reasonable basis for classification of persons who seek the privilege of crossing police lines."[14]

Ideally, response professionals would like to deal with media representatives who regularly cover their beats and are knowledgeable in these particular fields. But in reality, beat specialists may not be the only ones who cover major terrorist incidents and may even be replaced by star reporters and prominent anchors, typically generalists that lack the special expertise of beat reporters. In other words, while the police and other response agencies tend to deal mostly with beat reporters in their day-to-day work, they must be prepared to face generalists and members of the national media elite when terrorists commit major acts of mass-mediated violence. Denying access to generalists from local news networks and from prominent national media organizations, including star journalists and anchors such as Tom Brokaw, Peter Jennings, and Dan Rather, is probably not a realistic option for response professionals. If they can resist the star appeal of nationally known news personnel, most political leaders in their jurisdiction are less likely to do so at a time that assures them of great media exposure. These facts make the issue of access one of the most difficult problems for the response community and one that needs to be solved with the specifics of each case in mind.

I still agree with suggestions that police departments should be proactive in this respect. According to Abraham H. Miller,

> Police agencies, as a matter of course, should develop clear guidelines governing the news media's access to the scene of terrorist incidents and clear rules governing

police lines and press identification passes. The media should be made aware of these guidelines and conditions before terrorist incidents and similar events occur. This step seeks to avoid the arguments and recriminations that can develop between individual reporters and police officers during the rush and confusion of violent incidents. Police departments, if they have the organizational capacity, should have contingency plans for dealing with events likely to draw national news media attention, particularly extensive television coverage (Miller 1982, 83, 84).

While there is always a chance that members of the public will hurry to terrorism sites, the celebrity cult surrounding television news anchors and correspondents is likely to draw even more citizens onto the scene. As a result, police officers will be harder pressed to provide effective crowd control that is often essential for recovery, rescue, and negotiation efforts.

*Recommendation #7: As a general rule, crisis managers should not go the "prior restraints" route. In almost all terrorist emergencies, curbing press freedom is not an option. However, in extraordinary cases, when information—if revealed—would result in a "clear and present danger" for human life or the national interest in very specific and most serious ways, response professionals must sometimes consider this extreme and highly controversial step.*

Suppose that a reporter has learned that a hostage rescue mission is in the making. Suppose that terrorists have killed several hostages after seeing news reports of a previous attempt that was eventually aborted. Suppose that the reporter has told his producer and editor about his scoop and has thus triggered debates inside his news organization as to whether or not to publicize the news. Suppose that crisis managers fear that the information will be publicized—sooner or later. Now, if there is a clear and present danger that additional hostages—or one single hostage—will die if the news of another rescue attempt is broadcast or published, response professionals and political leaders must consider calling a judge for a restraining order. And they have a good chance of obtaining it.

This is not a likely scenario, but it is not an impossible one either. In the past, hostage situations have lasted for many months or years. In the new millennium, the extremely militant Abu Sayyaf, a terrorist group demanding independence from the Philippines, held hostages for many months on several occasions, threatened numerous times that rescue efforts by the Filipino Army would cause the execution of hostages, and actualized these threats on several occasions.

One can easily imagine other horror scenarios. Suppose that the CIA and/or other agencies have learned that a terrorist group plans a biological, chemical, or nuclear attack on an American city or region. Suppose that the intelligence has a few credible but also less convincing elements. Suppose that, as a precaution, measures to prevent a strike or, if that fails, respond to such an assault are secretly put in place. Suppose that the secret is leaked to a journalist who tries to verify the scoop as his news organization ponders the question of whether or not to publicize the information. It is not farfetched to assume that the news of an imminent attack with weapons of mass destruction would result in hysteria, panic, unorganized mass flight, or loss of life. Here, a case could be made for prior restraint and preventing the alarming news from being publicized.

For all the emphasis on freedom of expression and freedom of the press, even in the United States with its unique First Amendment rights, these fundamental and most precious liberties are not absolute. Nobody expressed this veracity better than Justice Oliver Wendell Holmes when he wrote for an unanimous Supreme Court,

> The most stringent protection of free speech would not protect a man in falsely shouting fire in a theatre and causing a panic. It does not even protect a man from an injunction against uttering words that may have all the effects of force. . . .
>
> The question in every case is whether the words used are used in such circumstances and are of such nature as to create a clear and present danger that will bring about the substantive evils that Congress has a right to prevent.[15]

In *Schenck v. United States*, however, Holmes and his brethren and the lower courts looked at a case after the fact: The controversial material had been published and those who published it had been indicted and found guilty of conspiracy to violate the Espionage Act of 1917. More than fifty years later, in *New York Times Company v. United States*, which arose out of the Pentagon Papers case, the Supreme Court ruled six to three against the government and its efforts to prevent the *New York Times* (and the *Washington Post*) from publishing internal government documents about the Vietnam War. In other words, this was an issue of prior restraint because the Nixon administration had asked the courts for an injunction directing the *Times* and the *Post* not to publicize classified material. But it is noteworthy that only two of the justices in the majority, Hugo Black and William O. Douglas, insisted that the First Amendment does not allow prior restraint in any circumstance. The seven other justices, albeit to varying degrees, recognized exceptions to the stringent meaning of freedom of expression and freedom of the press in the American context. Justice Potter Stewart, for example, wrote that prior restraint was permissible under the U.S. Constitution if disclosure would "surely result in direct, immediate, and irreparable damage to our Nation or its people."[16]

While those rare and exceptional cases in which the dissemination of information represents a clear and imminent danger to people are most likely during wars, one can argue that terrorism is in this sense a type of warfare. To this end, M. Cherif Bassiouni, a legal scholar, has applied the "clear and present danger" doctrine and other landmark rulings specifically to terrorist situation and has concluded,

> Despite the strong presumption of unconstitutionality, prior restraint may be constitutionally permissible where specific harm of a grave nature would surely result from media dissemination of certain information. Although general reporting of terrorism would lack the contextual immediacy required to justify suppression, the same may not be true during contemporaneous coverage of ongoing incidents, particularly in hostage situations. Numerous scenarios are imaginable in which prior restraints may be justified to save lives (Bassiouni 1981, 40).

Again, only in extreme situations when there is no doubt that the pending publication of certain information will lead to irreparable harm—most likely to hostages and law enforcement and other response professionals—is the prior restraint route a realistic option for those who manage and respond to terrorist acts.

*Recommendation #8: Encouraging media guidelines for reporting terrorist incidents may be prudent; however, trusting that news organizations will follow their guidelines is not.*

Following the Hanafi hostage drama in 1977, the outspoken Patrick Buchanan charged that "American TV has become patsy, promoter and paymaster for political terrorists—their preferred vehicle of communication."[17] Buchanan was not the only one who criticized media organization for the excessive amount and, more importantly, the kind of coverage they devoted to the incident. Critics inside and outside the media were especially concerned about live interviews with the hostage-holders inside the occupied buildings and their sympathizers outside. As they offered the Hanafis a public forum to air their grievances, media organizations all over the country and abroad seemed to give sect members an incentive not to negotiate a quick end to the situation but to exploit this opportunity for unlimited publicity. According to one observer,

> What did Khaalis [leader of the Hanafi sect] obtain for his efforts? Media exposure, in otherwise unreachable proportions. There was continuous live television coverage; domination of virtually the entire first section of the *Washington Post* for two days; and transatlantic phone interviews. The event transformed the Hanafi Muslims from a little-known group, even within Washington, to the focal point of national and international media coverage (Miller 1980, 83).

Nobody was more aware of this sudden fame than Hanafi leader Hamass Abdul Khaalis, who became very selective during the hostage drama as to the news organizations with which he would communicate. He turned down radio and TV stations with limited audiences, telling them that they were not worth talking to. At one time, he declined to give an interview with a Texas radio reporter after learning that his station had only twenty thousand watts, informing the newsman that he would not talk to radio stations with less than fifty thousand watts (Jaehning 1978, 723). Moreover, by revealing on the air details about law enforcement officers' actual moves and anticipated actions, news organizations provided up-to-date information to the Hanafis that may have hampered early efforts to resolve the crisis and endangered the well-being of innocent bystanders and response professionals.

One result of the Hanifi incident was that several news organizations, among them wire services, daily newspapers, and TV and radio networks, developed internal guidelines for reporting terrorist situations. Among the first media organizations to enact such codes was United Press International. Its guidelines were representative for these kinds of blueprints, pledging not to jeopardize lives, not to become part of an unfolding terrorist incident, and not to participate in negotiations. But these guidelines were, and still are, altogether broad, leaving ample room to circumvent the specific prohibitions with phrases such as, "In all cases we will apply the rule of common sense" or "We will judge each story on its own and if a story is newsworthy cover it despite the danger of contagion" (Miller 1982, 146–147).

In the more than twenty years since the first guidelines for terrorism coverage were adopted, far more dramatic, far more lengthy, and far more deadly terrorism has plagued the United States abroad and at home. Neither formal guidelines nor informal newsroom agreements on how to handle the coverage of terrorist incidents has eradicated excessive and potentially harmful reporting. If anything, the growing competition in the media market and the trend from hard news to infotainment news has led to more aggressiveness in pursuing the sensational, dramatic, tragic, and frightening aspects of news in general and in the area of terrorism incidents in particular. Even in news organizations with the best intentions to adhere to self-imposed guidelines, these codes of behavior and reporting fly out of the window in the face of major incidents, when the competitive juices flow especially energetic in the struggle for ratings, circulation, and, most of all, corporate profit imperatives.

More recently, thoughtful media professionals have developed far more detailed and stringent guidelines. An excellent example of unambiguous prescriptions for responsible reporting of terrorist incidents, hostage situations, and similar incidents is provided by Bob Steel of the Poynter Institute. Unlike the provisions in most guidelines of this kind, Steel's fifteen points are precise and not watered down by general statements that result in loopholes.[18] If news organizations would follow these sorts of guidelines, they would be far less likely to become unwitting accomplices in terrorist schemes.

It certainly makes sense to encourage news organizations to consider and discuss how to cover, or not to cover, terrorist situations regardless of whether the results are formal guidelines or simply a better understanding of the problems surrounding this sort of coverage. Over time, such practices and measures could affect terrorism coverage for the better. But unless all news organizations sign on to what critics will call self-censorship, the competitive tendencies will prevail and prevent meaningful changes.

*Recommendation #9: By showing their human face in dealing with terrorism's victims and their loved ones, members of the response community will help others—and themselves.*

When terrorists strike, response specialists must deal with victims as well as with their families, friends, neighbors, and the larger public. On one level, crisis managers and everyone else involved in dealing with an act of terror are expected to be cool, rational, and detached enough to effectively handle whatever has to be done. On another level, however, the same people are expected to be sensitive to the feelings of the immediately affected people and responsive to their needs. In no other area of the emergency response field are both gratitude and resentment more easily and more vehemently expressed than in the real or perceived treatment of victims and their families. The visuals of exhausted emergency workers who dug victims out of the rubble of the Murrah Federal Building in Oklahoma City, the compelling pictures of grief-stricken rescuers carrying dead children from the scene of unspeakable terror, the sensible words of officials speaking for the police and fire departments and other organizations added up to a mass-mediated composite of a crisis response community with a human face that was comforting to the injured, to the families of victims, and to the nation. The unspoken message here was that of men and women who went beyond the call of duty in their difficult work and were at all times a part of a community in shock and pain.

Because of the scope of the 2001 terrorism, the heroics of the rescuers were even more visible. Although losing hundreds of their colleagues when the World Trade Center collapsed, members of New York's fire and police departments worked relentlessly, around the clock in efforts to save lives, even when there was no longer any hope. These rescuers' selfless efforts, witnessed by New Yorkers and Americans in the hours, days, weeks, and months after the 9–11 terror, forever changed the perceptions of the men and women in New York's fire and police departments. Perhaps nothing expressed this genuine admiration more than Halloween Day 2001, when many boys and girls dressed up as firefighters and police officers, and Christmas of that year, when children wished for fire engines and police cars from Santa. And there were other groups that conveyed this spirit of absolute compassion—the teams of FEMA, the iron workers, the members of the National Guard, and even the search dogs that pushed on in spite of their badly cut feet. In a way, New York's darkest hour became its finest; New York became a community that closed ranks behind the shining example of emergency response specialists who revealed the human face behind their first rate professionalism.

But there have also been instances when victims of terrorism, their families, and even the public at large may not see the human face of response professionals, and this causes them to react critically. Following the catastrophic bombing of PanAm Flight 103 over Lockerbie, Scotland, for example, both the airline and the U.S. State Department were harshly criticized by the victims' families for not providing prompt information and assistance to those who wanted to travel to the crash site. Most of all, even years after the incident, families of the Flight 103 victims complained bitterly about the insensitivity of the State Department personnel that they encountered. Eventually, the Department of State conceded that there was a need "to build a more integrated approach . . . sensitizing our people to dealing with such tragedies, and the need for compassionate follow through. . . . [W]e can never forget that we are participating in a life-shattering event for these families, and that we must proceed with utmost care."[19]

All organizations, public and private, need to realize that terrorism, like other crises, calls for both professional and human response. To show compassion by deed for the victims of terrorism and their loved ones is certainly the most important imperative here, but to translate this reality into a media reality is another. Certainly, the victims of terrorism and/or their loved ones will be thankful when they encounter compassionate response professionals. But beyond this, it is also important that crisis managers and those who speak for the emergency response community project this compassionate and comforting image via the media to a traumatized public. Public perception is not shaped by reality but by the pseudoreality reflected in the mass media.

*Recommendation #10: Last but not least, terrorism response professionals can circumvent the traditional news media and communicate directly with each other and, more importantly, with the public by using the Internet.*

Terrorism response professionals would not have to think about how to handle media relations, i.e., how to assure factual reporting or how to react to potentially damaging incident-related media revelations, if they could circumvent the fourth estate and directly communicate with the public. But while the traditional print and electronic media are alive and well and still the dominant mode of transmitting news and public information, the Internet offers the emergency and terrorist response community a means to inform, warn, and instruct the public during and after incidents without having to pass the scrutiny of gatekeepers in the traditional news media.

Also, in major indents, when television and radio stations are knocked off the air, part of the citizenry may still be able to access the Internet via battery-powered computers. This scenario is not as obscure as it might seem at first. When a terrorist bomb exploded in the garage of the World Trade Center in 1993 and rocked the building's twin towers mightily, it knocked out most of New York's broadcast transmitters on the top of the towers. As a result, only WCBS, which maintained a back-up system on the Empire State Building, was able to broadcast over local airwaves. Otherwise, television coverage was available only for those who had access to cable channels.

But whether or not the traditional media function is normal, terrorist response professionals will be most successful in getting their own messages across to the public if they utilize their Web sites. It may well be that the vast majority of Americans will first turn to television and radio when terrorists strike, and that others will prefer the Web sites of their favorite news organizations to inform themselves, but if law enforcement and other response agencies inform the public of their own sites, chances are that many citizens will access these sites for the most authoritative emergency information. Such Internet sites need to be updated often and diligently and are additional means to provide media organizations around the country and the world with new and archived press releases, statements, warnings, clarifications, etc.

Finally, the Internet provides an ideal means for response professionals to communicate with each other, especially when geographically far apart. While the traditional media has been helpful in the past in alerting emergency specialists to the needs of a particular incident, the Internet can serve as a more specialized means of communication between response professionals in ways that the traditional news media cannot. Here, for sure, the jargon of specialists is perfectly fine and makes for shorter and quicker communication, action, and cooperation.

While this chapter addresses questions of public information and media relations during terrorist crises from the perspectives of public officials and emergency response specialists, implicit in this discussion is also the kind of stance that the news media should take in such situations. To be sure, the media has a responsibility to fully inform citizens of important events and developments. Governmental power—especially authority in extraordinary situation—needs monitoring and robust checks to prevent abuse of power. If there are abuses, the media must ensure that they are revealed. But the media must also remember their responsibility to the public interest and public good as first articulated in the Canons of Journalism in the 1920s and reemphasized in updates of these professional guidelines for the fourth estate. A responsible press must not only insist on factual and full information but must also recognize in extraordinary cases that certain revelations in the news could have devastating consequences for rescue personnel and the victims of terrorism.

## Notes

1. For more on media coverage, changes in public opinion, and new congressional hearings with respect to Waco, see Brigitte L. Nacos, *Terrorism and the Media: From the Iran Hostage Crisis to the Oklahoma City Bombing* (New York: Columbia University Press, 1996), Preface to the Paperback edition.

2. Interview with Lou Michel, 9 April 2001.

3. After the *Boston Globe* published a story that, according to anonymous official sources, the killings were crimes of passion, the New Hampshire Attorney General reacted with a press release and the categorical statement that "investigators do not hold the belief attributed to them." For more on this topic, see Jim Fox, "Small town, big story," *Brill's Content* (June 2001): 70–71.

4. Howard Kurtz, "For every cool head, a thousand overheated muffins," *Washington Post*, 29 October 2001, C1.

5. Kurtz, C1.

6. Kurtz, C1.

7. Quoted here from Andrew Kirtzman, "Mayor dodges death and calms the city," *New York Daily News*, 21 October 2001.

8. Kirtzman, "Mayor dodges death and calms the city."

9. Kirtzman, "Mayor dodges death and calms the city."

10. The incident in 1977 ended when President Jimmy Carter agreed to speak to Corey Moore by phone if he released his remaining hostage unharmed and if he surrendered to police. Moore laid down his weapons and surrendered after he heard the President on television promising to keep his end of the arrangement.

11. 408 U.S. 665; 1972.

12. 381 U.S. 1; 1965.

13. 9 Cal. App. 3d 448; 1970.

14. 9 Cal. App. 3d 448; 1970.

15. *Schenck v. United States*, 1919 (249 U.S. 47).

16. *New York Times Company v. United States*, 1971 (403 U.S. 713).

17. This remark was attributed to Buchanan in *TV Guide* (26 March 1977): A5.

18. Bob Steel, "Guidelines for covering hostage-taking, crises, prison uprisings, terrorist actions." The guidelines were posted by the Poynter Institute in July 1999 at http://www.poynter.org/dj/tips/ethics/guidelines.htm [accessed 1 April 2002].

19. Cited in the "Report of the President's Commission on Aviation Security and Terrorism," Washington, D.C.: U.S. Government Printing Office, 15 May 1990, 102.

# 7

# Conclusion

IN EXPLAINING MEASURES to deny terrorists financial resources following the attacks on the United States on September 11, 2001, President George W. Bush and Secretary of State Colin Powell called money the "lifeblood" and the "oxygen" of terrorism.[1] While large sums of money were certainly helpful in preparing, organizing, and staging the major anti-American acts of terror in the 1990s and early 2000s from the first World Trade Center bombing to the second attack on the same building and the Department of Defense outside Washington, D.C., terrorists have in the past and will in the future commit horrific acts of violence for a great deal of attention without spending large amounts of money. This is not to say that there should not be strong efforts to follow the money trail; on the contrary, after the events of 9–11, bin Laden's money trail was one of the more successful methods used to identify and find members of the al-Qaeda terror network. But, as I describe in the previous chapters, publicity—far more than financial resources—is as essential for terrorists as the air they breathe. Terrorists perform their violent street theater not, or not only, to harm their immediate victims but to obtain the attention of mass publics that they could not reach without the media communicating their deeds and carrying their messages.

Inadvertently, then, the media play a central role in the calculus of political violence and are put into positions where they can magnify or minimize these kinds of acts and their perpetrators, or, of course, they can provide coverage that avoids either one of those extremes. And here the scorecard of the news media is mixed, both with respect to terrorism and anti- and counterterrorism.

To begin with, nonviolent anti- and counterterrorist measures are chronically under-reported unless these initiatives come in the wake of major terrorist incidents, such as the Oklahoma City bombing, the attacks on the U.S. embassies in Kenya and Tanzania, or the suicide bombing of the USS Cole. It is true that policy makers are quick with hearings and policy prescriptions after major acts of terrorism, but they fail to follow through with ongoing anti- and counterterrorist planning. These patterns, however, should not be copied by a press that takes its traditional role as a watchdog of government seriously and protects the public interest by prodding public officials for sustained attention and policy innovations in this important area of public safety. While otherwise eager to run with controversial political practices, the mainstream media displayed little appetite in the past to investigate and report on transactional politics, lobbying, and turf battles surrounding the generally complex details of counterterrorist preparedness programs. Only time will tell if the shock of the 9–11 attacks permanently eradicated news organizations' complacency in this respect.

Contrary to the lack of reporting on less than glamorous issues of terrorist prevention, the news has traditionally devoted a great deal of attention to acts of political violence. Indeed, as detailed in chapter 3, by devoting extraordinary broadcast time and column inches to even minor violence and elevating them to the level of spectacular reality show, the mass media, especially television, play into the hands of terrorists. Thus was the case when a small bunch of anarchists caused disturbances in the streets of Seattle during the World Trade Organization's meeting in 1999, when the violent minority received most of the media coverage—at the expense of peaceful demonstrators. By reporting in such unbalanced ways, the news media encourage propaganda by the deed. Thus, following their publicity success during the street battle with police in Seattle, anarchists organized more serious violence during subsequent international meetings.

No one would argue that the multi-pronged terrorism attacks on September 11, 2001, did not deserve the total media attention that they received in the following weeks or that the subsequent anthrax scare and the military counterterrorist campaign in Afghanistan should not have been reported more prominently than other domestic and international matters. Indeed, in chapter 2, I have described how the news coverage of the 9–11 horror and the reactions in the struck areas, in the United States, and abroad was exemplary in many respects—particularly in the first hours and days after the catastrophe, when television, radio, and the Internet provided the necessary information to a traumatized public at home and abroad. In the same way that New York's Mayor Rudy Giuliani and his emergency response professionals were models of hands-on crisis managing under the toughest of circumstances, and President George W. Bush transformed himself into a domestic and international leader, the press provided, in so many ways, public spheres that brought the directly affected communities, the nation, and large parts of the international community together in their shared horror and their willingness to assist in one way or another.

But there were also early signs of the media, especially television, returning to the overkill practices of their infotainment formats when there simply was not enough real news to fill their around-the-clock special terrorism programming. While the classic broadcast networks returned to their normal programs several days after 9–11, the all-news cable channels continued to cover the terrorist nightmare and its aftermath exclusively or almost totally. In the process, there were excesses that magnified a horror that was unprecedented to begin with. Even months after 9–11, these networks found daily opportunities to play and replay the destruction of the World Trade Center towers under the guise of all kinds of reviews and documentary types of programs. There was hardly a time when surfing through these channels did not produce the images of the falling WTC buildings, the Ground Zero site in downtown Manhattan, the plight of victims and survivors, or the large looming "evil one," Osama bin Laden.

As laudable as the we-are-all-in-this-together contributions of the media were in many respects, by dwelling endlessly on the outburst of patriotism and the idea of national unity without paying attention to other important matters in the political realm, the media helped to create an atmosphere in which criticism of the various crisis-related policy initiatives in Washington was mostly absent from the mass-mediated public debate. When people like Attorney General John Ashcroft questioned the patriotism of those on the right and left of the political spectrum who were critical of some aspects of his anti- and counterterrorist policy prosposals, there was not a massive outcry in the media on behalf of civil liberties—most of all freedom of expression.

Assuredly, the unlimited access the news media granted the President was not unusual during a serious crisis situations; this allowed the President to lead public and elite opinion at home and enlist support abroad. But despite George W. Bush's relentless public appearances, the news media's obsession with a figure that combined the appeal of the personified terrorist evil and worldwide celebrity resulted in disproportional news attention for Osama bin Laden, his causes and grievances, and the threats he and his supporters wanted publicized.

The most devastating terrorist act drew more attention to the role of new communication technology by facilitating the players in international terrorist organizations and conspiracies. Internet sites emerged as popular sources of information in the face of the 9–11 horrors and the subsequent anthrax attacks.

These events also pointed to the Web of hate with its extremists' sites, chat rooms, message boards, and e-mail facilities as powerful persuader, seducer, and recruitment mechanism for terrorist propaganda and action. Perhaps there is hope that more people—especially parents of impressionable children—have learned of this dark side to the information highway and have built up their defenses against hate in cyberspace.

In its last edition of 2001, the *New York Times* informed its readers that, starting with New Year's Day 2001, the newspaper would no longer publish the extra section "A Nation Challenged" that it had introduced on September 18, 2001, one week after 9–11, and published for more than three months. In explaining this move, the newspaper wrote,

> The events of Sept. 11 and their aftermath—terrorism, war, trauma and recovery—have become woven into all aspects of national and international life. The New Year provides an occasion to reflect that evolution by incorporating the coverage into the newspaper's main sections.[2]

Leaving open the reinstatement of the section in the face of "another overwhelming news development, transcending all boundaries," the editor of the *New York Times*—unlike television's all-news networks—signaled, more than three-and-one-half months after 9–11, a return to normalcy in terms of the news format, promising at the same time sustained attention to the premier national security problem posed by terrorism. The same day, the *Times* concluded its "Portraits in Grief," about eighteen hundred victims of September 11, whose families and friends had agreed to interviews. The editor assured, "As new names emerge or more families make themselves available, The Times expects to publish additional profile pages from time to time."[3] These short profiles accompanied by photographs had touched the hearts of readers across the country. As one observer explained,

> The peculiar genius of it was to put a human face on numbers that are unimaginable to most of us. As you read those individual portraits about love affairs or kissing children goodbye or coaching soccer and buying a dream house, it's so obvious that every one of them was a person who deserved to live a full and successful and happy life.[4]

Not meant as obituaries but as snapshots describing particular aspects of the portrayed men and women, these features never exploited the horror of the victims and the grief of those they left behind, but, rather, they celebrated their lives. Within these pages, then, the *New York Times* set high standards for the way the news media should handle the delicate job of covering the victims of incidents of very public violence.

While the chapters of this book focus mostly on the links between terrorism, the mass media, the general public, and governmental decision makers and far less on the victims of political violence, I am certainly aware that terrorism's most devastating effects are on the immediate victims, their families, their friends, and their acquaintances, as well as on those who are directly involved in rescue and recovery efforts. In the past, I have written about the media and about how hostages, other victims of terrorism, and their loved ones can exploit and be exploited by the media for their special interests (Nacos 1996b).

My conversations with some of the men who were at the World Trade Center site shortly after the towers collapsed and with one particular New York City firefighter, Keith Johnson, who was still volunteering to dig with others in the recovery teams at the Ground Zero site more than three months later, confirmed my own impression that with all the excesses in reporting, especially in the electronic media, the news did not reflect the full horror of the 9–11 terrorism. As one volunteer firefighter told me, "The press sanitizes reality."[5] While a blessing on one hand, it may be a handicap on the other, if one considers that understanding the full extent of the horror may be essential for the determination and patience required to stamp out all kinds of political violence. As he took some amateur photographs at Ground Zero before his job there was done, one rescuer said, "We must never forget this."[6]

## Notes

1. President Bush made this analogy in remarks on 24 September 2001, and Powell made his remarks during a White House briefing on 7 November 2001, according to Federal Document Clearing House transcripts available from Lexis-Nexis.

2. Editor's Note, "About 'A Nation Challenged,'" *New York Times*, 31 December 2001, B1.

3. "About 'A Nation Challenged,'" B1.

4. Kenneth T. Jackson, a professor of history at Columbia University, is quoted here from Janny Scott, "Closing a scrapbook full of life and sorrow," *New York Times*, 31 December 2001, B6.

5. Interview with Thomas Simmons, 27 November 2001.

6. Interview with Wayne Thorsen, 28 November 2001.

# Bibliography

Adams, James. 2001. "Virtual Defense." *Foreign Affairs* 80.3 (May/June): 98–112.

Adams, William C., ed. 1981. *Television Coverage of the Middle East.* Norwood, N.J.: Ablex Press.

Alali, A. Odasuo, and Kenoye Kelvin Eke, eds. 1991. *Media Coverage of Terrorism: Methods of Diffusion.* Newbury Park, Calif.: Sage.

Alger, Dean. 1998. *Megamedia: How Giant Corporations Dominate Mass Media, Distort Competition, and Endanger Democracy.* Lanham, Md.: Rowman & Littlefield.

Allison, Graham T., et al. 1996. *Avoiding Nuclear Anarchy.* Cambridge, Mass.: MIT Press.

Altheide, David L. 1982. "Three-in-One News: Network Coverage of Iran." *Journalism Quarterly* 59:482–486.

———.1987. "Format and Symbols in TV Coverage of Terrorism in the United States and Great Britain." *International Studies Quarterly* 31:161–176.

Arquilla, John, and David Ronfeldt. 1999. "The Advent of Netwar: Analytical Background." *Studies in Conflict and Terrorism* 22:193–206.

Arquilla, John, and Theodore Karasik. 1999. "Chechnya: A Glimpse of Future Conflict?" *Studies in Conflict and Terrorism* 22:207–229.

Bagdikian, Benjamin. 2000. *The Media Monopoly, 6th Edition.* Boston: Beacon Press.

Baker, Gerard. 1999. "Starbucks wars: The Seattle riots demonstrate the failure of mainstream US politics to provide an outlet for protest." *Financial Times,* 4 December, p. 10.

Bassiouni, M. Cherif. 1981. "Terrorism, Law Enforcement, and the Mass Media: Perspectives, Problems, Proposals." *The Journal of Criminal Law & Criminology* 72.1:1–51.

Baudrillard. Jean. 1993. *The Transparency of Evil.* London: Verso.

Bennett, Lance W. 2001. *News: The Politics of Illusion.* New York: Longman.

Bennett, Lance W., and David L. Paletz, eds. 1994. *Taken By Storm: The Media, Public Opinion, and U.S. Foreign Policy in the Gulf War.* Chicago: University of Chicago Press.

Bok, Sissela. 1998. *Mayhem: Violence as Public Entertainment.* Reading, Mass.: Perseus Books.

Brody, Richard A. 1991. *Assessing the President: The Media, Elite Opinion, and Public Support.* Stanford, Calif.: Stanford University Press.

Bryant, Jennings, and Dolf Zillmann, eds. 1986. *Perspectives on Media Effects.* Hillsdale, N.J.: Laurence Erlbaum.

Catton, William R., Jr. 1978. "Militants and the Media: Partners in Terrorism?" *Indiana Law Journal* 53:703–715.

Chase, Alston. 2000. "Harvard and the Unabomber." *Atlantic Monthly* 285.6 (June): 41–65.

Chomsky, Noam. 1988. *The Culture of Terrorism.* Boston, Mass.: South End Press.

Cook, Timothy E. 1994. Domesticating a Crisis: Washington Newsbeats and Network News after the Iraqi Invasion of Kuwait. In *Taken by Storm: The Media, Public Opinion, and U.S. Foreign Policy in the Gulf War,* edited by W. Lance Bennett and David L. Paletz. Chicago: University of Chicago Press.

Cotter, John M. 1999. "Sounds of Hate: White Power Rock and Roll and the Neo-Nazi Skinhead Subculture." *Terrorism and Political Violence* 11.2 (Summer): 111–140.

Crelinsten, Ronald D. 1997. "Television and Terrorism: Implications for Crisis Management and Policy-Making." *Terrorism and Political Violence* 9.4 (Winter): 8–32.

Crenshaw, Martha, ed. 1983. *Terrorism, Legitimacy, and Power: The Consequences of Political Violence.* Middletown, Conn.: Wesleyan University Press.

———, ed. 1995. *Terrorism in Context.* University Park, Penn.: Pennsylvania State University Press.

Danitz, Tiffany, and Warren P. Strobel. 1999. "The Internet's Impact on Activism: The Case of Burma." *Studies in Conflict and Terrorism* 22:257–269.

Delli Carpini, Michael X., and Bruce A. Williams. 1987. "Television and Terrorism: Patterns of Presentation and Occurrence, 1969 to 1980." *Western Political Quarterly* 40.1:45–64.

Dempsey, James X. 2000. "Counterterrorism and the Constitution." *Current History* (April): 164–168.

Denson, Bryan. 2001. "Eco-terrorist group prolific: The Earth Liberation Front's attacks rack up extensive damages." *The Oregonian,* 11 January.

Denson, Bryan, and James Long. 1999a. "Eco-terrorism sweeps the American West." *The Oregonian,* 26 September.

———. 1999b. "Ideologues drive the violence." *The Oregonian,* 27 September.

Edelman, Murray. 1977. *Political Language: Words that Succeed and Policies that Fail.* New York: Academic Press.

———. 1988. *Constructing the Political Spectacle.* Chicago: University of Chicago Press.

Ewen, Stuart. 1996. *PR! A Social History of Spin.* New York: Basic Books.

Fallows, James. 1996. *Breaking the News: How the Media Undermine American Democracy.* New York: Pantheon Books.

Finkel, Michael. 2000. "The Child Martyrs of Karni Crossing." *The New York Times Magazine* (24 December).

Friedman, Thomas L. 2002. "No mere terrorist." *New York Times*, 24 March, sect. 4, p. 15.

Gabler, Neil. 1998. *Life the Movie: How Entertainment Conquered Reality*. New York: Alfred Knopf.

Geranios, Nicholas K. 1999. "Anarchists occupy building to protest WTO." *Associated Press*, 3 December.

Gerbner, George, and L. Gross. 1976. "Living with Television: The Violence Profile." *Journal of Communication* 26.2:173–199.

Gordon, Avishag. 1997. "Terrorism on the Internet: Discovering the Unsought." *Terrorism and Political Violence* 9.4 (Winter): 159–165.

Graber, Doris. 1997. *Mass Media and American Politics*. Washington, D.C.: Congressional Quarterly Press.

Greenberg, Joel. 1996. "Rabin assassin's testimony: 'My goal was to paralyze him.'" *New York Times*, 24 January.

Guelke, Adrian. 1998. "Wars of Fear: Coming to Grips with Terrorism." *Harvard International Review* (Fall): 44–47.

Hallin, Daniel L. 1986. *The 'Uncensored War': The Media and Vietnam*. New York: Oxford University Press.

Hendrickson, Ryan C. 2000. "American War Powers and Terrorism: The Case of Osama bin Laden." *Studies in Conflict & Terrorism* 23.3 (July-September): 161–174.

Herman, Edward, and Gerry O'Sullivan. 1989. *The Terrorism Industry: The Experts and Institutions That Shape Our View of Terror*. New York: Pantheon Books.

Hickey, Neil. 1998. "Money Lust: How Pressure for Profit is Perverting Journalism." *Columbia Journalism Review* (July/August).

Hoffman, Bruce. 1995. "'Holy Terror': The Implications of Terrorism Motivated by a Religious Imperative." *Studies in Conflict & Terrorism* 18.4 (October/December).

———. 1997. "Why Terrorists Don't Claim Credit." *Terrorism and Political Violence* 9.1 (Spring): 1–6.

———. 1998. *Inside Terrorism*. New York: Columbia University Press.

Hollihan, Thomas A. 2001. *Uncivil Wars: Political Campaigns in the Media Age*. Boston: Bedford/St. Martin's.

Iyengar, Shanto. 1991. *Is Anyone Responsible? How Television Frames Political Issues*. Chicago: University of Chicago Press.

Iyengar, Shanto, and Donald R. Kinder. 1987. *News That Matters*. Chicago: University of Chicago Press.

Jacobs, Lawrence R., and Robert Y. Shapiro. 2000. *Politicians Don't Pander: Political Manipulation and the Loss of Democratic Responsiveness*. Chicago: University of Chicago Press.

Jaehning, Walter B. 1978. "Journalists and Terrorism: Captives of the Libertarian Tradition." *Indiana Law Review* 53:717–744.

Jenkins, Brian M. 1987. "Der internationale Terrorismus." *Aus Politik und Zeitgeschichte* B5:17–27.

Johnson, Larry C. 2001. "The declining terrorist threat." *New York Times*, 10 July, p. A19.

Kaplan, Jeffrey. 1995. "Violence in North America." *Terrorism and Political Violence* 7.1: 44–95.

Katz, Daniel, et al. 1954. *Public Opinion and Propaganda*. New York: Dryden Press.

Kegley, Charles Jr. 1990. *International Terrorism: Characteristics, Causes, Controls*. New York: St. Martin's Press.

Kellerman, Barbara. 1984. *The Political Presidency: Practice of Leadership*. New York: Oxford University Press.

Keohane, Robert O., and Joseph S. Nye Jr. 1998. "Power and Interdependence in the Information Age." *Foreign Affairs* 77.5 (September/October): 81–94.

Kernell, Samuel. 1985. *Going Public: New Strategies of Presidential Leadership, Third Edition*. Washington, D.C.: Congressional Quarterly Press.

Kupperman, Robert, and Jeff Kamen. 1989. *Final Warning: Averting Disaster in the New Age of Terrorism*. New York: Doubleday.

Kuzma, Lynn M. 2000. "Trends: Terrorism in the United States." *Public Opinion Quarterly* 64.1 (Spring): 90–105.

Laqueur, Walter. 1987. *The Age of Terrorism*. Boston, Mass.: Little, Brown and Company.

———. 1999. *The New Terrorism: Fanaticism and the Arms of Mass Destruction*. New York: Oxford University Press,.

Lemann, Nicholas. 2001. "The Quiet Man." *The New Yorker* (7 May): 56–71.

Linsky, Martin. 1986. *Impact: How the Press Affects Federal Policy Making*. New York: W. W. Norton.

Lippmann, Walter. 1949. *Public Opinion*. New York: Free Press.

Livingston, Stephen. 1994. *The Terrorism Spectacle*. Boulder, Colo.: Westview Press.

MacArthur, John R. 1993. *Second Front: Censorship and Propaganda in the Gulf War*. Berkeley, Calif.: University of California Press.

Macdonald, Andrew. 1996. *The Turner Diaries, Second Edition*. New York: Barricade Books.

Margalit, Avishai. 1995. "The Terror Master." *New York Review*, October 15.

Martin, David C., and John Walcott. 1988. *Best Laid Plans: The Inside Story of America's War Against Terrorism*. New York: Harper & Row.

McMullan, Ronald K. 1993. "Ethnic Conflict in Russia: Implications for the United States." *Studies in Conflict and Terrorism* 16.3 (July/September): 201–218.

Michel, Lou, and Dan Herbeck. 2001. *American Terrorist: Timothy McVeigh & the Oklahoma City Bombing*. New York: Regan Books.

Miller, Abraham H. 1980. *Terrorism and Hostage Negotiations*. Boulder, Colo.: Westview Press.

———. 1982. *Terrorism, the Media and the Law*. Dobbs Ferry, N.Y.: Transnational Publishers.

Nacos, Brigitte L. 1990. *The Press, Presidents, and Crises*. New York: Columbia University Press.

———. 1994a. *Terrorism and the Media: From the Iran Hostage Crisis to the World Trade Center Bombing*. New York: Columbia University Press.

———. 1994b. "Presidential Leadership During the Persian Gulf War." *Presidential Studies Quarterly* 24.3 (Summer): 563–575.

———. 1996a. "After the Cold War: Terrorism Looms Larger as a Weapon of Dissent and Warfare." *Current World Leaders* 39.4 (August): 11–26.

———. 1996b. *Terrorism and the Media: From the Iran Hostage Crisis to the Oklahoma City Bombing.* New York: Columbia University Press.

———. 2000. "Accomplice or Witness? The Mass Media's Role in Terrorism." *Current History* 99 (April): 174–178.

Nacos, Brigitte L., Robert Y. Shapiro, and Pierangelo Isernia, eds. 2000. *Decisionmaking in a Glass House: Mass Media, Public Opinion, and American and European Foreign Policy in the 21st Century.* Lanham, Md.: Rowman & Littlefield.

Neustadt, Richard E. 1980. *Presidential Power: The Politics of Leadership from FDR to Carter.* New York: Macmillan.

*New York Times.* 1996. "Chechen chief threatens attacks against Europe." 7 February.

Nimmo, Dan, and James E. Combs. 1985. *Nightly Horrors: Crisis Coverage in Television Network News.* Knoxville: University of Tennessee Press.

Nye, Joseph S., Jr., and William A. Owens. 1996. "America's Information Edge." *Foreign Affairs* 75.2 (March/April): 20–36.

O'Sullivan, John. 1986. Media Publicity Causes Terrorism. In *Terrorism: Opposing Viewpoints,* edited by Bonnie Szumski. St. Paul: Greenhaven.

Page, Benjamin I. 1996. *Who Deliberates? Mass Media in Modern Democracy.* Chicago: University of Chicago Press.

Page, Benjamin I., and Robert Y. Shapiro. 1989. Educating and Manipulating the Public. In *Manipulating Public Opinion,* edited by Michael Margolis and Gary A. Mauser. Pacific Grove, Calif.: Brooks/Cole.

———. 1992. *The Rational Public.* Chicago: University of Chicago Press.

Paletz, David L., and Alex P. Schmid. 1992. *Terrorism and the Media.* Newbury Park, Calif.: Sage.

Patterson, Thomas E. 1993. *Out of Order: How the Decline of the Political Parties and the Growing Power of the News Media Undermine the American Way of Electing Presidents.* New York: Knopf.

Picard, Robert G. 1991. News Coverage as the Contagion. In *Media Coverage of Terrorism,* edited by A. Odasuo Alali and Kenoye Kelvin Eke. Newbury Park: Sage.

Pillar, Paul R. 2001. *Terrorism and U.S. Foreign Policy.* Washington, D.C.: Brookings.

Pluchinsky, Dennis A. 1997. "The Terrorism Puzzle: Missing Pieces and No Boxcover." *Terrorism and Political Violence* 9.1 (Spring): 7–10.

Pratkanis, Anthony, and Elliot Aronson. 1992. *Age of Propaganda.* New York: W. H. Freeman.

Ranstorp, Magnus, and Gus Xhudo. 1994. "A Threat to Europe? Middle East Ties with the Balkans and their Impact upon Terrorist Activity Throughout the Region." *Terrorism and Political Violence* 6.2 (Summer).

Rapoport, David C. 1997. "To Claim or Not to Claim; That is the Question—Always!" *Terrorism and Political Violence* 9.1 (Spring): 11–17.

Reich, Walter, ed. 1990. *Origins of Terrorism: Psychologies, Ideologies, Theologies, States of Mind.* New York: Cambridge University Press.

Reeve, Simon. 1999. *The New Jackals: Ramzi Yousef, Osama bin Laden and the Future of Terrorism.* Boston, Mass.: Northeastern University Press.

Richardson, Louise. 1999. "Terrorists as Transnational Actors." *Terrorism and Political Violence* 11.4: 209–219.

Riley, John. 2000. "Sorting it all out." *Newsday,* 1 November, p. A45, A61.

Ronfeldt, David. 1999. "Netwar Across the Spectrum of Conflict: An Introductory Comment." *Studies in Conflict and Terrorism* 22:189–192.

Rose, Richard. 1991. *The Postmodern President, Second Edition.* Chatham, N.J.: Chatham House.

Rubin, Bernard. 1985. *When Information Counts: Grading the Media.* Lexington, Mass.: Lexington Books.

Rubenstein, Richard E. 1987. *Alchemists of Revolution: Terrorism in the Modern World.* New York: Basic Books.

Said, Edward W. 1981. *Covering Islam: How the Media and the Experts Determine How We See The Rest Of The World.* New York: Pantheon.

Scheuer, Jeffrey. 1999. *The Sound Bite Society: Television and the American Mind.* New York: Four Walls Eight Windows.

Schlesinger, Philip, Graham Murdock, and Philip Elliott. 1983. *Televising 'Terrorism': Political Violence in Popular Culture.* London, U.K.: Comedia.

Schmid, Alex P., and Jenny de Graaf. 1982. *Violence as Communication: Insurgent Terrorism and the Western News Media.* Beverly Hills, Calif.: Sage Publications.

Seib, Philip. 2001. *Going Live: Getting the News Right in a Real-Time, Online World.* Lanham, Md.: Rowman & Littlefield.

Shanahan, James, and Michael Morgan. 1999. *Television and its Viewers: Cultivation Theory and Research.* New York: Cambridge University Press.

Sontag, Deborah. 2000. "Israel acknowledges hunting down Arab militants." *New York Times,* 22 December, p. A12.

Stern, Jessica. 1999. *The Ultimate Terrorist.* Boston, Mass.: Harvard University Press.

———. 2000. "Pakistan's Jihad Culture." *Foreign Affairs* (November/December).

Stern, Kenneth S. 1996. *A Force Upon the Plain: The American Militia Movement and the Politics of Hate.* New York: Simon & Schuster.

Tulis, Jeffrey K. 1987. *The Rhetorical Presidency.* Princeton, N.J.: Princeton University Press.

Van Atta, Dale. 1998. "Carbombs & Cameras: The Need for Responsible Media Coverage of Terrorism." *Harvard International Review* (Fall): 66–70.

Verhovek, Sam Howe, and Joseph Kahn. 1999. "Talks and turmoil: street rage; dark parallels with anarchist outbreak in Oregon." *New York Times,* 3 December, p. A12.

Vetter, Harold J., and Gary R. Perlstein. 1991. *Perspectives on Terrorism.* Pacific Grove, Calif.: Brooks/Cole Publishing.

Walsh, Kenneth T. 1996. *Feeding the Beast: The White House versus the Press.* New York: Random House.

Weiman, Gabriel, and Conrad Winn. 1994. *The Theater of Terror: Mass Media and International Terrorism.* New York: Longman.

Whine, Michael. 1999a. "Cyberspace—A New Medium for Communication, Command, and Control by Extremists." *Studies in Conflict and Terrorism* 22:231–245.
———. 1999b. "Islamist Organizations on the Internet." *Terrorism and Political Violence* 11.1 (Spring): 123–132.
Wieviorka, Michel. 1993. *The Making of Terrorism.* Chicago: University of Chicago Press.
Wilkinson, Paul. 1997. "The Media and Terror: A Reassessment." *Terrorism and Political Violence* 9 (Summer): 132–134.
———. 2001. *Terrorism versus Democracy: The Liberal State Response.* London: Frank Cass.
Wolfsfeld, Gadi. 2001. "The News Media and the Second Intifada." *The Harvard International Journal of Press/Politics* 6.4:113–118.
Yankelovich, Daniel. 1991. *Coming to Public Judgment.* Syracuse, N.Y.: Syracuse University Press.
Zaller, John R. 1992. *The Nature and Origins of Mass Opinion.* New York: Cambridge University Press.
Zanini, Michele. 1999. "Middle Eastern Terrorism and Netwar." *Studies in Conflict and Terrorism* 22:247–256.

# Index